HARVARD HISTORICAL STUDIES, 141

Published under the auspices
of the Department of History
from the income of the
Paul Revere Frothingham Bequest
Robert Louis Stroock Fund
Henry Warren Torrey Fund

The Lara Family

CROWN AND NOBILITY IN
MEDIEVAL SPAIN

SIMON R. DOUBLEDAY

HARVARD UNIVERSITY PRESS
Cambridge, Massachusetts
London, England   2001

Library of Congress Cataloging-in-Publication Data

Doubleday, Simon R.
   The Lara Family: crown and nobility in medieval Spain / Simon R.
   Doubleday.
      p.   cm.—(Harvard historical studies; 141)
   Includes bibliographical references and index.
   ISBN 0-674-00606-2 (alk. paper)
   1. Lara family.   2. Castile (Spain)—History.   3. Nobility—Spain—Castile.
   I. Title.   II. Series

DP60.L3 D68 2001
946'.302—dc21   2001016916

Acknowledgments

Summer delights the scholar
With knowledge and reason.
Who is happy in hedgerow
Or meadow as he is?
—*Austin Clarke (1896–1974), "The Scholar"*

The road to Lara could not have been more delightful. For this, I first thank Thomas Bisson, whose graduate seminar opened my eyes to the possibilities of medieval Spain, and whose guidance has been invaluable at every step. To Charles Donahue of Harvard Law School I express my warmest appreciation; his generosity in time and attention went far beyond the bounds of necessity. Two grants from the Department of History at Harvard and the Real Colegio Complutense made possible my first summer of research in the hedgerows, meadows, and archives of Spain. Subsequent research was financed in part by the Program for Cultural Cooperation between Spain's Ministry of Culture and United States' Universities, and I could not have completed the project without the support of Dean Bernard Firestone and the Hofstra College of Liberal Arts and Sciences.

I am immensely indebted to Simon Barton, as much for his friendly suggestions and criticisms as for his pioneering scholarship; without him, there would have been many more errors of fact and identification. In Madrid, Reyna Pastor, Carlos Estepa Díez, and Isabel Alfonso Antón of the Consejo Superior de Investigaciones Científicas welcomed me with an enthusiasm I will never forget; their expertise, at a critical juncture in my research, was indispensable. Cristina Jular

Pérez-Alfaro has been an endless source of advice, assistance, and good humor, and Julio Escalona Monge is one of very few people to share my absorption in the history of the Lara family. Ana Rodríguez López, José Antonio Jara Fuente, and Ignacio Álvarez Borge have all been extraordinarily helpful, while Carmen Alonso was unstinting in her thirteenth-hour efforts to track down dusty tomes and recent articles. The excellent cartographic work was completed by Marco Antonio Rio Otero, of the University of Santiago de Compostela. At Harvard University Press, Elizabeth Suttell expertly guided this book through the early stages of publication, while Maria Ascher's editorial comments were quite brilliant. Without their support and guidance, it would have been much harder to evoke "the stone plain where the saints live"—the summer paradise of Austin Clarke's scholar. Yet some things on this plain, like the castle on the ridge at Lara, are still hard to make out, and many aspects of medieval Spain remain elusive. My greatest debt lies with all those friends and family members who have transmitted their passion for losing and finding oneself in a world which, in the end, can only be imagined.

Contents

Maps

The Lara Family

Introduction

Approaching Lara from the south, on the rough country lane that leads off the main road to Burgos, the traveler may discern a solitary shape at the end of the ridge which stands guard over the village. It is at first difficult to identify this shape. By turns, it seems to be a tree, a rock, a spire, or an ancient obelisk. High above the wheat fields and the stone plain, it overlooks the kind of landscape that Antonio Machado once described:

> A yellow roughness in the land,
> like the raw weave of country clothes,
> meadows dusted with new grass
> where scrawny sheep are browsing . . .
>
> Then rocks and still more rocks,
> stone barrens, craggy spurs—
> the haunt of lordly eagles—
> rock rose and bramble,
> upcountry herbs and briarbush and buckthorn.[1]

No longer the haunt of the lordly, Lara today is a place of considerable poverty. As late as 1981, only four out of twenty-seven villages in the so-called *Tierra Lara* had running water. The local economy, based primarily on cereal cultivation and supplemented by pastoral farming, is precarious; the natural disadvantages of rocky land and harsh climate are aggravated by a severe labor shortage. Like many pueblos in Old Castile, Lara has lost many of its inhabitants to the allure of urban opportunity. A flood of emigration over the past century has reduced the population from 5,666 in 1920 to 1,151 in 1980.[2] Yet Lara was not always a provincial backwater. Archaeological evidence suggests its importance as an urban center in the first several centuries after Christ, before a decline in the late Roman period.[3] Its necropolis indicates a sizable population, and the fact that the town moved down from the high ridge it had occupied reflects a confidence brought by peace and stability.[4] The population would later be concentrated in smaller nuclei, however;[5] and in the long phase of dislocation that followed the Arab-Berber invasion of the early eighth century, it was the windblown ridge above the village which became the focal point of Lara. At the end of the tenth century, as the Christian *reconquista* advanced toward the Duero river, Lara was captured by troops under the command of Gonzalo Fernández, count of the dynamic Leonese frontier region of Castile; and on the tip of the ridge known as "The Molar," a castle was constructed.[6]

Little remains of the castle today, except one crumbling, towering gateway; it is this lonely shape that rises high above the village. The ruined castle of Lara, visible from afar, is also conspicuous in the early medieval history of Castile as a whole. During the tenth century, it provided the focus for an *alfoz*, a small administrative district, with an unusually vibrant history.[7] The first sovereign count of Castile, Fernán González, son of the count who had conquered Lara, was probably born in the castle in 910, and after his mother relinquished control of the area he governed it until his death in 970.[8] The history of this period has been embellished by mythology, and notably by the story of the Seven Infantes of Lara, one of the most colorful legends of medieval Spain. It is this romance of treachery, love, and revenge, spanning the gulf between Lara and Córdoba, which accounts for the village's modern name, Lara de los Infantes.[9] Sadly, the historical basis for the romance appears weak; the history of the *alfoz* of Lara between the later tenth and later eleventh centuries is still obscure. We can say little more than that after Fernán González's death, Lara seems to have remained part of the inheritance of the counts of Castile for several generations. It was annexed by the Navarrese in the early eleventh century under Sancho the Great (1000–1035), and finally reverted to Castilian rule after Sancho's division of his dominions among his sons.[10] But toward the end of the eleventh century, the picture becomes much clearer: by the early 1080s, lordship over the area had fallen into the hands of one Gonzalo Núñez, the first known lord of the noble family that would one day come to be known as the Laras.

THE LARAS were among the most powerful noble families in Castile and León for about three hundred years: from the late eleventh century, when they rose to the pinnacle of power as royal favorites, to the middle of the fourteenth, when they faced a dramatic confrontation with the crown. The chapters that follow do not aim to provide an exhaustive history of the family. Little attention is paid here to their role as patrons of religious foundations, for example, or to the complex webs of marriage and clientage relationships which they established. For the sake of narrative coherence, I have also avoided pursuing the branch of the Lara family that established itself in Narbonne in the twelfth century. Instead, this study is primarily concerned with the tumultuous interaction between the crown and a great aristocratic family. Its approach is therefore more thematically specific than Simon Barton's excellent study, *The Aristocracy in Twelfth-Century León and Castile* (Cambridge, 1997); and in an effort to trace a change in the dynamics of power, it covers a longer chronological span. Part I, "Symbiosis," traces a phase lasting from the eleventh century to the thirteenth, a phase characterized by the Laras' escalating influence at court, heavy reliance on the administrative *tenencias* that were distributed by the crown, and surprisingly modest patrimonial power. Part II, "Confrontation," looks at the way in which the Laras were affected by a fundamental alteration in the dynamics of power in Castile and León during the reigns of Fernando III and Alfonso X.

Coincidentally, it is also about three hundred years since the publication of the only previous full-length work on the family, Luís de Salazar y Castro's *Historia genealógica de la Casa de Lara* (Madrid, 1696–1697). Salazar's four volumes are the tour de force of a brilliant genealogist. He had become the official Chronicler of Castile in 1685, and the next year joined the order of Calatrava, whose archives he used exhaustively. Together with his selection of documents relating to the family, published as the *Pruebas* (1694), and the autograph manuscripts at the Real

Academia de Historia, Salazar's *Casa de Lara* remains an extraordinarily useful source—one which, in the following chapters, will be mined for information more often than factually contradicted.[11] Yet it reflects a deeply conservative *mentalité*, inclined rather to idolize aristocracy than to analyze its underpinnings. The work lacks perspective on the changing social and political structures of medieval Castile, and any indication of change is overwhelmed by an impression of monolithic grandeur. The evolving foundations of aristocratic power are as obscure in Salazar's volumes as genealogical relationships are clear, and it is this evolution which is the primary concern of the present study. He nevertheless offers a welcome antidote to the unabashed hostility toward the nobility that is exhibited almost universally by royal chronicles and, in consequence, a large number of twentieth-century historians.

The negative historiographic view of the nobility derives in part from uncritical reliance on the intrinsically subjective materials produced under the aegis of the monarchy. The point was made powerfully by Otto Brunner in writing about the medieval Germanic lands:

> Medieval chronicles were written with an essentially moralizing intention, one informed by the ideal image of the just ruler as presented in the "mirrors of princes." And among the most prominent means of imputing unethical or unjust motives was the incessantly repeated accusation of "brigandage," the wickedness of plunderers and "robber knights." Almost every age of medieval narrative sources contains stereotyped complaints about "thieves and plunderers," "arson and looting," which modern historians then faithfully repeat.[12]

More recently, in the context of late medieval Castile, Miguel Ángel Ladero Quesada has suggested that the image of a rapacious nobility may be traced to a conscious political agenda on the part of the crown. Jealous of its powers, like local urban oligarchies, the emerging royal state drew upon antiseigneurial rhetoric in order to encourage a collective association of monarchy with freedom.[13] Royal chronicles, therefore, need to be treated with a good deal of caution; we should not judge the actions of the medieval aristocracy by the standards of proto-absolutism, or as if these actions took place within the context and behavioral expectations of a modern state. Changing patterns of power offer a more valuable framework for analysis than implicit belief in the moral inadequacy of the nobility.

The faith that the rise of monarchy over aristocracy was an inherently positive process has been pervasive, although the tide has begun to turn. But in reality the aristocracy was no more acquisitive than the crown: both pursued the almost inevitable logic of an intensely hierarchical society, seeking to advance their own interests by the accumulation of political, social, and jurisdictional authority. While the crown might act as a force for order and justice, it was not an inherently progressive institution: the representative assembly known as the Cortes, for instance, originated not in any new democratic vision but from a need to reinforce the base of political support for the king. Royal policies such as Alfonso X's pursuit of the imperial crown in the thirteenth century reflect just as much personal ambition as any aristocratic vendetta. In the final analysis, one might claim that the medieval nobility never approached the socially destructive power of the early modern monarchy, which would drive sixteenth-century Spain into economic stagnation, ethnic disaster, and catastrophic famine.

I

SYMBIOSIS

1

The Chains of Love

$\mathcal{I}$N ONE OF THE MOST striking images in Spanish litera-
ture, a frightened nine-year-old girl tells a knight on his journey into
exile that her family cannot give him shelter, for the king has decreed
that anyone doing so shall have his property seized and his eyes gouged
out. The citizens live in fear of the monarch; the dictates of the royal
anger, *ira regia*, cannot be contravened. So the much-loved knight,
Rodrigo Díaz, "El Cid," victim of malicious rumor, continues his ride
to the borders of the kingdom and beyond, to plunder and vanquish the
Moorish enemies of Castile, amass fortunes for his loyal retinue, and
win back the favor of the king he has offended. Without royal grace, he
must remain an exile, deprived of security and status. In this sense, the
Poema de Mio Cid is an accurate reflection of the dynamics of power in
Castile during the High Middle Ages.[1] Throughout the eleventh and
twelfth centuries, the king was the polestar of Castilian society, and in
large part the fortunes of a nobleman depended upon royal favor.

El Cid's king, Alfonso VI (reigned 1065–1109), had inherited a form
of kingship in which his authority was heightened by his role as active
commander of campaigns against the Moors and as distributor of the
wealth born of war. The most recent general study of the medieval
Spanish nobility describes the king as "the source of all riches, all pro-
motion, all downfall."[2] Equally, Georges Duby categorized Castile as a
"warrior economy," in which kings were enriched by tribute payments
(parias) imposed on the weak, fragmented Muslim kingdoms that had
emerged after the collapse of the Spanish caliphate in the first third of

the eleventh century. One of the hallmarks of this economy, according
to Duby, was the redistributive function of the crown: "Every gathering around a ruler appears as the high point of a regular system of free
exchange, permeating the whole social fabric and making kingship the
real regulator of the economy in general."[3] It is quite true that in the
ninth and tenth centuries the nobility had expanded in numbers and influence. Some powerful noble families had been able to establish control over great frontier territories; hence the secession of the counts of
Castile.[4] But neither in Castile nor in León had royal authority fragmented in the dramatic fashion of the French monarchy. There had
been no sudden collapse of public order into a violent new world of un-
trammeled local exploitation by knights and castellans, as there had
been north of the Pyrenees around the year 1000, nor did the nobility
confront the monarchy so directly at this stage.[5] The kings of Castile
and León, whose realms were reunited in 1072, had successfully retained the exclusive right to coin money, to adjudicate over a range of
particularly serious crimes, to own mined products, and to build fortresses. They could eject subjects from the kingdom, call magnates to
the royal host, or summon them to the court.[6] Royal prestige was
magnified further by an aura of the divine, associated partly with the
anointing of the king by the church.[7] This was perhaps especially true
for Alfonso VI, conqueror of Toledo—a city with enormous symbolic
value for Spanish Christendom.[8] Alfonso's reign, in fact, seems to have
marked a reaffirmation of royal authority and an effort to loosen the
chains between noble families and the territories where they had become dominant.[9]

The long-term delegation of public powers to private lords was limited in this period, a fact which generations of Spanish historians used
as evidence of the distinctive truncation of feudalism in most of the
peninsula until the late Middle Ages. This, of course, brings us to infa-
mous conceptual territory. Feudalism was understood, by historians in
the older tradition, to be a juridical relationship between members of
the social elite; it was characterized by an inextricable conjunction of
homage, links of vassalage, and the grant of hereditary fiefs in return
for military service, involving the devolution of jurisdictional powers
by the crown. Since this was a pattern that appeared to dominate the
feudal heartland of northwestern Europe and since these characteris-
tics were less prominent in Castile and León, historians maintained

that these regions were not properly feudalized and that, particularly before the twelfth century, the aristocracy was weak compared with its counterparts in other western European countries. The population was seen as consisting of small peasant proprietors, managing to avoid the oppressive fate of other European peasantries because of the unique circumstances of the *reconquista*.[10] Today, conversely, it is almost universally argued that Castile was *thoroughly* feudal. One historian even claims that power was "born feudalized"; in this view, a feudal monarchy and nobility emerged concurrently in the later tenth and eleventh centuries, so that by the beginning of the twelfth century the free peasantry had virtually disappeared.[11] The change in the scholarly consensus rests partly on a much broader definition of feudalism. This has its origins in the writings of Marc Bloch, who redefined the term as a global phenomenon embracing the whole of society, and in Marxist thought, where the term is used to designate agrarian systems based on extra-economic coercion and limitation of peasants' legal and personal freedoms. And indeed, by the eleventh century landholding entailed not only the leasing of land—which became increasingly important as the commercial economy of northern Castile developed—but also jurisdictional powers over the local inhabitants. These powers included the right to maintain law and order, organize military service in royal campaigns and the lord's private forays, impose labor services to be performed on his demesne, and finally to collect a wide range of taxes. This income, paid sometimes in cash but more frequently in kind, would be collected at the building known as the *palacio;* for this task, a wealthy lord might employ an administrator called a *merino*.[12] In the new, broader definition, there is absolutely no doubt that Castile and León were feudal societies by the dawn of the High Middle Ages—a fact which to some historians is almost aggravatingly self-evident. "The concept of Spanish feudalism in this sense," Peter Linehan has said, "assumes an air of sublime meaninglessness which renders it innocuous to some of the old juridical die-hards, risible or exasperating to others, according to temperament."[13]

It is quite true that the feudalism debate often seems to revolve around frustrating terminological argument more than any fundamental disagreement about social realities.[14] Both schools argue, for instance, that the territorial and jurisdictional power of the nobility steadily increased over the course of the Middle Ages. Yet the realignment of perspective has fostered an important new understanding of this social group. Recent work has suggested that as Castilian and Leonese society was "feudalized," the nobility—far from being inhibited by a powerful monarchy—attained a position of social dominance much earlier than was once believed. This may have occurred as early as the tenth century, precisely because the nobility's relationship with the crown was complementary and mutually reinforcing.[15] Throughout the Middle Ages, but particularly before the mid-thirteenth century, the royal court was in fact a fountain of aristocratic power. The dynamic of power at this stage was overwhelmingly one of symbiosis: the traditional duties of military aid and political counsel, and the temporary delegation of royal authority, bound magnates tightly to the king, who in turn provided generous rewards in land, money, office, and lordship.

For a nobleman aspiring to the heights of wealth and power, frequent presence at court was a prerequisite. This implied a peripatetic existence for noble families such as the Laras, since the court traveled tirelessly through the realm, to establish, expand, or exploit royal authority.[16] The leading members of the Lara family, in the eleventh and twelfth centuries, would have led a life that was necessarily as migratory as that of the king. At court, the Laras would have mingled with other members of the upper nobility, as well as with the royal family and the ecclesiastical elite. Their presence at court can be traced in the lists of subscribers—which is to say, those nobles and prelates who were present at the royal court and whose names appear (written by a scribe) at the foot of documents issued by the king. These lists, in which lay lords appear after ecclesiastical lords, represent a form of confirmation and consent, if not necessarily actual witnessing of the issuance of the document, and they provide a good reflection of both the composition of the court at a given moment and its internal hierarchy. The role of noblemen at court was in large part advisory, although they might also exercise legislative or judicial functions.[17] But their presence was also symbolic, a sign of loyalty; and loyalty paid. As the royal court flourished, moving gradually further from its primitive feudal roots toward greater institutional elaboration, access to the king became more and more lucrative. The rewards of loyalty might occasionally include high ecclesiastical office—a bishopric or an abbacy. Beginning, however, with the devotion that Alfonso VI showed to the house of Cluny, and his choice of a Frenchman to fill the reestablished see of Toledo, the crown showed a remarkable predilection for foreigners in making ecclesiastical appointments. Even when a bishopric went to a Castilian, the candidate was likely to be drawn from the ranks of mid-echelon royal servants.[18] Far more important for the nobility, therefore, were secular positions such as those of *alférez* (standard-bearer, as well as commander of the king's bodyguard and the army in the field in the absence of the king himself) and *mayordomo* (the chief steward, responsible for the management of the king's household and expenses). Both of these positions, but particularly the former, usually occupied by a young man, would be held repeatedly by upcoming members of the Lara family.[19] The role of *alférez* was a coveted prize in the career of a noble, not least because the late eleventh and twelfth centuries saw a reinvigoration of military activity. Many of the Laras would also carry the title of count (*comes*), which remained prestigious. Since it was not hereditary, it was an important mark of royal grace; the king appears to have had considerable choice in awarding the honor, and some capacity to withdraw it.[20] However, it probably no longer designated any precise function in royal administration, and seems instead to have become purely titular by the twelfth century.[21]

The greatest fruits of royal favor in the eleventh and twelfth centuries, and the pivotal administrative positions in Castile and León, were *tenencias*. In broad terms, tenancies consisted of the temporary delegation of royal lordship in a specific town or area: the exercise of jurisdictional, military, or financial authority, and receipt of some of the corresponding income. The tenant might supervise the collection of taxes, hear cases on appeal, or raise cavalry and infantry from the town or territory under his command. He was often assisted in his role by an *alcaide*, commander of the castle, and a *merino*, an administrator who was appointed from among the local citizens. As in the tenancies of Aragón, his authority in the locality was by no means absolute: over the course of the twelfth century, his jurisdiction was often challenged, and sometimes eclipsed, by the *alcaldes* (mayors and municipal judges) established by new local *fueros*.[22] (*Fueros* were documents recording municipal or regional laws, customs, or privileges.) Eventually, by the thirteenth century, the tenancies would fall into decay as their functions were gradually superseded by royal agents such as the *merinos* and *adelantados*. At the beginning of our period, however, they continued to be the basic unit of royal power. The lord of a tenancy might variously be known as *princeps terrae, dominus terrae, dominus villae, tenens castelli,* or *tenens terrae.*[23] Problematically, the words *tenens* and *tenente* do not become common until the 1130s; earlier, the perplexingly vague terms *dominante, imperante,* or simply *in* (*in Lara, in Asturias,* and so forth) are more common. It is notoriously hard to pinpoint the meaning of these terms or the precise nature of individual tenancies at this stage, perhaps because the nature of the authority itself was sometimes very nebulous. The line between public and private jurisdiction must often have been blurred, especially in the case of long-term tenancies. But the terms in question almost certainly do not refer to genuine patrimonial property, because in most cases the places they concern changed hands rapidly and were not transmitted along family lines. Nor, for the same reasons, do they seem to refer merely to a general preponderance in the area. Instead, it is likely that the terms corresponded to some form of tenancy, and the more specific designation *tenens* is often used for the same places in the next generation. Many tenancies crystallized around the districts called *alfoces,* which had been the basis of administration in Castile since the ninth century.[24] A good number (including Lara) formed around castles that may previously have been the focal point of *alfoces.*[25] The *alfoces* were units of fiscal dependency and obligation, as well as instruments for the collection of legal fines or military taxes like *fonsadera.* Other tenancies were organized around urban centers, including the key frontier towns of Segovia, Ávila, and Toledo; frontier tenancies of this kind were typically entrusted to a man in his prime, before he graduated to a tenancy in a more secure area of the heartland.[26] For the king, this system was an essential means of mobilizing an army, although in contrast with the more clearly defined responsibilities of tenants in the crown of Aragón, few high-ranking tenants assumed a regular military role; most must have valued their position largely for financial reasons.[27]

Did the distribution of tenancies by the crown merely correspond, as some have suggested, to preexisting patterns of noble landholding? The question is pivotal in discussing the dynamics of twelfth-century power. Unfortunately, the sparseness of the sources makes it very difficult to assess the full extent of lands held by a given individual, so any answer must remain tentative, especially in a case study such as this. Without doubt, there were instances where this pattern occurred. The patrimonial power of some nobles—Suero Vermúdez, for example, and the Froilaz clan—was very considerable.[28] For the crown, therefore, it must often have made practical sense to adapt to local dynamics, and the power of the monarchy was not such that it could invariably ride roughshod over other interests.[29] But it will be argued here that the king did *not* necessarily have to bow to the inevitable; in the case of the Laras at least, the distribution of tenancies was governed by their influence at court more than by independent territorial strength. There are, in fact, good reasons for believing that this may have been reasonably typical. In the chapters to come, the evidence will be examined in detail, but a few general remarks may be made right away. First, it is surely significant that Castilian and Leonese tenancies were never hereditary and were rarely retained for more than a few years; the rapidity with which they were rotated among different members of the nobility appears to reflect the strength of the monarchy and its capacity for political flexibility. Second, many of the Laras' tenancies appear to have been geographically unrelated to their patrimonial base, suggesting that some other dynamic was at work in the distribution of royal patronage. And third, as far as the evidence allows us to say, the unparalleled success that the family enjoyed in acquiring important tenancies cannot be explained by any very marked patrimonial supremacy over other lineages. In fact, they established patrimonial control over only one substantial estate on the peninsula (Molina) in the whole course of the twelfth century.

For now, their accumulation of patrimony was slow, piecemeal, and fragmented, and in this respect at least they resembled most other noble families in Castile and León. The territorial and jurisdictional dominance of the nobility over other inhabitants of the two kingdoms was perfectly visible, but it would not reach its full development for another three centuries. Noble landholding was always unstable before the creation of *mayorazgos* (entailed estates) in the later Middle Ages. Inheritance patterns were still predominantly cognatic, equal importance being attached to male and female lines, and Visigothic law dictated that all heirs, both male and female, should receive an equal share.[30] Sources suggest that although there was a long-term tendency toward favoring sons, egalitarian division of the inheritance among many or all offspring was fundamental in the twelfth century and continued to be so into the thirteenth.[31] Partition of property among vari-

ous heirs meant that lands that had been profitable in the tenth century were no longer so in a later period.[32] Of course, the Laras were
substantial landowners. A certain level of landed wealth was, in effect,
a *sine qua non*, necessary in order to enter the elite pool of candi-
dates from which tenants were chosen. But within this elite, patrimony
would prove to be a surprisingly weak basis for tapping royal power in
the twelfth century.

THE COURT OF THE KING, not the country estate, was the gateway to
the heights of power—and royal favor and disfavor alike could dictate a
noble family's fortunes. It was royal favor that raised up the first individual we may confidently identify as a member of the Lara family: a
courtier of Alfonso VI named Gonzalo Núñez (d. circa 1106). His ancestry is famously elusive. It now seems fairly clear, however, that Gonzalo was linked closely—perhaps by his marriage—to the Alfonso family, whose territorial base was near the Leonese border in the Tierra
de Campos. This family would subsequently give rise to some of the
most important lineages of the region (such as Osorio, Villalobos, and
Froilaz).[33] The most probable scenario is that Gonzalo was married to
Goto, daughter of María Gutiérrez, who was in turn the daughter of
Gutierre Alfonso.[34] His father-in-law would then have been Nuño
Álvarez (d. circa 1065), a nobleman who had been a witness of royal
charters from 1038 onward and had probably been tenant of Amaya.
The Álvarez family, in turn, was based between the Arlanzón and
Duero rivers; this may account in part for the Laras' subsequent
strength in the area.[35] What remains much less clear is Gonzalo's own
parentage. The simplicity of Spanish naming patterns in the High
Middle Ages means that we do know his father was named Nuño;[36] it
has indeed been suggested that he was son, rather than son-in-law, of
Nuño Álvarez, but this claim seems problematic.[37] Among other possible fathers are two members of the Salvadores lineage, who by the
1060s had established their influence over a sweeping area near Burgos,
including Lara itself.[38] There do appear to be close ties between the
Laras and the Salvadores family well into the twelfth century, but we
still lack the evidence to make any precise paternal connection.[39] We
can quite safely dismiss the assertion by Salazar y Castro that Gonzalo
had *married* into the Salvadores family.[40] Finally, there is even less evidence that Gonzalo Núñez's father was, as Salazar contends, a noble-

man named Nuño González, directly descended from the sovereign count of Castile, Fernán González.[41] In sum, the link with the Alfonso family is at present the connection that may be stated most confidently.

Beyond the issue of ancestry lies the related question of patrimony. The evidence allows us to say that Gonzalo Núñez possessed a number of properties in Castilla Vieja, Campos, and Asturias (see Map 1). Notably, he and his wife Goto owned the monastery of Santa María de Piasca, which had been linked with the Alfonso lineage, and *divisas* (shares of an inheritance) in a number of neighboring villages. In 1095 the couple granted these holdings to the great Leonese monastery of Sahagún, along with *divisas* in other villages, mostly in the fertile

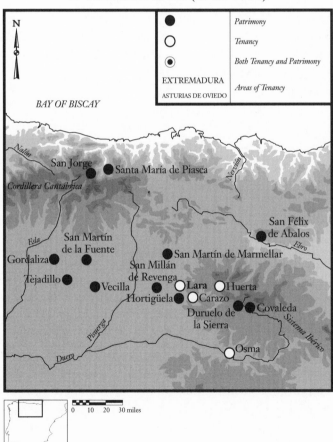

1. Gonzalo Núñez (d. ca. 1106)

farming land of Campos, which may similarly have been inherited from the Alfonso family.[42] He had property rights in Hortigüela, near Lara;[43] and a little further southeast, the villages of Duruelo de la Sierra and Covaleda, together with the abandoned church of San Millán de Velilla, which lay between them.[44] He granted all three places to the monastery of San Millán de la Cogolla in 1095, and made two other donations of ecclesiastical property.[45] We may perhaps see these donations as part of a more general process whereby large numbers of privately owned churches and monasteries were being granted to the church under the influence of the Gregorian reform movement.[46] Certainly, these possessions could not have comprised anything like the full extent of Gonzalo Núñez's patrimony; we are aware of them only because they were donated to the church, and only a small proportion of a noble's land would have been alienated in this way. But even given the dangers of arguing from silence, it is likely that his patrimony was vastly inferior to the well-documented territorial holdings of the Laras in the later thirteenth or fourteenth centuries. Equally, there is nothing to suggest that it outstripped the patrimony of great families like the Trabas of Galicia, or the Ansúrez clan of León, whose political preeminence—whatever their territorial power—would decline rapidly in the coming decades.

Instead, Gonzalo Núñez looks very much like a royal protégé: a man raised to great heights by virtue of the king's good graces. He appeared as a witness of a small number of royal diplomas as early as the mid-1070s, and a much larger number in the next two decades, almost certainly indicating that he was present in the royal entourage for long stretches of time.[47] We can only imagine the qualities that might have endeared him to the king: unwavering loyalty, perhaps, as well as good humor, sharp political instincts, and a robust appetite for the hunt. One thing, however, is quite clear: Gonzalo was a trusted and talented warrior, at a time when the need for such men was greater than ever. Alfonso VI's triumphant capture of Toledo had begun to seem more and more like a Pyrrhic victory: it had catalyzed an immense Muslim counterattack in 1086 by the Almoravids, the intolerant rulers of a huge northern African empire. The Christian kingdoms were now thrown back on the defensive, as Alfonso VI desperately tried to stem the tide. Serendipitously or otherwise, a new crusading ethos was also emerging in Spain.[48] For an ambitious nobleman like Gonzalo Núñez, the situation presented a golden opportunity: the prestige that might be acquired through successful service in royal campaigns was enormous. In 1093 Don Gonzalo participated in a royal campaign as far to the west as Portugal.[49] Two years later, he played a leading role in the unsuccessful attempt to stop the Almoravids from capturing the prosperous city of Huesca (in Aragón), presumably having been sent at the command of Alfonso VI, who was anxious to aid the Aragonese.[50] The rewards of this loyal activity are duly reflected in a document of 1098, in which Alfonso makes reference to his "beloved Gonzalo Núñez."[51]

Gonzalo, then, was probably a "new man"—a nobleman promoted in status as part of a conscious royal policy designed to renovate the elite. From the ninth-century *potentes* who, it has been said, were "made" as deliberately by the Asturian kings as a new Anglo-Norman aristocracy was made by William the Conqueror, to the *privados* favored by the Hapsburgs, Spanish political history is marked by repeated waves of such renovation. There were recurrent attempts to create a new body of potentates, bound more tightly in loyalty to the king than the old ruling class.[52] The Laras' novelty, like their subsequent ascendancy in Castile, makes them inherently distinctive; the sources of their influence are not, in other words, entirely representative of the nobility as a whole. On the other hand, there are plenty of parallel cases. Alfonso VI had elevated the Traba family of Galicia in a similar way, and new men virtually monopolized major positions in secular administration in the region. The most outstanding example is Count Raymond of Burgundy, to whom Alfonso married his daughter Urraca; Raymond was entrusted with the macro-tenancy of Galicia in 1079, soon after arriving at court, and he would retain it for no less than twenty years.[53] In fact, the same process was occurring at almost exactly the same time, for almost exactly the same reasons, in the embryonic kingdom of Portugal. Here, the demands of military activity against the Almoravids at the turn of the twelfth century accelerated the emergence of a new elite at the court of Afonso Henriques at Coimbra, who gave a special role to members of families of the second rank.[54] One suspects that this was precisely the principal reason for Gonzalo Núñez's ascent. His good fortune was later consolidated by the arrival at court of his two sons, Pedro González (d. 1130) and Rodrigo González (d. circa 1143), at least one of whom was granted the office of *alférez*.[55] The young Lara brothers then sealed their success by marriage alliances with other aristocratic families.[56]

Don Gonzalo was rewarded, like many faithful courtiers, with valuable tenancies like Carazo, Huerta, and Osma. Much more remarkable, however, was his prolonged tenancy of Lara, which he held for at least fourteen years, 1081–1095.[57] This was wholly exceptional; and it has sometimes been suggested that he received Lara not as a tenancy at all, but as a heritable patrimony acquired through kinship with the powerful Salvadores family. However, as we have seen, the evidence that Gonzalo Núñez de Lara was related to this family is still unclear; and it is not certain that Lara had ever been a patrimonial possession of the Salvadores family in any case.[58] The fact that Gonzalo Núñez first appears in control of Lara in 1081, two years before Gonzalo Salvadores' death, certainly undermines the possibility. It is most likely that Gonzalo Núñez held Lara as a long-term tenancy, held and exploited as if it were a patrimony; the patrimonialization of tenancies appears to have been widespread in this period.[59] If there was any form of kinship between the Laras and the Salvadores family, this association is likely to have been important primarily in the search for royal favor. In any case, the exceptionally prolonged tenure of Lara would eventually have a significant impact in molding the family's identity: the appellative "de Lara" appears in documents as late as the middle of the fourteenth century. It has been argued that the twelfth century marks the first use of surnames among medieval Castilian noble families, often on a toponymic basis, indicating a sense of cohesion which had not been present in the eleventh century.[60] However, in the late eleventh and twelfth centuries, the styling "de Lara" seems to have been used only by those members of the family who actually held the tenancy. The Lara family would not develop a clear sense of lineage until the end of the twelfth century, and would not think of themselves as "Laras" until the thirteenth century at the earliest. For now, Lara is likely to have been most important for the family not in a psychological or cultural sense, but in an economic one. The *alfoz* of Lara included, in the twelfth century, a number of once-separate villages: Barbadillo (10 kilometers to the southeast), Carazo and perhaps Salas (both about 15 kilometers to the southeast).[61] It was admittedly not so extensive as suggested by a document purportedly issued in 931 by the countess Momadona and her son, Count Fernán González, determining the boundaries of the lordship so as to include no fewer than sixty-six villages.[62] It is now widely agreed that the document is forged, probably created under the aegis of the *concejo* of Burgos in the thirteenth century after the absorption of Lara by the city.[63] But the tenancy of Lara was sometimes coupled with tenancy of other nearby districts such as Huerta (close to the eastern frontier), so there may have been some legitimacy to the eastern frontier claimed by the diploma; the same may be said regarding the southern boundary.[64] The tenancy of Lara would certainly have been lucrative, and would have dwarfed any of Gonzalo Núñez's patrimonial holdings. The dramatic rise of the Lara family was, it would appear, due less to autonomous patrimonial power than to influence at court; and this courtly influence was to reach new heights in the reign of Alfonso VI's daughter, Urraca.

QUEEN URRACA (reigned 1109–1126) has been maligned ever since her falling out with the first archbishop of Compostela, Diego Gelmírez, whose heated resentments were immortalized in the *Historia compostellana*.[65] For many historians, her reign represents a period of anarchy, unrest, and even "feudal revolution."[66] However, others have persuasively argued that the queen was both active and, in some respects at least, effective; certainly, even in her reign, royal favor remained fundamental.[67] The importance of her favor is made wonderfully clear in Gelmírez's chronicle, in reference to Pedro González de Lara: "This Count Pedro, so it was rumored, used to indulge in extremely strong chains of love with Queen Urraca, and from her held Castile and no small part of Campos."[68] It is not clear precisely when his relationship with Urraca began, but it is likely to have been shortly after his nearest rival died in 1111. Count Gómez González had been favored to marry the queen by a majority of the bishops and nobles of the realm after the death of Urraca's first husband, Count Raymond of Burgundy, in 1107. When, in 1109, she married Alfonso I *el Batallador* of Aragón (reigned 1104–1134), many of the Castilian elite rose in opposition, clustering around Count Gómez. As her marriage began to collapse, the count felt contentedly that he had wedlock within his grasp and "began to conduct the wars of the kingdom," but died in battle against the Aragonese.[69] Beginning around 1112, Pedro González de Lara inherited Urraca's favor and the dominance this brought. The report of the affair is echoed in the thirteenth-century chronicle *De rebus Hispania*. "Count Pedro of Lara, while he displayed undue private familiarity with the Queen, which he hoped to strengthen through marriage, was preeminent over all people, and began to exercise the office of king, and to rule everyone as a lord."[70]

The relationship serves to underline, in a particularly literal fashion, the intimacy of power in twelfth-century Spain. Pedro González's presence at court may be traced in royal diplomas from the first moments of the reign, when he appears with the office of *alférez*,[71] but his closeness to Urraca visibly promoted his career.[72] From 1107, he appears in the diplomas with the title of count.[73] He took further advantage of his virtually constant presence at Urraca's side to acquire a variety of tenancies in Castile and Campos, and to maintain control of the tenancy of Lara, which was evidently coming to be regarded almost as a family possession.[74] His power was unrivaled, and if the surviving diplomas are representative, his influence was even greater in the second half of the reign, partly because of the death of the great Leonese count Pedro Ansúrez around 1117.[75] Only determined opposition by other noble families kept his power within bounds, preventing him from gaining a strong foothold in León or Galicia. This opposition emerged as a direct response to Pedro's liaison with the queen: "The other magnates, not supporting the lady's infamy, began to resist him, and to impede the plan of marriage."[76] The *Primera crónica general* suggests that the magnates, believing that their rightful access to the monarch had been denied, felt it essential to establish a new king: Urraca's son by her first marriage, Alfonso Raimúndez.[77] Armed resistance reached a climax early in 1119, when Pedro González was seized and briefly imprisoned by Guter Fernández de Castro. Thus began the great rivalry between the Lara and Castro families, which would be one of the main features of Castilian politics in the twelfth century.[78] Yet for now, opposition was only a temporary inconvenience. By 1119, the challenge had been defused by a deft political compromise, and Pedro's position was secure.

As in the previous generation, his patrimony seems likely to have been of merely secondary importance (see Map 2). We know that he was lord of the villages of Jaramillo Quemado and Tardajos; like his father, he also had holdings in the fertile land of Campos, quite possibly a reflection of the Laras' descent from the Alfonso family.[79] But there is no evidence that his patrimonial supremacy was remotely equivalent to his political power. The same is true of his younger brother, Rodrigo (see Map 3). As we might expect, given the importance of partible inheritance, Rodrigo González had holdings of more or less equivalent size. Some of his property was, again, in Campos.[80] Far to the north, in Asturias, he had property in Arce and the little mountain village of San

2. Pedro González (d. 1130)

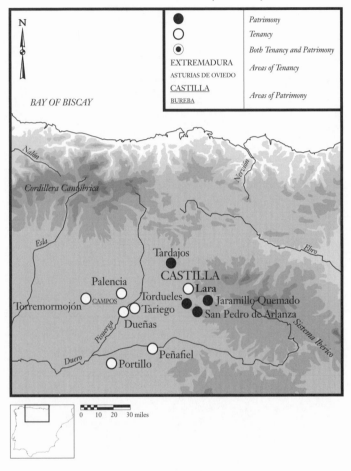

Mamés de Polaciones;[81] to the east, he had land in the region of La Bureba.[82] Finally, farther south, he owned property in Peñaranda de Duero. But his rapid rise to prominence, like his acquisition of tenancies, would be largely dependent on his brother's political success. In fact, one of the most striking elements of the Laras' experience in this early stage is the importance of horizontal and especially fraternal bonds: in an age before the full development of primogeniture and the linear transmission of entailed estates, brotherly love and loyalty was often the axis of aristocratic behavior. In the next two generations, Lara brothers would also come to dominate Castilian political life. It is striking that Rodrigo had been almost totally absent from court before

3. Rodrigo González (d. ca. 1143)

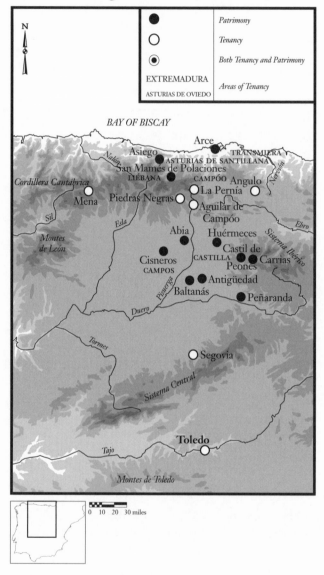

1117, and became a frequent witness of royal charters just at the point when Pedro's influence reached a plateau in 1119.[83] His rise to royal favor was then secured in the early 1120s by new chains of love: a marriage to Urraca's young half-sister, the *infanta* Sancha.[84] There was a strong correlation between his influence at court in the second half of the reign and his possession of tenancies. Among these was the tenancy of Asturias de Santillana, which probably involved jurisdictional and military authority over a number of places in the north of the peninsula, and may well have been intended as a safeguard against Aragonese pretensions. More briefly, he acquired the tenancy of Toledo, by far the largest city in the kingdom.[85]

During the final years of Urraca's reign, a semblance of stability was restored to Castile. In 1124, both Pedro and Rodrigo González, who were clearly devoted followers of the queen, confirmed diplomas issued by her young son Alfonso Raimúndez (child of her marriage to Raymond of Burgundy) in which he was already styling himself king.[86] Yet any hopes of lasting harmony were immediately dispelled when she died on 8 March 1126. Ironically, the traditional view of her reign as a period of anarchic disruption is usually matched by agreement that her son, now enthroned as Alfonso VII (reigned 1126–1157), was responsible for the reimposition of royal authority: darkness was supposedly followed by light.[87] In reality, half a dozen years of peace in the closing stage of the queen's reign were now followed by a half-dozen of turmoil. On the very day after Urraca's death, Alfonso arrived at León to find that the fortress of the city was refusing to recognize him: the rebels' hopes lay "in Count Pedro of Lara and his brother Rodrigo González, Castilians who preferred to have war rather than peace with the king."[88] The king's forces stormed the fortress, but the two Lara brothers held out against royal authority in Asturias de Santillana, the region which formed one of Rodrigo's key tenancies.[89] Salazar y Castro, writing in the late seventeenth century, suggested that Pedro González aimed at nothing less than independent sovereignty. "Among mortals, there is nothing so commendable, or so hungered for, as the status of recognizing the authority of no one, and depending solely on God and one's own judgment."[90] Claiming that in Spain, only Portugal, Albarracín, and Molina ever managed to establish such sovereignty (one might surely add the renegade county of Castile), Salazar added that the *príncipes* of the house of Lara were among very few ever to attempt it. Pedro González, in his view, was the first who "showed himself desirous of that prerogative." In support of his claim, he refers to a diploma of 1128 in which Pedro refers to himself as count of Lara "by the grace of God." This, Salazar states, was something that no other Castilian subject dared to do, with the exception of Pedro's own descendants and, in 1170, a lord of Vizcaya.[91] However, it is not at all clear that the phrase indicates any subversive aspiration to autonomy. When Pedro González's eldest son Manrique used the formula *Malric Dei gratia comes* in 1148, for example, he clearly enjoyed the good graces of the king.[92] The need to rely on the intensely hostile royal chronicle in fact makes the Laras' strategy almost completely impenetrable. However, it is not hard to hazard a guess. The queen's death had left them facing a sudden loss of hegemony at court and the accession of an unsympathetic monarch whose Galician supporters would probably be rewarded at their expense.[93]

It is possible that Pedro González wished to place his son by Urraca, Fernando Pérez, on the throne, but more likely that he aspired to the accession of Alfonso I *el Batallador*, with whom Urraca had maintained a cordial relationship for the last decade of her life.[94] The Aragonese king still maintained his aspirations to imperial control over Castile. As Bernard Reilly observes, as long as Urraca had been queen, Pedro González and Alfonso I had been natural enemies; now that she was dead, and Alfonso Raimúndez in control of most of Castile, they were natural allies.[95] For now, Pedro and his brother returned grudgingly to court, but twice in the next three years Pedro would passively support the Aragonese.[96] First, in July 1127, when Alfonso VII summoned an army to intercept Aragonese forces on their way to Castrojeriz, Pedro's recalcitrance seems to have forced the Castilian king to agree to terms. "Count Pedro of Lara, who was in the first regiment of the king of León, did not want to fight against the king of Aragón, because his heart was with him, and he [Pedro] had discussion with him."[97] Again, when *el Batallador* was menacing the frontier early in 1129, the Laras were humiliatingly unresponsive: "Count Pedro of Lara and his brother Count Rodrigo and their people and allies did not want to go in support of the king of León."[98] The tension between the king and Pedro González reached the boiling point in 1130, when Alfonso VII seized and imprisoned Count Pedro and his son-in-law Count Bertran of Risnel because "they were disturbing the kingdom."[99] Showing the kind of fraternal solidarity that was characteristic of the Laras in the twelfth century, Rodrigo González rebelled immediately, but the two prisoners were kept in chains until their castles and towns were surrendered. Paramount among Pedro González's lost possessions was the tenancy of Lara, which appeared later the same year in the hands of

Ordoño Gustios, probably yet another "new man," a member of the lesser nobility who had been elevated to undermine the power of the older aristocracy.[100] Count Pedro fled immediately to Aragón, seeking the aid of *el Batallador*, who was busy besieging Bayonne in an attempt to expand his control over the Basque Country.[101] But no sooner had he reached the Aragonese camp at Bayonne than he challenged the Count of Toulouse to hand-to-hand combat. "And they went out to war like two strong lions, and Count Pedro was wounded by Count Alfonso and, falling from his horse, broke his arm and died some days later."[102]

Once the metaphorical chains of favor binding the Laras to the crown had been broken, the family was left virtually powerless. They found themselves forced to watch the rise of new protégés like Ponce de Cabrera and Ponce de Minerva—Catalans, no less, who had arrived in 1127 in the retinue of Alfonso VII's bride, Berenguela. The newcomers' ascent is a perfect illustration of the power of royal patronage. "Landless outsiders when they arrived," writes Simon Barton, "they were nonetheless able, by dint of service to the crown, to become leading figures on the stage of Leonese-Castilian politics."[103] The Laras' fall, conversely, was paralleled by that of the Flaínez clan, which had been among the most powerful Leonese families at the turn of the century but which, deprived of royal favor, was now reduced to purely local importance.[104] The leading noble families did not enjoy the depth of patrimony that they would have by the end of the thirteenth century, and their political autonomy was correspondingly limited. Rodrigo González de Lara, for example, was simply incapable of sustained resistance after his brother's death. Falling upon him and other rebels in Asturias de Santillana, the king seized their castles, set fire to their properties and cut down their vines and orchards. Seeing that he could avoid the king "neither in castles, nor in mountains, nor in caves," Rodrigo was obliged to negotiate with him.[105] We are told that during the course of their talks by the Pisuerga River, Alfonso VII became angry with Rodrigo and seized him by the neck; they fell from their horses, and the count's soldiers fled in terror. Rodrigo was now placed in iron chains—the chains of disfavor—and held until he yielded his honors and castles. The king then "dismissed him, empty and without honor."[106]

2

The Revels of War

$\mathcal{D}$ESPITE THE LARAS' REBELLION early in the reign of
Alfonso VII, their relationship with the monarchy was only occasionally confrontational in the twelfth century, because they relied on their
closeness to the crown and lacked the resources necessary for prolonged opposition. Equally, the centralization of government, which
would destabilize the world of thirteenth-century politics, was not yet
a royal ambition. From the king's perspective, a good working relationship with the Laras was still valuable, particularly in matters of war.
It was probably during Alfonso VII's reign that the ideal of crusade
took root in Spain, advancing under the banner of St. James, whose
mythical persona was now transformed from peaceable fisherman into
Matamoros, the imperious Moorslayer.[1] Alfonso himself led twenty-
nine military expeditions, culminating in the triumphant conquest of
Almería in 1147.[2] As in other western European kingdoms, war stimulated the royal military structure and mobilized more fiscal resources,
so that it became even more important for the nobility to obtain a
piece of the royal pie.[3] Specifically, the reign catalyzed the emergence
of frontier militias in royal barracks towns like Ávila, Segovia, and
Salamanca; and the tenants of these places (who were often known
as *alcaldes*) took on a particular importance in organizing their military mobilization and campaigns.[4] Members of the Lara family would
repeatedly be favored to fill these tenancies; and indeed it was the
intensification of Castilian military activity in the south that allowed
the Laras to recover their earlier prominence in the kingdom.

The Almoravids, who ever since their arrival in Spain in 1086 had brought a new degree of aggression to Christian-Muslim relations, had lately stepped up their offensive campaigns in the Tagus valley, destroying the castle of Aceca in 1130. During the following year, they killed the governor of Toledo, who was replaced in 1132 by Rodrigo González de Lara. Rodrigo had returned to the royal court earlier in the year, admitting his fault to the king, and was immediately granted "great honors in Extremadura and Castile," among them the tenancies of Segovia and Toledo.[5] Alfonso's magnanimity is remarkable, but there was a good deal of pragmatism involved, too. Rodrigo González had previously held the tenancy of Toledo under Urraca; and like his father, who had been sent to fight the Almoravids at Huesca, he was evidently perceived as an outstanding military leader.[6] He wasted no time in confirming this reputation. In June 1132, Rodrigo led a devastating campaign down the Guadalquivir valley, as far as the outskirts of Seville itself, setting fires, cutting down orchards, and seizing immense quantities of booty: gold and silver, costly clothing, horses and asses, oxen, cows, and other cattle.[7] The long-term rewards were even greater: within three years, he had also been granted the tenancy of Asturias and received a major patrimonial grant from Alfonso VII.[8] These were heady days for the Castilian monarchy and a good moment for a nobleman in royal service. In 1135, King Alfonso was formally crowned emperor in León cathedral, solemnizing a Castilian-Leonese pretension to lordship over the other Christian kingdoms that had been forming since the end of the previous century.[9] Success in Andalucía brought buoyant confidence, and began to reverse the slow exhaustion of war profits that had occurred after the Almoravid invasion. The "warrior economy" and the redistributive function of the king were therefore revitalized. Markedly more than in Catalonia, the nobility remained dependent on royal service.[10]

The other side of the coin of royal favor became clear in 1137, when Rodrigo's fortunes failed to survive an acrimonious dispute with the king. We do not know the cause, although it is possible that the king perceived him as being dangerously well connected: following his earlier wedding to a daughter of Alfonso VI, he had married again, this time to Estefanía, daughter of Count Armengol VI of Urgell.[11] After learning that Alfonso's patience toward him was rapidly deteriorating, Rodrigo surrendered Toledo and other cities and towns he held. He then left for the Holy Land, where he is said to have built a castle and given it over to the Knights Templar. Returning over the Adriatic, he eventually landed again on Spanish shores, staying for a time with Ramón Berenguer IV of Barcelona, before traveling on to the courts of Navarre and Valencia, whereupon he contracted leprosy.[12] After a brief return to his Castilian homeland, the dying Rodrigo made a final journey to Jerusalem, and remained there until his death in about 1143.[13]

Rodrigo's return to royal service had been a false dawn for the Laras. But in the 1140s, as the authority of the Almoravids in Andalucía began to disintegrate under internal pressure, Castilian campaigns in the south accelerated again, bringing yet greater opportunities for military heroism. Recounting the capture of a number of Andalusian towns, including Andújar and Baeza, the *Poema de Almería* rhapsodizes about one hero in particular: Manrique de Lara (d. 1164), the eldest son of Pedro González:

> He was pleasing to everyone and at the same time to the
>   emperor,
> so that he shone among the Saracens and the Christians.
> Outstanding in repute, he was loved by all;
> liberal and generous, he was never miserly to anyone.[14]

Manrique's ability to be pleasing to the emperor-king, by feats of arms and chivalric largesse, was vital to the unexpectedly swift recovery of the Lara family in the middle of the twelfth century, after the rebellions of the preceding years. His liberality, generosity, and charm brought prominence and prestige; and Manrique inherited, above all, the reputation for military skill that his uncle Rodrigo had earned. This, of course, brought him tenancies. It has been suggested that Alfonso VII's reign marked the beginning of a process whereby tenancies were held on a long-term basis, but even if this is so, royal favor remained absolutely critical.[15] Manrique had already held the pivotal frontier towns of Ávila and Toledo in the mid-1130s, while he was prominent in the royal court, as well as serving as *alférez* between 1134 and 1137.[16] After a lacuna of several years, lasting until 1142, his regular presence at court allowed him to begin accumulating more border tenancies: Medinaceli and the little town of Madrid were added to Ávila and Toledo in the mid-1140s (see Map 4).[17] Since he never acquired the office of *alférez* again, it was probably as tenant of Toledo

4. Manrique Pérez (d. 1164)

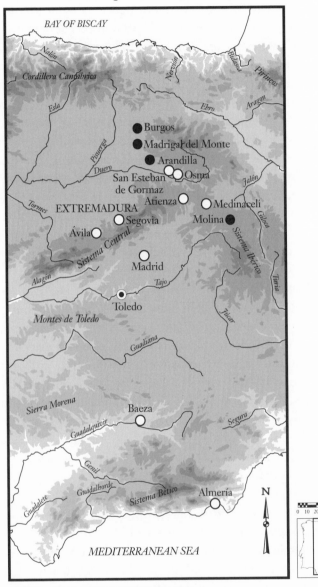

BAY OF BISCAY

Nalón

Cordillera Cantábrica

Nervión

Bidasoa

Pirineos

Esla

Ebro

Aragón

Pisuerga

● Burgos

● Madrigal del Monte

Duero

● Arandilla

○○ Osma

San Esteban de Gormaz

Jalón

Tormes

EXTREMADURA

Atienza ○

○ Medinaceli

Jiloca

○ Segovia

Molina ●

Ávila ○

Sistema Central

Sistema Ibérico

Alagón

Madrid ○

Tajo

Turia

⊙ Toledo

Júcar

Montes de Toledo

Guadiana

Sierra Morena

Baeza ○

Segura

Guadalquivir

Genil

Guadalete

Guadalhorce

Sistema Bético

Almería ○

N

MEDITERRANEAN SEA

0 10 20 30 miles

●   *Patrimony*

○   *Tenancy*

⊙   *Both Tenancy and Patrimony*

EXTREMADURA

ASTURIAS DE OVIEDO   *Areas of Tenancy*

that he assumed a leading role in military campaigns of this decade. Having been designated a count in 1145, he was present at the first conquest of Córdoba (1146), and the absorption of Baeza and Cala- trava early the next year.[18] The culmination of his military career, how- ever, was his role in the conquest of the port city of Almería (1147– 1148), and in this context the poet of the campaign describes how Manrique flourished in arms and "reveled in war."[19] His leadership in these celebrated campaigns, which benefited from an implosion of Almoravid imperial power, can only have strengthened his immense prestige at court and accelerated the cycle of the family's success. He was granted immediate tenancy of Baeza, and retained control of it for a full ten years before a successful Muslim counterattack. Such was the extent of Manrique's jurisdiction that he appointed an *alcalde* to admin- ister the tenancy in his stead; in fact, he developed a private officialdom that also included his own *mayordomo*, an *alférez*, and, rather unusually, a professional notary.[20]

One of the more hagiographic modern appraisals of Manrique— written in the 1920s—claims that he was "the greatest politico-military figure of the entire Middle Ages," and suggests that he was the most shining example of vassalic or ministerial loyalty in the whole course of Spanish history.[21] Such a view, coming as it does from an author who interweaves pseudo-history with the claim that the Primo de Rivera dictatorship is essential for Spain and that Catalonia is an open prison, should remind us of the dangers (and political implications) of glorify- ing military exploits. Nonetheless, it should also remind us of the im- portance of individual personality and talent, a factor that is sometimes lost in the contemporary focus on family structures.[22]

The role of individuality is demonstrated inversely by the relative insignificance of Álvaro Pérez (d. 1172), the second in the triumvirate of Lara brothers in the mid-twelfth century and by far the least promi- nent. Álvaro, who is curiously invisible in the reign of Alfonso VII, en- joyed relatively few tenancies, fleetingly and belatedly, mostly after the mid-1160s (see Map 5).[23] He would not have enough prestige to be ad- dressed as a count until as late as 1166.[24] Their youngest brother, Nuño Pérez (d. 1177), on the other hand, was extremely active under Alfonso VII, holding the office of *alférez* between 1145 and 1155.[25] His rela- tionship with Manrique is, in fact, the second of two great brotherly partnerships that would characterize the history of the Laras in the

5. Álvaro Pérez (d.1172)

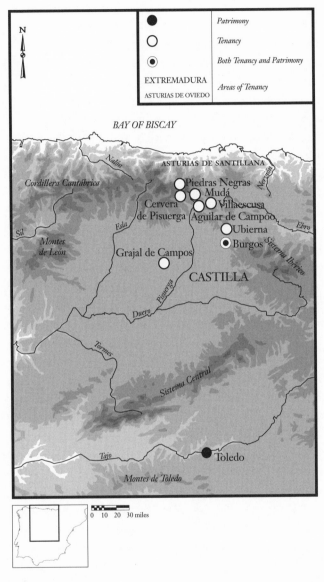

twelfth and early thirteenth centuries. In his capacity as *alférez*, he had joined Manrique at the conquests of Baeza, Calatrava, and Almería, before being taken hostage and imprisoned in Jaén.[26] He was evidently ransomed soon after, however, and we may imagine he took special pleasure in the act of besieging Jaén in 1150.[27]

It is, once again, unlikely that the Laras' ascendancy at court was driven by preexistent territorial power. Manrique possessed a few houses in Burgos;[28] some property in Toledo;[29] some lands to the west of Molina, which were alienated in 1151 and 1153;[30] and probably the properties in Arandilla and Madrigal alienated by his wife, Ermesenda, after his death.[31] He also held one major estate, Molina, on the Aragonese frontier, but it appears to have been his position as royal *alférez* that allowed him to acquire it. In the *fuero* (or law code) which he granted to the town, Manrique states: "I found a greatly deserted place that I wish to be populated."[32] One suspects that he took the virtually abandoned town and territory of Molina with little or no resistance, perhaps as early as 1134, when he had first held the office of *alférez* and when Castilian forces had advanced on Zaragoza.[33] Alfonso VII may then have formally granted Molina to the *alférez* who had captured it as a reward for his service in the Zaragoza campaign.[34] The *fuero*'s modern editor rejects what he sees as a fanciful story told by a fourteenth-century chronicler, in which Manrique's possession of Molina is explained as the result of a dispute between the kings of Castile and Aragón.[35] However, King Alfonso's decision may quite well be attributed to the continual Castilian-Aragonese friction that was focused on the border zone. According to the surviving text of the *fuero*, which is dated 1154, Manrique instructed the inhabitants of Molina: "You shall always have a lord from among my sons and grandsons, one that is pleasing to you and will do good for you; otherwise you shall have no lord."[36] It might seem at first that Molina was perceived as what would become known as a *behetría de linaje*—by later romantic tradition, a place whose inhabitants were able to choose any lord from a given lineage. But it was treated as if it were a freely alienable patrimonial possession. After Manrique's death in 1164, his wife, Ermesenda, received half of the lordship, and his son, Pedro Manrique, the other half; then, in 1175, Ermesenda herself partitioned her share, granting half to the Order of Calatrava and the other to her grandson García Pérez Manrique.[37] This fragmentation and alienation would have been impossible in a *behetría de linaje*. There is perhaps good reason for us to be suspicious of the text. If this portion of the *fuero* had indeed been written in 1154, the two divisions would have contravened it. Instead, it bears the imprint of a later age. Although the twentieth-century editor of the text assumes that it is an accurate copy of the original, he suggests that it probably dates from the end of the thirteenth century or the beginning of the fourteenth.[38] If one were, in fact, to date the text to around 1290, there would be a good explanation for its redaction and, indeed, adaptation. By this time, the Lara family would be urgently concerned with reinforcing their position on the Aragonese frontier. The marriage in 1290 of Juan Núñez II de Lara to Isabel, heiress of Molina, created a powerful stimulus for the forgery of evidence purporting to show that Molina had always been a *behetría de linaje* and was therefore an inalienable possession of the Laras. The late thirteenth-century redaction is replete with references to the de facto independence of the lordship of Molina, an independence that would be crucial for the Laras in these far more confrontational years. It specifies that inhabitants are obliged to perform service in the count's host but not that of the king, and that no heraldic symbol should be displayed other than those of the count or *concejo*.[39] These concerns would make far more sense in a document of the 1290s, when Juan Núñez II clashed violently with Sancho IV of Castile, than in a document of 1154 ostensibly produced by a noble whose career had been built from the start upon service in Alfonso VII's military campaigns.

FRONTIER TENANTS in the kingdom of Castile and León would have grown increasingly nervous in the mid-1150s, as a new Islamic movement originating in Morocco—the Almohads—displaced the crumbling power of their predecessors, the Almoravids, in the south. Devout, militant, and purposeful, the Almohads recaptured Manrique de Lara's tenancies of Almería and Baeza in 1157, and over the coming decades they would press farther and farther toward the heart of the peninsula. The same year marked the death of Alfonso VII and brought an end to the phase of Christian expansionism that had characterized his reign. Following the emperor's death, the twin realms of León and Castile were partitioned in accordance with his wishes: León passed to his younger son, Fernando II (reigned 1157–1188), and Castile to his short-lived eldest son, Sancho III (reigned 1157–1158), who was then succeeded by the child-king Alfonso VIII (reigned 1158–1214). However, the partition, which would last until 1230, further undermined the security of the two kingdoms, allowing noble families to set one realm against another.[40] This became immediately apparent during the vicious struggle for preeminence between the Laras and the Castro family that occurred in the minority of Alfonso VIII. Early in Alfonso's reign, according to the thirteenth-century *De rebus Hispaniae*, the body of Gutierre Fernández de Castro was summarily disinterred by his vengeful rival, Manrique de Lara, who had managed to gain custody of the young king. Manrique, says the chronicler, was determined to hasten the return of tenancies held from the crown, which Sancho III had allegedly agreed to freeze for a fifteen-year period; he threatened to charge Gutierre Fernández posthumously as a traitor if Gutierre's nephews did not comply.[41] The tale is in fact chronologically impossible; yet the ferocious competition for control of the king, which the chronicle describes, was an important feature of this era.[42] The Lara family's proximity to Alfonso VIII was lucrative, and they fought hard to intensify their ascendancy at court, feeding the fires of a long struggle with the Castro family for control of the king. As the story of Manrique's unsavory exhumation shows, making sense of this period entails careful distillation of the chronicles. Their accounts of how the Laras had managed to acquire custody of the king in the first place are again both implausible and revealing. They relate that Alfonso VIII had initially been entrusted to the care of Gutierre Fernández de Castro; the Laras are said to have politely advised him to surrender this privilege to Manrique, whose popular support in Extremadura, they said, would enable him to quell unrest in the kingdom. The lord of Castro, duped by the Laras' ostensible public-spiritedness, granted them possession of the child-king, and Alfonso VIII was first placed in the custody of a relative of the Laras, García Garcés de Aza. But when the Lara brothers saw that García Garcés could not afford this responsibility, they had the king handed over to the avaricious Manrique.[43] In its details, the narrative is unpersuasive—Gutierre Fernández, for instance, behaves with improbable naiveté—but the underlying principle is transparent. There could be no better evidence of the clarity with which the Lara family and others recognized the importance of personal access to the king.

Deprived of custody, the Castros then turned desperately for assistance to the king of León, as the Laras would do a half-century later when their control of the young King Enrique I was ended by his sudden death. This was a natural tactic, in view of the various marriage alliances between the Castros and the Leonese Alfonso family, and it seemed to work. The Leonese defeated Nuño Pérez in battle in July

1160 and occupied a large area of the frontier region of Castile then known as Extremadura (including Ávila and Segovia).[44] The events as recounted in the chronicle are as follows: Both the kingdom in general and Manrique in particular are then driven to such a financial crisis that Manrique is forced to surrender the young king in vassalage to Fernando II of León. They travel to Soria, and Fernando arrives to meet them; but as the transfer is about to occur, young Alfonso is rescued on horseback by a young knight who spirits him away to the castle of San Esteban de Gormaz. The people of Soria go off in hot pursuit, but Nuño Pérez intercepts him and has whisked him off to Atienza by the next morning.[45] For once, the swashbuckling narrative may be at least partly true: in September 1162, Manrique concluded a peace treaty with the king of León in which he was indeed obliged to surrender control of Alfonso, and according to one source was immediately granted custody again.[46] The dramatic removal of the child-king to the castle of San Esteban (which, like Atienza, was held by Manrique) may in reality have occurred with the full consent of Fernando II. Quite possibly, Fernando had granted physical custody of Alfonso to the Laras in return for a symbolic act of homage whereby his imperial overlordship was recognized. In the wake of the treaty, Manrique and his brothers witnessed a number of Leonese diplomas while Fernando II styled himself king "in Toledo, Extremadura, Castile, León, Galicia, and Asturias."[47]

Having regained physical custody of the king, the Laras "inseparably and faithfully adhered to him."[48] Manrique, who had been "in charge of the business of the kingdom" as early as 1158, is described in a diploma of 1161 as "the king's servant";[49] along with Nuño Pérez, he appears as "administrator of the king's business" in 1163,[50] and was still enjoying this role in early 1164.[51] In the course of a military campaign during the summer, designed to capture stubborn Castro tenancies in the Transierra, Manrique was killed during an unsuccessful siege of the town of Huete.[52] To rub salt in the wound, Nuño Pérez was also captured. Yet the family's momentum was not easily halted. During a release to attend to his brother's funeral, Nuño Pérez escaped, and immediately assumed unrivaled prominence at court.[53] To their enemies, the Laras must have seemed like a Hydra: no sooner had one ghastly head of the family been removed than others appeared in its stead. Interestingly, it was a brother, rather than a son, who took Manrique's place;[54]

in an age before transmission of land through primogeniture reached its full development, fraternal bonds would be important again and again. Just as Pedro and Rodrigo González had dominated Castile early in the 1120s, so Pedro's three children dominated in the 1160s.

Nuño Pérez's supremacy in the kingdom after Manrique's death was widely recognized. On 1 March 1165, Pope Alexander III addressed him directly, informing him that since the excommunicated bishop of Osma had not appeared before him, the bishop should be replaced; Don Nuño was evidently perceived as the de facto ruler, and sole regent, of the kingdom.[55] He confirmed royal diplomas frequently from the beginning of the reign until his death, appearing high in the lists of witnesses, and from 1162 onward enjoyed the status of count.[56] He retained his elevated position as "administrator of the king's affairs" into the 1170s; and from the beginning of 1168, the diplomas formulaically describe him as performing this role faithfully.[57] Most striking of all is a reference to Nuño Pérez in 1174–1175 as "tenant of the court of King Alfonso," a term which may be unique in the history of Castile.[58] The *Crónica Latina de los reyes de Castilla* states that through their control of the king, Manrique and Nuño had each attempted to subordinate all other considerations to their own honor and self-interest.[59] This view is not entirely without foundation: Nuño enjoyed a substantial proportion of his tenancies in these years, and was also able to ensure an important role for his eldest son, Fernando Núñez (d. 1219), who, rather unusually, appears with the title of count during his father's own lifetime.[60]

Did any of Nuño's tenancies derive from independent, patrimonial strength? In a few cases, this is possible, and the family's territorial influence does seem rather more substantial in this period than it had been a generation or two earlier. Characteristically for the twelfth century, Nuño Pérez's lands were extremely diffuse (see Map 6). He was lord of Gama on the north coast;[61] Sarracín, south of Burgos, which he granted to the monastery of Arlanza in exchange for Huérmeces, northwest of Molina;[62] Alcabón and Aceca, near Toledo;[63] and some houses in Toledo itself.[64] But the correlation between patrimony and tenancies occurs in the area near the Leonese border. It was here, for example, that he founded the hospital of Puente Itero.[65] In this area, he also possessed land in Zorita and Perales;[66] Cisneros and Villela;[67] and,

6. Nuño Pérez (d. 1177)

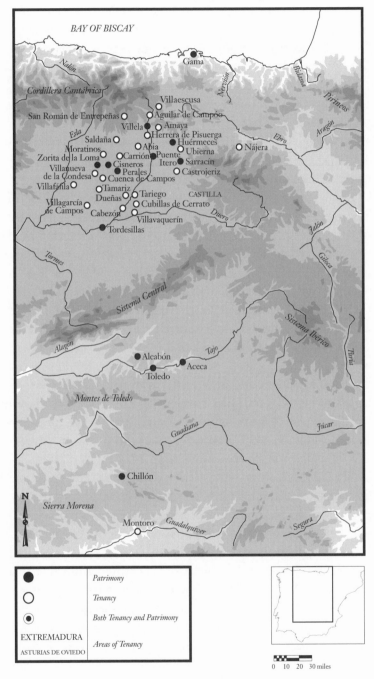

BAY OF BISCAY

Cordillera Cantábrica

Nalón

Norbón

Bidasoa

Pirineos

Gama

Villaescusa

San Román de Entrepeñas

Aguilar de Campóo

Villela

Amaya

Herrera de Pisuerga

Aragón

Ebro

Esla

Saldaña

Abia

Huérmeces

Nájera

Moratinos

Ubierna

Zorita de la Loma

Carrión

Puente

Villanueva de la Condesa

Cisneros

Itero

Sarracín

Perales

Castrojeriz

Villafáfila

Cuenca de Campos

Tamariz

Tariego

CASTILLA

Villagarcía de Campos

Dueñas

Cubillas de Cerrato

Duero

Cabezón

Villavaquerín

Jalón

Tordesillas

Giboca

Tormes

Sistema Ibérico

Sistema Central

Turia

Alagón

Toria

Alcabón

Tajo

Aceca

Toledo

Montes de Toledo

Júcar

Guadiana

Chillón

N

Sierra Morena

Montoro

Guadalquivir

Segura

●	Patrimony
○	Tenancy
◉	Both Tenancy and Patrimony
EXTREMADURA	Areas of Tenancy
ASTURIAS DE OVIEDO	

0   10   20   30 miles

farther south in the borderlands, several places near Tordesillas.[68] Some
of these properties may have been inherited from his father, Pedro
González, who had also been influential in this area, and again it is possible that the location of Nuño's tenancies reflected this patrimonial
pattern. But causal connections are hard to prove; it is also conceivable
that some of the properties had been acquired because of a reverse process, a result of his influence as a tenant in this region. Patrimony
might accrue directly from royal favor, as in the case of Chillón, valuable for its mercury mines, which he received in a grant from Alfonso
VIII "for the many great services that you, Count Nuño, have both de-
votedly and faithfully shown to me."[69]

The question about patrimonial power is also worth asking in the
context of Pedro Rodríguez (d. 1183), who as son of Count Rodrigo
González was usually dubbed *filius comitis*.[70] Pedro seems to have been
the inheritor of his father's moderate patrimonial interests in northern Castile (see Map 7). He had properties to the east of the bay of
Santander;[71] further inland, in a number of places close to Villarcayo;[72]
and, finally, in Huérmeces.[73] It is true that his tenancies—Bureba,
Castilla la Vieja, and Nájera—were also located toward the north.
However, the geographical correlation is close only in very broad, regional terms. There is even less of a correlation in the case of his
nephew, Pedro Manrique (see Map 8). In the old Castilian heartland,
Pedro Manrique (d. 1202) had a variety of properties: some houses in
Burgos;[74] some possessions in nearby Los Ausines;[75] and, further to the
south, in Cogolludo and Carabanchel, along with two properties near
Toledo which he sold to the cathedral in 1177.[76] On the basis of this
and other sales, at least two historians have made the extrapolation that
he was not a good administrator, although it is equally possible that he
simply viewed his patrimony as the source of a small, quick profit.[77]
Meanwhile, he was entrusted with important frontier tenancies along a
line stretching from Lara and San Esteban, through Atienza and the
Transierra, to Toledo and Cuenca. It is admittedly possible that his
possessions in Molina made him a natural choice to serve this leading
role on the southeastern frontier. However, apart from Molina itself his
patrimonial possessions in this region are less than spectacular.[78] We
should associate his tenancies largely with the influence of his father,
Manrique, who had paved the way for the son's own success at court.[79]

The Laras' preeminence in the kingdom was certainly not unchal-

7. Pedro Rodríguez (d. 1183)

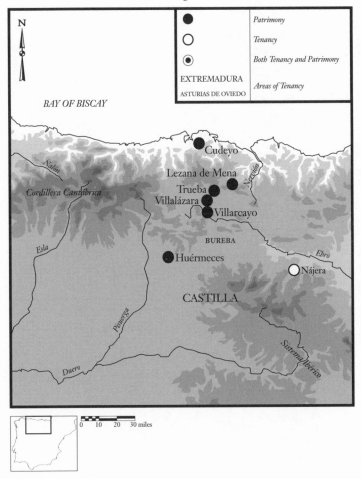

lenged: Nuño Pérez faced rebellions by the Castros in 1167 and again in 1169. On the second occasion, during an attempt to regain control of castles held by the Castros, he was captured at Zorita and imprisoned before being released as a result of a Castilian counter-offensive. Earlier, in 1165, Fernando II of León had also renewed hostilities. After reaching peace with the Portuguese, he attacked the Castilians, who were led by Nuño Pérez, pursuing them to Medina de Rioseco, where he laid siege. Once again (for at least the fourth time in his life), Nuño was imprisoned, and once more he barely escaped.[80] However, after the Castilians recaptured Toledo from a Leonese garrison in 1166, the

8. Pedro Manrique (d. 1202)

Legend:
- ● Patrimony
- ○ Tenancy
- ◉ Both Tenancy and Patrimony

Areas of Tenancy

EXTREMADURA
ASTURIAS DE OVIEDO

0 10 20 30 miles

Map labels:

MEDITERRANEAN SEA

BAY OF BISCAY

ASTURIAS DE OVIEDO

EXTREMADURA

TRANSIERRA

Narbonne

Ter, Llobregat, Segre, Cordillera Costero-Catalana, Cinca, Pirineos, Gállego, Aragón, Ebro, Bidasoa, Navelión

Jalón, Giloca, Medinaceli, Molina, Sistema Ibérico, Turia, Cañete, Cuenca, Tragacete, Bonilla, Bérbeta, Hita, Cogolludo, Arienza, Huete, Valtablado, Carabanchel, Barciles

Burgos, Los Ausines, Lara, Alcózar, Osma, Hontoria de la Cantera, San Esteban de Gormaz

Pisuerga, Duero, Dueñas, Cabezón, Toro, Esla, Tormes, Salamanca, Sistema Central, Añover de Tajo, Toledo, Montes de Toledo, Tajo

Babia, Luna, León, Cordillera Cantábrica, Nalón, Sil, Montes de León, Ciudad Rodrigo

N

Leonese ceased to be a serious menace; during the early 1170s, before his death at the siege of Cuenca (1177), Nuño Pérez even reappeared as a witness of Leonese royal diplomas.[81] The stage was set for the betrothal of his widow, Teresa, to Fernando II himself, in 1178, and a donation by the Leonese king to his intended bride—remarkably enough, given for the "good services" he had received from Teresa and her husband.[82] Fernando II had evidently come to recognize that opposition to the Laras within Castile was not broad enough or deep enough to support his intervention.

Opposition, for now, was limited for at least two reasons. First, the webs of personal power relations which were spun at the royal court tended to produce a factional pursuit of interests and therefore factional opposition; this contrasted with the broader type of political association which would emerge in the thirteenth century. Noble alliances extending beyond the family or a restricted geographic orbit appear to have been rare in the twelfth century. In practical terms, this meant that Nuño Pérez was facing an easily isolated, and easily defeated, enemy. Second, he does not appear to have pursued his own interests with quite the reckless abandon that would characterize the Laras in the early thirteenth century. The rival Haro family remained prominent at court during the years of Lara domination, and two Lara sons even married Haro daughters.[83] The family's ascendancy would remain stable as long as it avoided exclusivity–and not a moment longer.

3

A Zenith and a Nadir

*I*N THE MUSEUM OF MEDIEVAL FABRICS, in the mon-
astery of Las Huelgas near Burgos, a cream-colored bonnet is on dis-
play, embroidered with dozens of russet-colored cauldrons. It dates
from the early thirteenth century and is almost perfectly preserved,
having been sealed for centuries in the raised stone tomb of Enrique I
of Castile (reigned 1214–1217). But the bonnet was not Enrique's. It is
thought instead to have belonged to Álvaro Núñez de Lara, and the
cauldrons may be the earliest representation of the family's heraldic
arms.[1] Fifteen-year-old Enrique had died suddenly, in the custody of
Álvaro Núñez, who was head of the family in the first two decades of
the century. The presence of the bonnet in the young king's tomb is a
graphic illustration of the Laras' political dominance at this stage; and
in a sense, it is also a symbol of the disaster that was to befall them. In
the aftermath of Enrique's death, the family would be flung from power
by a wave of domestic opposition, defeated in battle, and forced to seek
refuge in the court of León.

A generation earlier, the fate of the Laras could not possibly have
been foreseen. An illustrious marriage between Pedro Manrique de
Lara and the *infanta* Sancha Garcés of Navarre (1165) had mingled the
blood of the family with that of El Cid himself; Sancha was the hero's
great-granddaughter.[2] Indeed, it has been suggested that many features
of the *Poema de Mio Cid*, which probably dates from the late twelfth
or early thirteenth century, bear the imprint of a pro-Lara agenda.
There is, for example, the vilification of the *infantes* of Carrión (ances-

tors of the rival Castros) and the disproportionate emphasis on a lord of Molina; the poem may even have been written by a member of the Laras' retinue, with the aim of advancing the family's position.[3] It is also possible that, as Simon Barton has argued, the poem can be read as a monarchical response to defections by Castilian nobles to the crown of León, and as an attempt to reinforce awareness of the rights and obligations of vassalage.[4] The Laras would certainly be among those who sought advantage in the dynastic division of Castile and León. After all, in both kingdoms, the power of the nobility was still predicated upon the strength of the crown. There was never a time in the late twelfth century when the Laras were not represented at the two royal courts, and rarely a moment when members of the family did not hold important tenancies.

The remarriage of Teresa, Nuño Pérez's widow, to Fernando II in 1178 meant that the couple's sons had effectively become adopted children of the Leonese monarch.[5] Hand-in-glove with the king, they gained prestige accordingly.[6] In this respect, as in so many others, they were excelling at a changing game; many of the Castilian élite gravitated toward León in the later twelfth century, as the radius of noble activity increased.[7] The rotation of tenancies was exceptionally pronounced in León, where these positions were becoming more widely used as instruments of royal authority.[8] To find a tenancy lasting more than a few years is unusual.[9] In general, the delegation of power embodied in the Leonese system of tenancies was carefully controlled by the monarchy, and there was markedly less continuity in tenancies than in the nonjurisdictional offices of *alférez* and *mayordomo*. But for the Laras, this was extremely good news. As Gonzalo Núñez (d. 1225) discovered to his advantage, personal access meant political reward;[10] he was showered with tenancies out of all proportion to the family's patrimonies in the kingdom.[11] He made far more appearances at the court of León than his brothers, was at his stepfather's side as early as the spring of 1180, and repeatedly surfaces in Leonese documentation in the following years.[12] In the mid-1180s, his uncle Pedro Manrique briefly joined him.[13] Gonzalo then returned to Castile in the mid-1190s and was again almost entirely absent between 1200 and 1204, but he was back in León for most of the next decade.[14] Accordingly, his tenancies brought a degree of territorial power in Galicia and León that was unprecedented and unrepeated in the family's history (see Map 9).[15]

As for Castile, the torch of courtly influence was carried first by

9. Gonzalo Núñez (d. 1225)

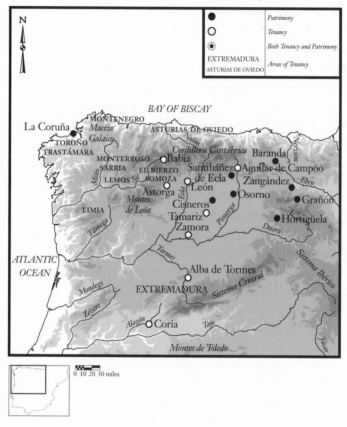

the elderly Pedro Rodríguez and his nephews Pedro Manrique and Fernando Núñez, both of whom were established courtiers.[16] During the 1190s, Pedro Manrique was joined by his younger son, Rodrigo Pérez, who became *merino mayor*.[17] Meanwhile, Fernando Núñez continued to witness royal diplomas through the turn of the century before becoming virtually a permanent fixture late in the reign;[18] he also served a number of terms as royal *alférez*.[19] The arrival of his younger brothers Gonzalo and Álvaro further reinforced his family's position. Gonzalo Núñez was more active in the kingdom of León, but was intermittently present at the Castilian court.[20] Finally, Álvaro Núñez (d. 1218), the last of the brothers to arrive at court, would establish the firmest foothold of all. After 1196, he appeared almost continuously as either a witness to royal diplomas or as the royal *alférez*.[21]

As in earlier generations, it is hard to find evidence that the Laras' strength as landowners was great enough to have dictated this ascendancy, though like many other noble families of the twelfth century they were gradually expanding their territorial and jurisdictional authority. Their lands remained fragmented, because patterns of partible inheritance were still strong.[22] The evidence for patrimony is strongest for the eldest brother, Fernando Núñez (see Map 10). Fernando had properties to the east of Santander, which he granted to the order of Santiago with the castle of Carabanchel.[23] He also had interests in Berlanga de Duero.[24] Many of his other properties seem to have been concentrated within a fifty-mile radius of Burgos, a fact that may reflect a concerted effort to consolidate territorial strength there.[25] Even so, much of the relevant evidence is indirect. For instance, his daughters Sancha and Teresa would make a large number of land sales to the bishopric of Burgos in the 1240s;[26] and his wife likewise made a substantial grant of property near Burgos (property that may also have belonged to her husband) to the cathedral.[27] Fernando's son Álvaro Fernández also alienated property in this region, granting a church in Boadilla del Camino to the bishop of Palencia.[28] There is less evidence of patrimony for the two younger brothers, Álvaro and Gonzalo Núñez. In addition to some shared properties—the result of partible inheritance—in the upper Ebro valley and in Tamariz, Álvaro Núñez (Map 11) held the town of Alhambra; Carcedo de Bureba;[29] Ribarredonda (possibly the place of that name just south of Medinaceli);[30] and Castroverde de Campos.[31] Gonzalo's properties included Grañón, Santibáñez de Ecla, Osorno, and some land in Cisneros.[32]

Turning briefly to a different branch of the family, the patrimony of Nuño Sánchez was more impressive. Even before he acquired the viscounties of Fenollet and Perapertusa (in 1226), he had the counties of Roussillon, Cerdaña, Conflent, and Vallespir—a major patrimonial base.[33] But like Pedro Manrique's lordship of Narbonne, they had negligible importance for Castilian affairs. Nuño Sánchez had inherited Narbonne by 1192. He spent most of the rest of the year there, but evidently had no great interest in personal control of it: in 1194, he granted it to his eldest son, Aimerico.[34] The history of Narbonne was henceforth almost entirely separate from the history of the Lara family. Although it was closer to the Castilian heartland than (for instance) Galicia, one has a sense that it was perceived almost as another world:

10. Fernando Núñez (d. 1219)

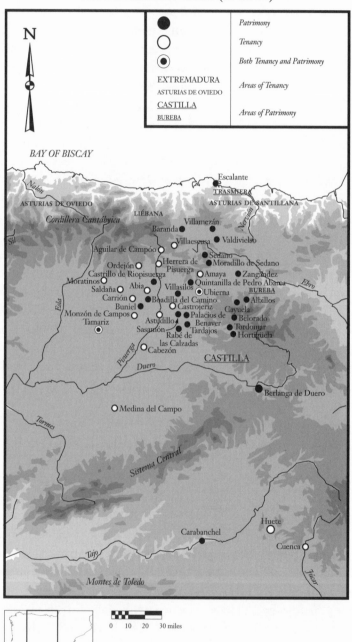

●	Patrimony
○	Tenancy
◉	Both Tenancy and Patrimony
EXTREMADURA ASTURIAS DE OVIEDO	Areas of Tenancy
<u>CASTILLA</u> BUREBA	Areas of Patrimony

N

BAY OF BISCAY

Escalante
TRASMIERA
ASTURIAS DE OVIEDO   ASTURIAS DE SANTILLANA
Cordillera Cantábrica   LIÉBANA
Natón
Nervión

Villamezán
Baranda
Villaescusa   Valdivielso
Aguilar de Campóo   Sedano
Herrera de   Moradillo de Sedano
Ordejón   Pisuerga
Castrillo de Riopisuerga   Amaya   Zangández
Moratinos   Quintanilla de Pedro Abarca
Saldaña   Abia   Villasilos   Ubierna   BUREBA
Carrión   Albillos
Buniel   Boadilla del Camino   Castrojeriz
Monzón de Campos   Palacios de   Cayuela
Tamariz   Astudillo   Benaver   Belorado
Sasamón   Tardajos   Tordomar
Rabé de   Hortigüela
las Calzadas
Cabezón

Sil
Esla
Pisuerga
Ebro

CASTILLA

Duero

Berlanga de Duero

Medina del Campo

Tormes

Sistema Central

Huete
Carabanchel
Cuenca
Tajo
Júcar

Montes de Toledo

0   10   20   30 miles

11. Álvaro Núñez (d. 1218)

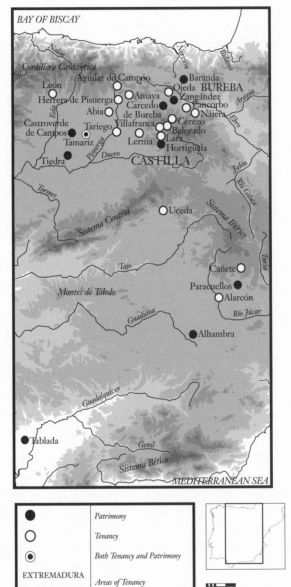

BAY OF BISCAY

Cordillera Cantábrica

León

Aguilar de Campóo

Baranda

Ojeda BUREBA

Herrera de Pisuerga

Amaya

Zangández

Pancorbo

Abia

Carcedo de Bureba

Nájera

Castroverde de Campos

Tariego

Villafranca

Cerezo

Belorado

Tamariz

Lerma

Lara

Tiedra

Hortigüela

CASTILLA

Uceda

Cañete

Paracuellos

Alarcón

Alhambra

Tablada

MEDITERRANEAN SEA

● Patrimony

○ Tenancy

◉ Both Tenancy and Patrimony

EXTREMADURA
ASTURIAS DE OVIEDO

Areas of Tenancy

0 10 20 30 miles

there is none of the cultural or political proximity which existed between Castile and the kingdom of León. In Castile itself, the Laras were simply not thinking in terms of grand patrimonial strategy at this stage. Molina, the jewel of Pedro Manrique's possessions after his father's death, never played as crucial a role for the family in the twelfth century as it would in the late thirteenth century. At the end of 1177, he and his second wife donated to the Order of Calatrava their lands, windmills, houses, and vineyards in Albaladejo, Cañete, and Cuenca.[35] A century later, this would be unthinkable: Cañete would be at the center of determined attempts by the Laras to develop a power base on the southeastern frontier. Clearly, Pedro Manrique's concerns were very different. It may be that his properties in Albaladejo and Cuenca were small, but both towns lay along this frontier, and there seems to have been no concerted effort to develop a major patrimony here.[36]

The situation is expressed neatly by Hilda Grassotti, who reflects on the idea that the thirteenth-century chronicler Rodrigo Jiménez de Rada may have been the first Castilian magnate, ecclesiastical or lay, to have used Jewish fiscal agents in the administration of his domains. Neither the Haros nor the Castros nor the Laras, she writes, had yet acquired the kind of estates in full ownership that would have made these officials necessary, and only in the early fourteenth century would the use of Jews in estate administration become frequent. "I tend to believe that these great lords were governors of districts—that is to say, *tenentes* or *seniores civitatum*—more than great proprietors."[37]

For now, access to the king, and to the offices and tenancies that he distributed, continued to be the basis of power. Gonzalo Núñez's fleeting presence in Castile (1195–1197) was almost immediately rewarded with the tenancy of Aguilar. Pedro Manrique held at least five Castilian tenancies in the late twelfth century, although this is a smaller number than one might expect given his long presence at court, possibly because his career largely predated the Laras' greatest influence there. The fact that his father had died very early in the reign, and had presumably been less of a formative influence on the young king than Nuño Pérez, may also have diminished his power at court relative to that of his cousins Fernando and Álvaro Núñez. Fernando Núñez, for instance, repeatedly appears with tenancies that had previously been held by his father (Nuño Pérez): Abia, Amaya, Cabezón, Castrojeriz, Herrera de Pisuerga, Moratinos, and Saldaña. It is even possible that in

Amaya and perhaps Abia, we are seeing a process of informal patrimonialization, a process that was fairly well advanced by the end of
the century.[38] Certainly, the good graces of the king remained vital, and
the chronology of Fernando's tenancies corresponds closely to his presence at court. It may be significant that some of his tenancies—like
Aguilar, Amaya, Castrojeriz, Herrera, Ordejón, and Ubierna—were located in the same radius around Burgos in which many of his patrimonies were concentrated. However, others—such as Abia, Cabezón,
Carrión, Monzón, Saldaña, and Moratinos—were in areas where there
does not seem to have been any equivalent patrimonial concentration.
The king retained control of the situation, rather than merely accom-
modating to it, and like the king of León he rotated tenancies with remarkable rapidity.[39] By the end of the reign, Álvaro Núñez above all
was relishing his role as a royal favorite. On 31 October 1212, in the aftermath of the great crusading victory over the Almohads at Las Navas
de Tolosa, Alfonso VIII granted the town of Castroverde to "Álvaro
Núñez, my beloved and faithful vassal, . . . in return for the many voluntary services which you have given to me and faithfully performed,
and have equally striven to perform every day until now; and furthermore in return for the service, which should be particularly com-
mended, which you rendered me on the field of battle when you held
my banner like a mighty man."[40]

The king's gratitude is easy to understand. If, from the perspective of
the Christian kingdoms, the victory at Las Navas had been the most
glorious in the history of the *reconquista*, crushing the dangers posed
by the fundamentalist Almohads, from a royal perspective it was also
an immense political boon. An earlier military catastrophe at Alarcos
in Castilla la Mancha (1195) and the slow pace of expansion under
Alfonso VIII had limited the property and tenancies which were avail-
able for redistribution to the nobility, and thus threatened the delicate
balance of power. The battle of Las Navas warded off this threat, so
that contemporaries might well have felt they were seeing the old symbiosis between crown and nobility acquire a new lease on life.[41] For
now, the balance of power was stable, and the Laras were riding high
on the success of the Castilian king.

YET IN THE SHORT, unhappy, and rather exhilarating reign of Enrique I (1214–1217), this balance was thoroughly upset. Following the

old king's death in October 1214 and that of his queen soon after, the regency fell to his elder sister. Berenguela, as queen of Alfonso IX of León (reigned 1188–1230), had been active in Leonese affairs before the marriage was dissolved by the papacy on the grounds of consanguinity, and now took on the pivotal role in the governance of Castile.[42] But her regency brought disproportionate influence to the bishop of Palencia and the archbishop of Toledo, and provoked indignation among the magnates: "a majority of the barons agreed that Álvaro Núñez should be the king's regent and should undertake the care of the kingdom."[43] In turn, the Laras, who had been gathering momentum rapidly under Alfonso VIII, now used their tutelage of the adolescent king to develop an exceptional ascendancy in Castile. As they did so, they gradually excluded other aristocratic families from their "natural" influence and from the tenancies that traditionally corresponded to this influence, further destabilizing the political situation. There can be little question of the family's ambitions. As early as April 1215, shortly after obtaining custody of the king, Álvaro Núñez was styling himself "count."[44] Equally, the *Crónica latina* draws a direct connection between the adoption of this title by his brother Gonzalo the following year and worsening conditions in Castile.[45]

At the same time, these actions in themselves were hardly extraordinary, and there are grounds for suspecting that the sins of the Laras have been considerably exaggerated. It is, to say the least, unfortunate that our understanding of these events is based on the account by the archbishop whose political preeminence was ended by the Lara family. Rodrigo Jiménez de Rada's *De rebus Hispaniae* is the almost exclusive source for the relevant chapters of the *Primera crónica general*, and in both narratives Álvaro Núñez de Lara emerges as the two-dimensional villain of the piece. The chronicles have flooded a good deal of modern historiography with their royalist sympathies, and there are plenty of reasons for being skeptical. In the first place, Peter Linehan has drawn attention to the Toledan agenda in the archbishop's chronicle, and to the propagandistic manipulation of the past that permeates it. His portrait of Jiménez de Rada is memorable. "Here was an archbishop with a warrior's eye to the main chance, shrewdly appreciative of the lie of the land, a historian for whom history *was* warfare, a master of camouflage, the perfect judge of the feint, connoisseur of the understatement, unblinking purveyor of the inconceivable."[46] Jiménez's determination to promote the interests of Toledo over Santiago and Seville is now as clear as his general aggrandizement of the crown.[47] But the archbishop also had a specific reason to despise the Lara family. In the later years of Alfonso VIII's reign, Jiménez had been audaciously expanding the temporal possessions of the see of Toledo, and in 1214 Berenguela had granted him jurisdiction over the territory surrounding the castle of Milagro. After the end of her regency, however, he received no further royal favors, and he remained on the political sidelines for the rest of the reign.[48] We should therefore be extremely wary of his description of the Edenic social harmony that allegedly flourished under the regency in which he had been instrumental, as well as the account in the *Primera crónica general* which is derived from it. Under Berenguela, he writes, "both the poor and the rich, both the clerics and the laymen, were all well protected in their estates, as in the time of King Alfonso, her father, until the turbulence of the *ricos hombres* placed discord and envy in this situation."[49]

What is important to note here is the implication that, in fact, a rather broad segment of the aristocracy was ill at ease with Berenguela's regency. After Álvaro Núñez gained custody of the king, he would retain the official support of a majority of the nobility, as well as the episcopate and the cities, for the rest of the reign. Some of these supporters would later need to invent what has been termed an *antilarista* history, a retrospective fiction of opposition to the Laras. Although his ambitions did alienate a number of nobles, Álvaro Núñez's forces were always more numerous than his opponents' during Enrique's reign; and even after the king died, the cities of Castilian Extremadura (Segovia, Ávila, Coca) remained loyal to Álvaro.[50] But the royalist chronicles clearly have an interest in downplaying any indication that the Laras enjoyed such widespread support. Jiménez de Rada's account of the way in which the early regency was ended plays down any impression of a consensus among the nobility: "[The Lara brothers] then began to fight to have the guardianship of the child-king, because if they had it they would be able to satiate the evil desires they had in their hearts against those who wished them evil, as their father had done in the childhood of King Alfonso, the father of this king, Enrique."[51]

The chronicler relates how in April 1215 Berenguela reluctantly ceded tutelage to Álvaro Núñez de Lara, stating that she did so only under pressure from the original guardian—a knight from Palencia—

who had been bribed by Don Álvaro with the offer of the small town of Tablada. One effect of this story is to undermine the impact of various indications that Álvaro Núñez was representative of a substantial sector of the nobility, but Jiménez de Rada cannot manage to conceal this entirely. Berenguela, he states, "had Álvaro Núñez and all the other great men of Castile come before her, and had them all swear that, unless they had her consent, they would not take land from anyone nor give land away, nor act against any neighbor, nor impose any tax in any part of the kingdom; and they all swore this and did homage there to Queen Berenguela."[52]

If we are to believe Jiménez de Rada, Álvaro Núñez then immediately embarked on a course of unmitigated evil, starting civil conflicts, exiling hidalgos, humbling grandees, imposing taxes on the rich, the monastic orders, and the church, and using the profits for his own ends.[53] It is just about possible that all of this is true; but the fact that each of Álvaro Núñez's sins neatly contradicts the specific terms of agreement with Berenguela again raises suspicion. There is one independent piece of evidence corroborating part of the story: on 15 February 1216, Don Álvaro issued an apology for his actions toward the church, promising never again to take *tercias* (shares of the ecclesiastical tithes) or to advise that they should be imposed.[54] But in view of the crisis which was to erupt in the reign of Alfonso X (1252–1284), when the church would clash repeatedly with the Learned King over the ecclesiastical taxes imposed to fund his imperial dreams, not even this policy seems inherently negative. It might well be interpreted as a structural conflict between secular and religious authorities. The real reason for secular opposition to Álvaro Núñez was the exclusion of influential aristocrats from the royal court. One case in point is Gonzalo Rodríguez Girón, who in 1216 was dislodged from the office of *mayordomo*, which he had held for eighteen years.[55] The tendency toward exclusion was later extended: the king ceased summoning to the Cortes either Queen Berenguela herself or her aristocratic supporters— Gonzalo Rodríguez, of course, but also Lope Díaz de Haro, Álvaro Díaz de Cameros, and Alfonso Téllez de Meneses, as well as Rodrigo Jiménez, archbishop of Toledo.[56] It was this policy which would now drive the country into civil war.

War seemed likely as early as the spring of 1216. In the diplomas, Álvaro Núñez appears as "regent of the whole land," and malcontents were increasingly defecting to Queen Berenguela; in May, her forces seized the castle of Autillo.[57] Tension brewed for a year, after which the situation deteriorated further: Gonzalo Rodríguez Girón and the Téllez family left the court. In April 1217 Álvaro Núñez, still styling himself "king's regent," launched a military campaign against the rebels.[58] This campaign was aimed at the lands of the Téllez family and the Girones, especially Campos and the castle of Autillo; the siege of this castle was lifted only when Álvaro Núñez heard that Alfonso IX of León (Queen Berenguela's husband) was planning to come to its aid.[59] Álvaro Núñez's relationship with the Leonese had long been strained. In 1209, he had taken part in military action against León;[60] and ever since Queen Berenguela and her son, Fernando, had left for the Leonese court in the spring of 1215, when Álvaro became regent in Castile, the relationship looked bleaker than ever. Álvaro's position rested almost entirely upon his personal access to the Castilian king, Enrique I, and upon Enrique's political strength. The grant of the town of Alhambra, in January 1217, was emblematic of the rewards he continued to reap.[61] But now disaster struck. In May, Don Álvaro arrived with Enrique I's entourage in the city of Palencia. Enrique was fifteen years old. While playing with some other young men of his age, so the chronicles tell us, he was struck on the head by a tile or rock accidentally dislodged from a roof by one of his friends; a few days later, after an unsuccessful and excruciating operation, he died.[62] His death brought an abrupt and total fall from power for the Laras, initiating a period of decline that would last until the middle of the century. In one fell swoop, it removed the fragile foundation of the family's hegemony: control of the king's person. For their opponents this was, to say the very least, extraordinarily fortunate.

Was the hand of fortune guided by Berenguela and her followers? The evidence is circumstantial, but there are enough curiosities surrounding the king's death to make the question worth asking. Quite apart from Berenguela's suspiciously good luck, the improbability of the boy's death, and the context of a civil war which had already begun to escalate, it is interesting that she is said to have found out about her brother's death almost instantly, despite the best efforts of Álvaro Núñez to hush up the affair.[63] At the very least, one might suspect the presence of spies. Jiménez de Rada himself in fact makes it clear that she had sent a spy on a previous occasion, allegedly to check on the condition of her brother.[64] This is one of a number of curious details even in a chronicle that is overwhelmingly favorable toward Berenguela and Fernando. Jiménez de Rada also claims, in the same passage, that Álvaro Núñez responded by having a letter forged, with the Queen's name and seal, stating that she planned to have the young king poisoned because Enrique hated her. The chronicle claims that the letter was indeed proven to be a forgery, and that the resulting anger of the people forced Álvaro to leave the archbishopric of Toledo. However, in view of the extraordinarily strong prejudices of this text, we should surely consider it a possibility that the letter was genuine. It may also be significant that the death took place in the immediate context of determined attempts by Álvaro Núñez de Lara to arrange a marriage between Enrique and the *infanta* Sancha, daughter of Alfonso IX of León. Under the terms of this alliance, Enrique, and not the sons of Berenguela, would have become heir to the kingdom of León.[65] Álvaro's efforts to arrange a Leonese marriage proved unsuccessful, but the negotiations do seem to have catalyzed a rapprochement with King Alfonso. Tensions were still high in the spring of 1217 because of Alfonso's support of Berenguela in her opposition to the Laras; but after reaching agreement with Alfonso in May, Álvaro Núñez became his *mayordomo*.[66] For both Enrique and the Laras, the prospect of a reunification of Castile and León under their aegis was a massive coup. Among their opponents, it would have provoked fear and outrage.

The Portuguese *Crónica geral de Espanha de 1344*, one of the very few sources sympathetic to the Laras, identifies the person who dropped or threw the tile (or rock): Iñigo de Mendoza.[67] The same identification is made in an earlier manuscript in the Biblioteca Nacional, which tersely describes how Enrique "died in Palencia from a tile which Iñigo de Mendoza threw on his head."[68] There was indeed an Iñigo de Mendoza present in the royal court a few months before Enrique's death; he witnessed a number of royal privileges granted in the spring of 1217.[69] Intriguingly, the Mendozas were related to the Haros, archenemies of the Laras.[70] For this reason, one may be skeptical of the view that the general silence in the chronicles, on the subject of the young man, is due simply to forgetfulness and inertia.[71] Still, if Iñigo was an intentional regicide, it does not seem that he was conspicuously rewarded for his actions by the new king, Fernando III; and the Portuguese chronicle is not always reliable.[72] While questions remain about the cause of

Enrique's death, any speculation about assassination must be very ten-tative. The consequence is far clearer: a total and abrupt end to the Lara family's influence at the court of Castile.

Increasingly desperate, having attempted fruitlessly to negotiate cus-tody of the young king Fernando, Álvaro Núñez turned for assistance to the king of León, with whom he had begun to establish an unexpect-edly cordial relationship. In an astonishing volte-face, Alfonso IX, who had been vigorously supporting Berenguela and Fernando III earlier in the year, began to build fortifications and launch military incursions against them; Jiménez de Rada places the blame squarely on the shoul-ders of Álvaro Núñez.[73] In any case, Leonese military intervention was ineffective. In the face of stiff resistance, Alfonso IX abandoned the at-tempt to capture Burgos and left the Laras to fend for themselves. The almost immediate result was the capture of Lara and Lerma, which had been held by Álvaro Núñez;[74] and on 20 September 1217, Álvaro was captured. He was imprisoned at Valladolid, and put to torture, only narrowly escaping execution, before being ordered to surrender his castles.[75] Once released, early in 1218, he resumed resistance alongside his brother Fernando, who had temporarily been forced to surrender his castles of Castrojeriz and Monzón before receiving them back as a vassal of the new king; but the brothers achieved little, and returned to the Leonese court.[76] Álvaro appears to have been able to persuade Alfonso IX to send forces into Castile a second time, but when the monarchs reached agreement, he was left fatally isolated.[77]

There are two accounts of Álvaro Núñez's death at Castrejón, a vil-lage west of Medina del Campo, where he had arrived in armed pursuit of his enemies Gonzalo Rodríguez Girón and Lope Díaz de Haro. Ac-cording to the archbishop of Toledo, he fell mortally sick while arm-ing himself for battle; for Jiménez de Rada, it must have seemed rhe-torically fitting that Don Álvaro should die in an act of ignominious treachery.[78] But there is a different cadence to the second account. Ac-cording to the more sympathetic *Crónica geral de Espanha de 1344*, Álvaro Núñez was struck dead by a projectile thrown from a city wall. If this tale is accurate, he had met a fate curiously reminiscent of that of King Enrique, whose reign had been his apogee.[79] His brothers did not long survive him, though León continued to provide sanctuary and even patronage for a while.[80] The peace of Toro (26 August 1218) be-tween Alfonso IX and his son, Fernando III of Castile, was a severe setback. It stipulated that Alfonso would not receive Gonzalo or Fernando Núñez in the kingdom of León until Christmas that year, and would expel them if they so much as set foot in León.[81] By February the two brothers were at Alfonso's side once more;[82] and Gonzalo was still in the entourage of the king of León in June.[83] But they appear to have outstayed their welcome, perhaps because of a renewed accord between the Castilian and Leonese kings. Fernando left the kingdom, and entered the service of the king of Morocco; he soon fell mortally sick, joining the Order of Saint John shortly before his death.[84] His body was brought back to Castile and buried at the hospital of Itero de la Vega, which his parents had founded.[85] In the autumn of 1221, Gonzalo, probably having instigated a rebellion by Gonzalo Pérez Manrique, also departed for Moorish territory.[86] He returned to the Castilian court in June 1224, but the reconciliation was brief. Leaving again for al-Andalus, he died the next year, in exile like his brother Fernando before him; his body was brought to Castile to be interred by the Knights Templar.[87] Within the space of half a dozen years, all three brothers had been buried; and the power of the Laras had apparently been laid to rest. Yet they would rise again within a generation, aspiring to a new territorial autonomy allowing them greater stability and more independence from the whims of courtly favor.

II

CONFRONTATION

4

The Road to Rebellion

𝒯HE MID-THIRTEENTH CENTURY is a luminous period in the mythology of Spanish history. It is an age of resplendent reconquests, of the capture of Córdoba and Seville; the age of a saint-king, San Fernando, canonized for his crusades in Andalucía; and the age of the most cultured of medieval rulers, Alfonso *el Sabio*. Finally, it is perceived as an era in which the crown gained the upper hand over its habitually turbulent nobles. But this view deserves closer examination. "Turbulence" has customarily been seen as the almost hereditary failing of a single element in medieval society: a uniquely self-interested nobility. Modern liberalism rightly discourages us from using the word to describe popular unrest, while a faith in the rise of the modern state makes it appear incongruous to speak of a turbulent monarchy. Yet our sense of a single, abstract, sovereign power with a monopoly on legitimate violence was foreign to the Middle Ages. Even the laws of King Alfonso's *Siete partidas*, despite their general tendency to exalt the power of the king, enshrined the right of the nobility to wage war against the king under certain conditions.[1] In fact, as Otto Brunner has explained in the context of the medieval Germanic lands, there was felt to be a multiplicity of powers enjoying the right to autonomous political action, acting if necessary against superior powers. "Historians, however, stand peculiarly helpless before these facts, because they approach them presupposing the modern state. . . . They allow only powers ostensibly representing 'the state' to act from 'political' motivations; the local powers, on the other hand, act out of 'greed and self-interest.'"[2]

Noble resistance in thirteenth-century Castile cannot be attributed to a moral failure unique to one estate, and still less to the personal idiosyncrasies of individuals. The dangers may be illustrated by a passage of creative genealogy in Salazar's history of the Laras. Confronted by the evidence of worsening relations between the crown and the Lara family in the late thirteenth century, Salazar mistakenly divides the great Juan Núñez I de Lara (d. 1294) into two distinct, and indeed contrasting, personae. Whereas his first Juan Núñez is characterized by "great composure in his habits, generous affability, heroic valor, and natural calmness," his second Juan Núñez (actually the same person) is "violent and repugnant."[3] In fact, the deterioration in relations between crown and nobility must be seen not as a reflection of imagined personality traits but as a reaction to the expansive assertion of royal lordship in an age of acute economic dislocation. This was, after all, an *age* of reaction, in which the lay nobility all across western Europe responded vigorously to the consolidation of the feudal monarchies; hence the noble revolts in France in 1226 and 1241.[4] The unrest that would break out in Castile during the 1270s also parallels the thirteenth-century baronial revolts in England—revolts that have enjoyed a comparatively respectable reputation. The baronial revolt of 1215, invoking pre-Angevin "ancient custom," anticipated various demands by the Castilian barons for a return to the customs of Fernando III's reign. As J. C. Holt has argued, the reaction which the Magna Carta embodied was a reaction to a more complicated system of royal government than had existed a century earlier; and in Castile, the rebellion was similarly directed against an expanding monarchical system.[5] The Laras were therefore caught up in a change far larger than themselves. Their relationship with the crown was not, of course, antithetical; the monarchy still sought the cooperation of the Laras, and of many other noble lineages, just as such families seized any chance to increase their influence over the king. But by the end of the thirteenth century, the dynamics of power had changed irrevocably. As the crown developed a certain level of administrative independence from the nobility, and as families like the Laras attempted to amass a patrimony large enough to allow them greater autonomy of their own, old bonds were stretched and snapped.

*   *   *

THE ASSERTION OF monarchical authority began in earnest in the reign of Fernando III of Castile (1217–1252), whose accession to the throne of León in 1230 would bring the definitive dynastic unification of the two kingdoms. It is particularly important to demythologize the events of this reign, since of course we are dealing with a king who was quite literally canonized. The usual dangers of accepting the royal chronicles at face value are magnified in the case of a king who has had tremendous symbolic value for generations of more recent Spanish historians. Indeed, the political use of San Fernando, which reached a peak in the Bourbon period, continued well into the Franco years (1939–1975), when he was presented as the epitome of order and strong government.[6] On its own terms, the image is quite justifiable. From the start of his reign, Fernando applied constant pressure on long-disputed frontier zones with León, Portugal, and Aragón, sought new forms of royal revenue, and developed the role of royal administrative agents, *merinos mayores*, and *merinos menores*.[7] But strong central government came at the expense of other interests, as much in the thirteenth century as in the twentieth. It was, specifically, the imposition of royal authority that gave rise to a long succession of aristocratic rebellions in this period.[8]

In the immediate aftermath of the Laras' defeat by Berenguela and Fernando in 1217–1218, there had been two rebellions, led by Rodrigo Díaz de Cameros and Gonzalo Pérez Manrique, respectively. The lord of Cameros was in all likelihood resentful about royal intrusions into his area of influence toward the eastern frontier of Castile. This apparently provoked the offer of the throne to Louis VIII of France by a group of nobles headed by Rodrigo Díaz.[9] After the rebellion, King Fernando reclaimed a number of northeastern Castilian tenancies that had belonged to the lord of Cameros, and granted many to the Haros, but, ironically, the Haros themselves would later rebel.[10] The uprising by Gonzalo Pérez in 1221, meanwhile, began with devastation of the Castilian territory bordering Molina and ended with a royal siege of Zafra. It might at first glance appear to be an individual act of desperation by a member of the defeated Lara family, and in the account by Jiménez de Rada it seems a rebellion of purposeless violence. But it should clearly be seen as an example of the gathering tension between the crown and important sectors of the nobility. Royal policy was delicately forceful, designed to reestablish control over the nobility while retaining its allegiance. Gonzalo Pérez Manrique did not lose property or tenancies as a result of his rising, remaining in possession of Molina until the end of his life.[11] But a marriage settlement was arranged whereby Gonzalo Pérez's granddaughter Mafalda would marry the *infante* Alfonso (the future Alfonso X) and inherit Molina after Gonzalo's death, thus ensuring the transmission of an important patrimony to the crown.[12] When Gonzalo Pérez died in 1239, Alfonso became lord of Molina.[13] Mafalda herself did not live much beyond the summer of 1241;[14] and the great lordship of Molina was absorbed quietly into the royal line.[15]

The king's policy toward the principal line of the Laras was characterized by the same gentle but resolute subjugation. Fernando III was determined to avoid a political recovery by the family; the mild punishments meted out to the rebellious Haros in 1233 and 1241 were part of a policy aimed at preserving that family's ascendancy over their Lara rivals.[16] Much later, in 1272, an indignant Alfonso X, facing massive rebellion by the nobles, would remind Nuño González of the dire predicament which the Laras had faced at this stage: "King Fernando [III] did not want to make you a knight or give you land, nor did he have any desire to show you favor. Rather, he wished ill upon you and all your lineage, because Count Fernando and Count Álvaro, your uncles, and Count Gonzalo, your father, when he began to reign, rose up against him and did great disservice to him, making a great war against him."[17]

There is plenty of evidence to suggest that the Laras had indeed been kept firmly in the background in the 1220s and early 1230s. The only references from the late 1220s to the illegitimate sons of Álvaro Núñez, for instance, suggest that they had been thrust into a non-Castilian orbit. In 1228, Fernando Álvarez received ecclesiastical property from his distant cousin Aurembiaix, countess of Urgell, and in the same year both he and his brother Gonzalo Álvarez subscribed an act of the countess in Montalbán, in southern Aragón.[18] There are also few references to the children of Gonzalo Núñez in this period.[19] It is likely that the Lara family maintained some independent patrimonial power in these politically barren years; but the myriad land sales made by the wife and daughters of the eldest son of the previous generation, Fernando Núñez, surely reflects the penurious isolation of the family in the 1230s. This may explain the foreign marriages made by his two daughters, Sancha and Teresa Fernández. Sancha was married to the Portuguese *infante* Fernando de la Serpa,[20] and Teresa to Ponz Huc of Empuries.[21] There is scarcely any sign of their brother, Álvaro Fernández, before 1235.[22]

The crucial factors in the family's recovery (factors with a long history) were the acceleration of the reconquest and conspicuous military service. Waging the Andalusian campaigns, which culminated in the capture of the great cities of Córdoba and Seville, required peace and participation from the nobles of Castile, and there was naturally an effort to harness the Laras' energies. Between 1235 and 1240, several members of the family appear at the court of Castile, albeit in a modest role far removed from the hegemony of the previous generation. Álvaro Fernández, who had not confirmed any royal privileges until 1235, did so frequently over the next five years.[23] The timing of his return to court may be directly connected with preparations for the campaign which culminated in the capture of Córdoba in 1236; and his rise in the court hierarchy should be linked to the role which he played in this campaign.[24] His cousin Diego González was also present at the court of Castile, confirming many privileges between 1235 and 1239, and he too was present at Córdoba.[25] This was equally true of two other cousins, Rodrigo and Fernando Álvarez, illegitimate sons of Álvaro Núñez. Rodrigo had a truly illustrious military career, infusing life into the family's flagging fortunes; he was present not only at Córdoba but also at the conquest of Seville, and his efforts there were eulogized by the *Primera crónica general*.[26] In the ensuing months, he was granted Tamariz and, more importantly, Alcalá de Guadaira, to which two of his children would succeed.[27] By the end of the 1240s, therefore, the Laras were beginning to develop the kind of momentum which would propel them back into the center of power in the reign of Alfonso X (1252–1284).

But one member of the family more than any other was responsible for this revival through royal service. After Diego's death, probably around 1239, the way was paved for his younger brother, Nuño González de Lara (d. 1275), who had spent most of the preceding years of the reign on the political periphery.[28] There is no evidence that Nuño González enjoyed a particularly great inheritance (see Map 12).[29] Instead, he owed much to the factor that had always been the secret of the Laras' success: personal closeness to the royal family. In this case the link was to the young Castilian *infante* Alfonso, with whom Nuño became a close friend. It is possible that he first came into con-

12. Nuño González (d. 1275)

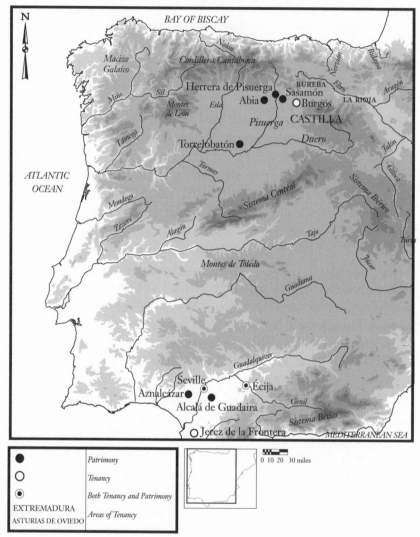

tact with Alfonso by being in the retinue of the queen's *mayordomo*, García Fernández de Villamayor, one of whose diplomas he confirms in 1228.[30] If so, the results were at first slow, doubtless because of Fernando III's determination to keep the Laras on the lower rungs of the ladder of courtly influence. Not until the early 1240s did Nuño González rise out of obscurity. But acting against his father's wishes, the young prince then took it upon himself to see to Nuño's interests. It was almost certainly the *infante* who introduced Nuño González to the royal court and ensured his uninterrupted presence between 1243 and 1252.[31] Alfonso's patronage would also explain why, in the diplomas, Nuño González rapidly assumed third place among lay subscribers, a status in the court hierarchy that he would never lose.[32] Alongside Alfonso, Nuño González participated in the conquest of Murcia in 1243–1244;[33] a successful attack against Arjona in 1244;[34] and, after helping the king at Jaén in 1245, an expedition to support Sancho II of Portugal (who was embroiled in civil war) in 1246.[35] In later life, during a political crisis of 1272, a beleaguered Alfonso would remind Don Nuño of these happier years. The king then "begged him as a friend and ordered him as a vassal to quiet his heart and serve him," reminding him that he had once granted Écija to hold as a tenancy on his behalf.[36] Écija was one of several towns that had surrendered to Fernando III between 1240 and 1241. King Fernando had first entrusted its tenancy to the *infante*, who proceeded to pass it on to Nuño González.[37] To a king who had spent the turbulent beginnings of his reign dismantling the web of Lara tenancies, this must have been infuriating. Through his friendship with the prince, Nuño González had managed to gain entry to the corridors of power from within.[38] Alfonso also managed to persuade his father to approve Nuño's marriage to the king's half-sister Teresa Alfonso, a daughter of Alfonso IX of León.[39] The king's grudging consent was probably encouraged by a need to muster support for the climactic campaign against Seville. Nuño González was present in the siege of the city, and was one of the "many good knights, *infantes*, and aristocrats" whom the king later rewarded.[40] As a result of his participation, he received the local estate of Corixad-Albat (later renamed Herrera).[41]

These were the small beginnings of the patrimonial expansion that would be a key part of the Laras' history in the later thirteenth century. This expansion matches a broader pattern of change among the nobility, whereby patrimony and patrimonialized jurisdiction were becoming more important as the defining elements of aristocratic power. Whereas in the twelfth century, aristocratic power had rested primarily on influence at court, it now began to rest primarily on autonomous control over land and the people who lived on it. Both factors were always important: influence at court remained highly desirable in the late thirteenth century, and conversely the nobility had already begun to absorb greater *dominio señorial* by the end of the twelfth.[42] What occurred now was a subtle, faltering, but unmistakable shift in emphasis. One embodiment of change was an increasing concern with the precise definition of property limits—a development that seems associated in part with the commercialization of agriculture in northern Castile.[43] Much more dramatic, however, was the rise of large noble domains. By the early fourteenth century, there were some estates (such as Vizcaya, which was to fall into the hands of the Laras) which resembled the great *mayorazgos* of the later Middle Ages. Reyna Pastor has written that the power of some heads of important lineages in the later thirteenth century was such that they constituted "states within a state."[44] Rural Andalucía gradually became a society of latifundia, and throughout the realms of Castile and León there was also an accentuation of jurisdictional lordship on the part of the nobility.[45] Landlords imposed not only rents on land leased from the demesne, which generally represented the heaviest burden for the peasantry, but also increasingly heavy "jurisdictional" rents levied on peasants who might even be occupying and working someone else's land.[46] There was an expansion of the types of feudal impositions in the thirteenth century. Alongside older taxes like the *yantar, fonsadera,* and *martiniega* came newer taxes like *monedas* and *servicios*—subsidies granted in the Cortes and subsequently imposed on the peasantry.[47] Finally, there was a greater emphasis on the royal concession of lifetime and hereditary privileges of jurisdiction over men.[48] Specifically, the term *merum imperium* ("full jurisdictional lordship"), introduced by Alfonso X in the *Siete partidas*, flourished over the next hundred years, despite royal attempts in the early fourteenth century to impede this process.[49]

What was the role of the great thirteenth-century reconquests in the course of this social transformation? Until recently, it was taken for granted that the dramatic territorial expansion of Castile and León in this period led directly to a spectacular increase in the landed fortunes of the aristocracy.[50] But recent work on the medieval Castilian nobility shows that with the exception of some members of the royal family, the magnates were simply not among the main beneficiaries of the southern reconquests. This fact, it is now claimed, helped to provoke a series of great noble revolts in the 1270s.[51] A good number of regional studies have pointed in this direction. It has been shown that the seigneurialization of Andalucía did not begin in earnest until the four-

teenth century, and that the nobility controlled only about a quarter of
the region in the late thirteenth century (this fraction was to double by
the end of the Middle Ages).[52] One seminal article has demonstrated
that the initial repopulation of Andalucía was designed to serve the interests of the crown: the great mass of settlers were not nobles but
peones, receiving enough property for the livelihood of their family and
the performance of military service as infantry. Although some parts of
the region were organized into noble lordships from the first moment,
the development of the aristocracy through the concentration of land
ownership was a gradual, belated process.[53] A more geographically specific analysis of the process reveals that in Seville, while some lands
went to members of the royal family, nobles, and prelates, much larger
areas were granted to knights, foot soldiers, and other lesser members
of the Castilian armies. In Córdoba, similarly, latifundia formed merely
a small minority of the new estates being created.[54] Finally it has been
claimed that there was actually an inverse correlation between prominence at the Castilian court and "compensation" in the south.[55]

The case of Nuño González de Lara, who was prominent at the
court of Alfonso el Sabio (1252–1284), seems to bear this out. There is
no doubt that he continued to enjoy a privileged position in this so-
phisticated setting for at least the first decade of Alfonso X's reign. He
subscribed a large number of diplomas between 1252 and 1256 (he was
almost invariably listed first among nonroyal lay lords) and a lesser
number in later years.[56] In Alfonso's service, he maintained the illustrious military role that he had first assumed in the 1240s, commanding a
royal army which defeated the discontented *infante* Enrique in a battle
near Lebrija in 1255.[57] He also assisted in the recovery of the rebellious
Mudéjar cities of Jérez in 1255, Écija in 1262–1263, and Matrera in
1263, as they tried with alarming determination to turn back the tide of
the reconquest.[58] Moreover, Nuño enjoyed the kind of important tenancies which had traditionally corresponded to courtly influence and
military protagonism: Seville;[59] Jérez de la Frontera;[60] Écija;[61] and, to
the north, Bureba, La Rioja, and Castilla la Vieja.[62] However, little of
the honor and favor that he received came in the form of patrimonial
grants. In view of the huge territories which had been opened up on the
Andalusian frontier, and which had been granted in vast quantities to
royal scions and military orders, this fact can hardly have been lost on
him. He was certainly granted one substantial estate (Corixad-Albat)

and a smaller property in Aznalcázar; a few houses in Seville, in 1258;[63] and some windmills in Alcalá de Guadaira.[64] He and his wife were able to give some other windmills in Alcalá to the Order of Santiago, in return for a house in San Miguel de Bobadilla, in December 1259;[65] and finally, his tenancy of Écija also seems to have allowed him to acquire some properties there.[66] But houses, windmills, and *bodegas* were little consolation. Many other nobles received substantial portions of land in Seville, and Nuño González's was by no means the largest.[67] The Laras gained a disproportionately small amount of land as a result of the reconquest, and would never become securely established in Andalucía.

It must have been aggravatingly clear that the determination to limit aristocratic strength, which had characterized Fernando III's reign, had by no means vanished into thin air. Of course, one would hardly place Nuño González among the ranks of the economically oppressed (he appears to have had three hundred knights in his retinue), but in aristocratic circles wealth was evidently perceived in relative terms.[68] His concern was anything but isolated. In particular, to judge from the sumptuary clauses in Alfonso's price regulations, there was rather widespread anxiety among the high nobility with regard to the ascent of the *caballeros villanos* (urban nobility). The threat of new social mobility provoked a closing of ranks at the highest level: in the late thirteenth century, lawsuits were being brought against parvenus claiming full privileges of nobility.[69] Furthermore, the influx of precious metals and the increase in salaries needed to attract peasants to Andalucía catalyzed spiraling inflation throughout Castile, and threatened seigneurial and tenurial revenues;[70] this was true even in the north, since demographic redistribution had serious ramifications throughout the kingdom.[71] King Alfonso attempted to control this inflation through price, salary, and export controls, and through devaluation of the coinage, but apparently in vain. This was, in fact, the first systematic debasement of coinage in Spain, and the first phase of inflation, for which we have clear evidence. A recent study has concluded: "With Alfonso X, a cycle of debasement and manipulation began in León-Castile that would continue down to the reign of the Catholic Kings."[72] There was an estimated overall inflation of 1,000 percent between 1268 and 1294 alone, and the cost of living was especially high in Andalucía.[73] One response was to seek even greater stipends from the monarchy, but the increase in the circulation of money resulting from large stipends in turn aggravated the effects of inflation.[74] Reyna Pastor argues that "one can speak of a new economy" (a destabilized, monetary economy) after the reconquests of the early thirteenth century.[75] The dislocating effects of this inflation should not be underestimated. A letter of 9 May 1272, written at the behest of a number of magnates, expressed alarm that "men are very short of money for their purchases, and for those things which they need every day."[76] By this stage, the political ramifications were clear. Economic crisis would feed an ever-intensifying aristocratic reaction against the new domestic aspirations of the Castilian monarchy.

THE NOBILITY'S ATTITUDE corresponds closely to the German *mentalité* described by Otto Brunner: there was felt to be a "Good Old Order," in which a variety of secular powers exercised jurisdiction and no single authority enjoyed internal sovereignty in the modern sense of the word. This order had to be preserved or restored, if necessary by force.[77] The Good Old Order was under intense challenge in the reign of Alfonso X, as political ideology moved away from the idea of a society based on feudal bonds to a new concept of corporate unity linking all men under the rule of the king. The idea of a unitary body politic, and the concept of the ruler as God's vicar, were essential parts of this ideological framework; Alfonso's law codes placed royal prescription over the traditional body of customary law.[78] This was not absolutism: the king was not above the law, and ideas of mutual obligation between king and people remained fundamental.[79] Still, we may trace in such an ideology the beginnings of the centralized authority characteristic of the modern state. The expansion of monarchy was colored by an effort to limit and transcend the close relationship with the nobility which had been characteristic of the eleventh and twelfth centuries. Alfonso X sought the support of urban elites as a counterweight to the aristocracy, granting exemption from taxes to the *caballeros villanos* and at the same time imposing sumptuary legislation on the higher nobility.[80] The royal tribunal was resurrected as an instrument for the enforcement of the new legal codes, and almost immediately evoked a negative reaction from the nobility, whose role in the judicial process had been unilaterally undermined. The nature and composition of the tribunal would be at the center of baronial grievances in the coming rebellion.[81]

Professional jurists played a key role in the tribunal, just as royal jus-
tices increasingly supplanted municipal *alcaldes*, who were more likely
to fall under the influence of local magnates.[82] Above all, the high nobility was increasingly excluded from positions of administrative influence. In the eleventh and twelfth centuries, aristocratic power had to a
great degree been monarchical power in disguise: the role of the high
nobility had been enormously enhanced by their role as tenants. Now,
alternative administrative mechanisms were being developed, and the
aristocracy was very gradually being squeezed out of the process. It
is true that the high nobility continued to dominate some of the
most important offices of state—*mayordomo mayor, alférez mayor, camarero mayor, justicia mayor,* and *canciller mayor*—although some of these
offices (particularly the first two) were traditional and honorific.[83]
Alfonso X could not possibly have dispensed with their services,
though one suspects that he fervently wished to, and even his *Siete
partidas* show some respect for the attributes of lineage and blood.[84] Yet
elsewhere the underlying attitude of the monarch is betrayed: "The
king cannot obtain good service every day from men who are noble and
powerful; for on account of their exalted rank, they will disdain constant service, and because of their power, they will venture to do things
which will result in his injury and degradation. For this reason he
should select men of moderate station."[85]

    This policy was applied to two of the most important new offices
in royal administration, *adelantado mayor* and *merino mayor.*[86] Nomina-
tion of these officials was often political, until the development of patrimonialization under the Trastámaras: that is to say, nominees were
frequently close confidants of the king.[87] The emergence of the
adelantados mayores and *merinos mayores* was an important step toward
centralization, bureaucratization, and royal authoritarianism. Many officials, such as the *merinos mayores*, depended less on noble magnates
than on the king, and the nobility lost its monopoly on territorial
administration and was consequently driven to rebellion.[88] Over the
course of the thirteenth century, it was the new *merindades* that became the key instruments of royal fiscal and jurisdictional control.[89]
Such mechanisms largely replaced the old system of tenancies that had
played such a large role in the history of the Castilian nobility in the
twelfth century.[90]

    The Laras' response would be violent and prolonged. For Nuño

González and Alfonso X, cooperation rather quickly gave way to re-crimination. To judge from Nuño's decreasing presence in the royal di-plomas, relations between the two men had been on a downward spiral since the late 1250s. The breakdown then seems to have been acceler-ated by tension over the defense of Jérez in 1264: in *cantiga* 345 of the *Cantigas de Santa María*, the king criticizes Nuño's allegedly irresolute behavior.[91] Still, even assuming that the *cantiga* faithfully represents Alfonso's attitude in the mid-1260s, it is hard to imagine that this was a fundamental cause for the deterioration. The same might be said of the tension that arose when, in 1267, Nuño González objected to Alfonso's decision to end his claims to vassalic service from the Portuguese. In seeking deeper problems, we should avoid the assumption that discon-tent among the nobility was individual and atomized, although this is sometimes the impression conveyed by the royal chronicles.[92] For all their hostility to Alfonso X personally, the chronicles are vigor-ously opposed to any challenge to the crown, and obscure the unity of baronial discontent. In reality, the way in which the nobles now asso-ciated and defined their interests, in broader and less factional ways, suggests the emergence of more truly political practices in this pe-riod—a process corresponding to the transition from lordship to gov-ernment in royal administration. A broad rebellious alliance now co-alesced under the leadership of Nuño González de Lara and the *infante* Felipe, at Don Nuño's town of Lerma, in February 1271.[93] It probably also included Nuño's two sons, Fernán Rodríguez (son of his cousin Rodrigo Álvarez), Lope Díaz de Haro, Diego López de Haro, Esteban Fernández de Castro, Fernán Ruiz de Castro, Simón Ruiz de Cameros, Álvar Díaz de Asturias, Fernán González de Saldaña, Gil Gómez de Roa, Lope de Mendoza, and Juan García.[94] The Aragonese chroni-cler Jerónimo de Zurita also emphasizes the involvement of urban *pro-curadores*;[95] their involvement is likely to have been stimulated by the fact that the Cortes remained, for the moment, an essentially regal in-stitution in which the grievances of the urban representatives were rarely raised or addressed.[96] The breadth of the alliance suggests that rebellion and civil war were becoming normal forms of politics by other means, serving to advance widely shared interests that could not be furthered effectively in any other way.[97]

The *Crónica de Alfonso X* traces the course of the rebellion in de-tail; and although its political sympathies are transparent, it is an uncommonly valuable source for tracing baronial resistance, since it frequently appears to be working directly from diplomatic sources. This is the case, for instance, when the chronicler quotes liberally from a letter written by Abu Yusuf, the leader of the powerful Marinid realm in Morocco, to Nuño González, in which a number of Don Nuño's specific complaints against Alfonso X are mentioned: "He made wrong demands on you, and created false coins for you, and broke the good law which you used in the past, so that your estates were changed and things became more expensive and merchants were ruined."[98] It would be hard to find better evidence for the importance of inflation in destabilizing Castilian society, undermining economic security, and leading toward broad-based rebellion.[99] The precarious economic situation was a vital catalyst for the unrest of these years. Nuño González's anxieties with regard to patrimonial security in an age of high inflation can only have been aggravated by the seizure of some of his property while he was engaged in a diplomatic expedition to Málaga.[100] The factor that Alfonso's most recent biographer sees as Nuño González's "most serious complaint," the king's determination to uphold Lope Díaz de Haro's rights in Vizcaya in the face of Don Nuño's aspirations to this territory, may be seen as part of this pressure for patrimonial resources.[101]

Although they might have been pressed by economic anxiety, it was in political terms that the rebels expressed their grievances in 1272, and their actions should be considered first and foremost a reaction to the growth of monarchical authority. The two types of concern are sometimes indistinguishable. When the rebels met the king's forces near Lerma and accompanied him to Burgos in September, they refused to enter the city walls; instead, Nuño González, acting as spokesman, presented a number of grievances and demands. Among these were complaints that the *servicios* imposed on them should be collected more rapidly and should never be made obligatory by law; that the *alcabala* raised in Burgos was unjust; and that the actions of *merinos* and royal tax collectors were harmful.[102] These grievances should be seen against the backdrop of increased competition for control of tax revenues, pitting king against nobility and Cortes;[103] they embody a mixture of purely economic discontent and special discomfort regarding the fiscal intrusions of the crown. But more fundamentally, it is resentment at the growth of royal government that provides the common thread in the rebels' demands. Other grievances were the imposition of the new royal laws (the *Fuero Real*), and the use of non-noble *alcaldes* to judge the nobility in the royal tribunal.[104] The demands were subsequently elaborated in the Cortes that Nuño González asked to be summoned on behalf of the other nobles; it opened on 29 September 1272. There was a stipulation that there should be two noble *alcaldes* in the royal tribunal, for instance, and a demand that the *merinos* be replaced by *adelantados*. Innovations in the tribunal seemed to infringe on the principle of trial by peers, and conflicted with the older concept of a balance of power between king and people.[105] The developing role of the *merinos* as agents of royal fiscality is well documented; the nobles considered the *merinos* an obstacle to the growth of their own lordships, and demanded their replacement by *adelantados* because these positions were associated with a higher rank of nobility.[106] Among other grievances, the earlier request that *servicios* should be imposed only under certain conditions was replaced by a demand that they should not be imposed at all. Again, one suspects that this had as much to do with hostility to the intrusive royal *merinos* as with strictly economic concerns.[107]

The chronicle's assertion that, during negotiations between king and rebels in the Cortes of 1272, "all those present realized that [Alfonso] was in the right and in accord with law and that Felipe and the magnates were making an uproar without reason" is charmingly implausible. The rebel magnates had voiced deep and widely shared concerns, and Alfonso's response was largely to accommodate them. Immediately after the first confrontation, he promised, for instance, that the nobility would enjoy the same *fueros* as in previous reigns (that is to say, above all, the *Fuero Viejo*) and would not be judged according to municipal *fueros* unless they so wished. He added that the *servicios* were extraordinary measures necessary to finance the campaigns against the Moors, his bid for the imperial title, and the nobles' own stipends, and would not be levied on a regular basis. He would drop the *alcabala* imposed on Burgos, and any abuses by *merinos* and royal tax collectors would be remedied.[108] After the rebels had reformulated their program in the Cortes, Alfonso pledged to fulfill their demands regarding *alcaldes* and *adelantados*, to avoid infringing older *fueros*, and to allow the nobles to exempt their vassals from *servicios* if they wished.[109]

The rebels, then, were reacting to royal innovation in the practice of government. This was to become even clearer in 1273, when, ensconced in the kingdom of Granada, they reformulated their program. They demanded, for instance, that the laws, privileges, customs, and *fueros* of Alfonso's realm should be the same as in his father's and grand-father's reigns, and that the situation with regard to the salt pits and iron mines should be the same as in his father's reign. Further, they insisted that *moneda* should be collected only once every seven years, as under his father and grandfather, that *montazgos* (pasturage tolls) should not be taken except as in his father's reign, and that the list of prohibited exports should be restricted to those of his father's time. Other demands, such as those for the abolition of the *diezmos* (import and export customs duties) and the *servicios*, differed only in that they merely implied, rather than explicitly stating, the desire for a return to the days of more limited royal government.[110]

Meanwhile, in the face of these challenges, the Laras were actively pursuing a new territorial strategy: the accumulation of large landed estates on the mountainous border with Aragón. Over the course of the next three generations, each principal lord of the Lara family would ac-quire—if all too briefly—a virtually independent new patrimony on this frontier, and for this patrimony each would fight the crown. The process had begun in 1260 with Nuño González's decision to arrange the marriage of his son, Juan Núñez I, to Teresa Álvarez de Azagra. Teresa was heiress of the bleak, weather-beaten frontier territory of Albarracín.[111] This was a greater estate than the Laras had ever pos-sessed. It extended far from the town itself toward the Valencian coast, and in fact was extensive enough to allow for transhumance between the summer pastures near the town and the temperate lowlands.[112] It also had great military and political value, by virtue of its location on the long border between Castile and Aragón, which has been described as the most important nursery of fortifications in medieval Spain.[113] One historian mistakenly suggests that when Juan Núñez I styled him-self "vassal of Saint Mary and lord of Albarracín," recognizing no supe-rior, this was a reflection of personal arrogance.[114] In reality, this styling literally went with the territory, and may be traced at least as far back as 1176; if independence is defined by conspicuous refusal to recognize allegiance, Albarracín was evidently perceived to be an unusually inde-pendent lordship.[115] The chronicler Bernat Desclot describes the city as lying "between four kingdoms—that is to say, between the kingdom of Aragón and the kingdom of Valencia, and between the kingdoms of Castile and Navarre"; this is also a striking reflection of indepen-dence.[116] The marriage, then, was part of a determined patrimonial policy pursued by the Laras in the century after the conquest of Seville, designed to increase territorial holdings and to develop them in strate-gically independent sites. It coincides with a phase in which Nuño González's subscriptions of royal diplomas became increasingly infre-quent, and suggests the emergence of a rift that was shortly to produce outright rebellion.

To COMBAT THE PRETENSIONS of the Castilian monarchy, the Laras also turned increasingly abroad. The fragmentation of sover-eignty on the Iberian peninsula came to be an essential element in their strategies. Over the next century, they were repeatedly able to exploit tensions between the different Christian kingdoms of Spain, as well as hostility between these kingdoms and the rising power of France; they would even turn for assistance to the potentates of al-Andalus. The in-ternational dimension of the Laras' history was not entirely new—they had turned to the court of León for sanctuary earlier in the century—but it now became vastly more important. Since the Leonese connec-tion was no longer open after the union of the kingdoms of Castile and León in 1230, it also necessarily took new directions.[117] The change of emphasis is clear in their relations with Aragón. As early as the twelfth century, the Laras had established close links with this kingdom through a marriage by Sancha Núñez (daughter of Nuño Pérez) to the Aragonese *infante* Sancho. Their son, Nuño Sánchez, would enjoy an illustrious career at the court of Aragón, participating alongside Pere II at the battle of Las Navas in 1212. He was similarly a regular member of the court of Jaume I (reigned 1213–1276) in the 1220s and 1230s, and participated actively in the conquests of Mallorca and Ibiza.[118] Even so, Aragón and Castile (unlike Castile and León) had usually re-mained discrete spheres of political action. Only now, in the more con-frontational climate of the late thirteenth century, would the kingdom of Aragón begin to take on real importance for the Laras. In the au-tumn in 1269, a remarkable conversation took place on the riverbank in Burgos between Nuño González and Jaume I of Aragón. King Jaume, who was in Burgos for the wedding of the Castilian *infante* Fernando de la Cerda, was riding along the esplanade when he was greeted unexpectedly by Nuño González, who offered to enter his service and to provide "a hundred or two hundred knights." The king then responded by assuring Don Nuño that he was well aware of the tension between the lord of Lara and Alfonso X, but advised him that "this is a better time than any other for healing the wound." The crisis was temporarily defused, and Nuño González's offer of service to the king of Aragón was turned down, but an important precedent had been set.[119] Shortly thereafter, he successfully entered the service of another Christian monarch, Henri I of Navarre (reigned 1270–1274), with whom the rebel nobles had been in contact since the previous year.[120]

Surprisingly, perhaps, it was the Moorish kingdom of Granada that provided the most important foreign connections for the Lara family. Muhammad I (reigned 1232–1273) had his own grudges against Alfonso X—the king of Castile had supported the rebellious governors of Málaga and Guadix, who belonged to the Banu Ashqilula clan—and he was receptive to the Laras' advances. The initial contact appears to have been made indirectly through Don Nuño's two sons, Nuño González II and Juan Núñez I, when Muhammad I met Alfonso X at Jaén in the summer of 1268: this contact catalyzed the emergence of a Castilian noble coalition.[121] As the rebellion began to escalate in 1271, the rebels had made further overtures toward Granada, urging Muhammad I to wage war on Castile and refusing to participate in Alfonso's campaign against Granada that year.[122] Active cooperation with Granada was not long in coming. After the breakdown of talks in the Cortes of 1272, it was in Granada that the rebels sought refuge; and alongside the *infante* Felipe, Nuño González defeated the insubordinate governor of Málaga.[123] The lord of Lara and his fellow émigrés, including his sons, soon gained the grateful cooperation of a new king of Granada (Muhammad II, reigned 1273–1302) in harassing Alfonso X.[124] This harassment was political rather than directly military in form. As a condition of peace, Muhammad II stipulated that Alfonso stop aiding the Banu Ashqilula. Since Alfonso was not prepared to do this, and was in turn demanding the ports of Algeciras and Tarifa (which Muhammad II was not prepared to surrender), negotiations dragged on for months and delayed his longed-for departure in search of election as Holy Roman Emperor. Juan Núñez I de Lara, who had already acted as an intermediary on at least one occasion, was sent back and forth between Granada and the Castilian court in Toledo, attempting to reach a compromise on Algeciras and Tarifa.[125] Alfonso was forced to come to terms. At an assembly in Almagro in March 1273, to which the noble exiles sent their messengers, he agreed to drop two of the six *servicios* that had been arranged in 1269, and to collect customs duties for only the next six years.[126] In July, the agreement was ratified in Seville. Alfonso promised that *moneda* would be collected only every seven years, that *diezmos* and *servicios* would be reduced, and that the king would provide additional stipends to those who accompanied him on his imperial journey. Finally, he agreed to confirm the *fueros* of Castile and León as they had been in the reigns of Alfonso VIII of Castile and Alfonso IX of León, abolishing the *Fuero Real.*[127]

Nuño González, having achieved a good number of his political goals through rebellion, returned contentedly to the royal court in Burgos in March 1274. Unfortunately, the peace treaty with Castile had been less acceptable for Muhammad II, who was obliged to pay two years' tribute (together with an additional lump sum for Alfonso's journey) and forced to accept a two-year truce with the Banu Ashqilula.[128] By way of compromise, a shorter truce was arranged in December 1273; but this did not assuage Muhammad's resentment. Doubtless encouraged by Alfonso's absence from Castile, he now appealed to the North African Marinids for military assistance. The Marinid leader, Abu Yusuf, first asked for and received what Alfonso X had been denied: the ports of Algeciras and Tarifa; then, in August 1275, his forces swept northeast up the Guadalquivir valley. On 7 September, Abu Yusuf's vastly superior army met the Castilian troops under Nuño González near Écija. Don Nuño's forces were destroyed. He himself was decapitated, and his head sent to his erstwhile ally, the king of Granada. Muhammad expressed satisfaction with the outcome of the battle but regret at the fate of Don Nuño—a man, he said, who had done much to make him king.[129]

5

Revolt, Rapprochement, and Rumor

𝒥N AN IMMEDIATE SENSE, the Laras' increased hostility to the crown in the last quarter of the thirteenth century was based on a dynastic issue. The crushing defeat of the Castilian army at Écija followed close on the heels of an even greater disaster for the kingdom, earlier in the summer of 1275: the sudden death of Alfonso X's heir, nineteen-year old Fernando de la Cerda.[1] A succession crisis of vast proportions ensued. For the next generation, conflicting claims to the throne by Fernando de la Cerda's son, Alfonso de la Cerda, and Fernando's younger brother Sancho (the future Sancho IV) would be a constant and explosive element in Castilian politics.[2] Into this drama the Laras were immediately drawn, for it had been to Juan Núñez I that the dying Fernando had entrusted the interests of his children, requesting him especially to ensure his son's succession to the throne.[3] The *infante* Sancho, on the other hand, was ardently championed by the Haro family. Jealous of the Laras' control of the new heir, the Haros encouraged Sancho's declaration of war against his father, Alfonso X, and would become prominent at the royal court as soon as Sancho was successfully installed as king. The Laras were naturally inclined to rebellion by their support for the La Cerdas' claim to the throne and their hostility to Sancho IV as a perceived usurper.

More fundamentally, however, the intensification of hostilities may be attributed to the erosion of the old symbiosis between king and nobility. The Laras' confrontation with the monarchy had been catalyzed by the administrative centralization initiated by Alfonso X, which destabilized the political sphere as a whole. Of course, the family was not interested in, or even capable of, independence from the monarchy: like other noble families, they aspired to collaborative government of a traditional, twelfth-century kind, as the rebellions against Alfonso had indicated. Their concern was to control the royal fountain of prosperity, rather than to destroy it, since enormous economic rewards could still be found in royal offices and stipends.[4] The search for family power meant alternating strategies of resistance and reconciliation; a very similar dynamic was characteristic of late medieval English history, although in Castile the nobility appears to have had more interest in participating directly in the administration of government.[5] Allegiances were fluid in the extreme; noblemen could easily be won over, and alliances against the king were rarely very stable. This was particularly the case in reigns when the royal program of centralization was muted or interrupted—for example, under Sancho IV (reigned 1284–1295) and Fernando IV (reigned 1295–1312). During this period, when the monarchy was gradually pushed into a more defensive position, broad-based aristocratic resistance tended to fragment easily into the factional pursuit of private interest, although the underlying challenges to symbiosis remained. In the case of the Laras, at least, tensions would come to focus specifically on the issue of patrimonial power.

CONFRONTATION WAS SPARKED over and over again by patrimonial concerns. In the late thirteenth and early fourteenth centuries, most outbreaks of violence between the Lara family and the crown can be traced directly to matters of land. The Laras sought the kind of territorial and jurisdictional power that would elevate them above new economic pressures and royal fiscal demands. In this context, the inflation of the late thirteenth century is again worth emphasis. There was a particularly sharp price increase between 1278 and 1281, and a substantial if less spectacular rise between 1294 and 1303.[6] Inflationary pressure is very likely to have stimulated changes in patrimonial strategy. One such change was the tendency toward the concentration of landed property in the hands of one member of the family. Primogeniture was now crystallizing, alongside a heightened sense of ancestry and lineage. The shift becomes marked among the descendants of Nuño González, whose extant seals, all featuring a shield with the Laras' emblematic cauldrons, reflect a more developed consciousness of ancestry.[7] The family's power in the three-quarters of a century between 1275 and 1351 was virtually coterminous with the three generations of first-born lords named Juan Núñez, and the very continuity in their names reflects a move away from the original patronymic system—a move that suggests structural change.[8] Juan Núñez I, II, and III each temporarily gained possession of a substantial estate (Albarracín, Molina, and Vizcaya, respectively) which was not matched in the case of any younger brothers. Although each of these estates was acquired by marriage rather than inheritance, the dominance of the eldest living son, thus contrived, was surprisingly new. The younger brothers of Juan Núñez I and Juan Núñez II each held very limited amounts of land. Salazar confidently (and in all likelihood correctly) asserts that Nuño González II inherited many places from his father, but has to admit that none of them are specifically mentioned in the documents.[9] Other than the fact that we know he was one of the *diviseros* of Caleruega, it appears impossible to identify any of the younger Nuño González's patrimonial holdings.[10] There is a similar fog surrounding the question of the inheritance of Nuño González III, the youngest brother in the next generation. He married the *infanta* Constanza of Portugal, who according to Salazar y Castro had interests in the towns of Vide and Alegrete, but there seems to be no evidence of an inheritance in Castile or León.[11] A sure reflection of the concentration of landholding in the hands of eldest sons was the absence of the kind of fraternal partnership that had been central to the Laras' activities in the twelfth and early thirteenth centuries. There had previously been one phase in which the cooperation of two brothers (Pedro González and Rodrigo González) had been crucial to the success of the Laras, and two phases in which a triumvirate of Lara brothers had acted together (Manrique, Nuño Pérez, and Álvaro Pérez in the 1160s, and Fernando Núñez, Álvaro Núñez, and Gonzalo Núñez in the 1210s). From the mid-thirteenth century, fraternal cooperation was considerably less conspicuous, presumably because the concentration of land in the hands of the eldest son undermined the importance of the support of younger siblings.

More dramatic than changes in patrimonial distribution within the family, though, was the strategy of aggressive territorial expansion that the Laras would pursue, with mixed success, over the next three generations. One historian has spoken of a more general "seigneurial offensive" beginning in the late thirteenth century and persisting in the years of economic and demographic crisis in the first third of the fourteenth, before reaching its climax under the new Trastámara dynasty.[12] This whole period witnessed an acceleration of the absorption of jurisdictional lordship by the nobility; and there are strong indications that aristocratic control of *behetrías* began to accelerate in the late thirteenth century.[13] The paucity of evidence makes it hard to be sure exactly how much, at this point, the Laras' patrimonial power in northern Castile resembled the extraordinary territorial influence which they were to accumulate by the mid-fourteenth century. We do know that Juan Núñez I inherited Torrelobatón from his father, and that, like his brother Nuño González II, he was one of the *diviseros* of Caleruega.[14] But a letter dated 31 March 1276 from Juan Núñez to his private *merinos* provides good evidence that the Laras shared much more fully in the "seigneurial offensive" (see Map 13): "From me, Juan Núñez, vassal of Saint Mary and lord of Albarracín, to all my *merinos* of Bureba, Castilla Vieja, Trasmiera, Asturias, Campóo, and Treviño, greetings. . . . I firmly command you all to guard and defend and assist all the places, towns, and vassals of the monastery of Oña."[15]

The document suggests the existence of a substantial number of private *merinos* exercising considerable power, and offers a rare glimpse of the structure of administration and jurisdiction whereby the Laras ruled their estates. There appears to have been an extensive network of officials collecting jurisdictional revenues and entrusted with important military responsibilities; the task of guarding "all the places, towns, and vassals" of the wealthy monastery of Oña was no small task. The provision of military as well as financial support had also been the function of the royal *merinos* of the later twelfth and thirteenth centuries. It is possible that some of Juan Núñez's officials had been absorbed from the ranks of the *merinos menores* of the royal jurisdiction; administrative imitation is also plausible. Certainly, Juan Núñez had at his disposal at least 300 knights, and probably many more, and it seems likely that the *merinos* were responsible for providing a large number of them.[16] This considerable military capacity, in itself, reflects the wealth born of patrimonial expansion; there is no indication that the Laras, or any other noble family, had been able to summon knights on anything remotely resembling this scale in the eleventh and twelfth centuries.[17] When

13. Juan Núñez I (d. 1294)

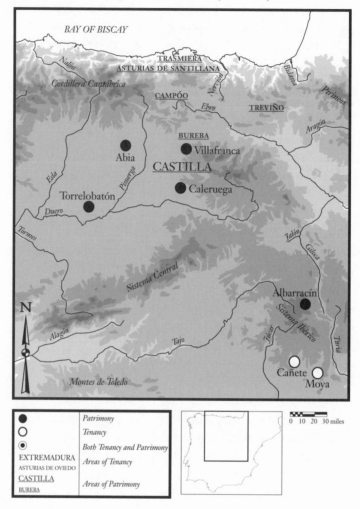

they had led an army, it had been as *alféreces* of the king; and indeed 300
knights would seem to be a decent estimate of the total number in the
entire royal army in this earlier period.[18]

Since the humbling of the family by Fernando III, however, the
heartland of northern Castile had played a relatively modest role in the
family's activities. This was surely related to the fact that landholding
in this region, characterized by its small scale and the complex nexus
of shared lordships, offered less potential for the development of the
great estates which were now necessary for the perpetuation of aristo-

cratic power. Even once the chronicles began to use "Lara" as a family name—suggesting some public consciousness of the shared ancestry of the family and their origins in Old Castile—the Laras almost never did so themselves in the diplomatic sources. Juan Núñez I identified himself almost exclusively as "lord of Albarracín." The real focus of his patrimonial strategies lay along the Aragonese frontier, where the Laras attempted desperately to create a series of more or less autonomous enclaves.[19] And no patrimony was more contentious than the lordship of Albarracín. The first phase of confrontation between the Laras and the monarchy in this period, from 1276 to 1289, seems to have crystallized quickly into a titanic struggle not for the rights of the La Cerdas but for control of Albarracín.

Before looking at the dynamics of this struggle, it is important to examine the international strategy that Juan Núñez was developing. To have any hope of success in confronting the crown of Castile, he needed to rely heavily on foreign support, and in doing so he needed to be creative. The connections that the Lara family had developed at the court of Granada in the previous generation had proved to be ephemeral. Indeed, in 1282, the *infante* Sancho allied with Granada against Juan Núñez I.[20] Abandoned by a great power to the south, Juan Núñez turned north—to the French, ever more active in peninsular affairs. Like relations with León at the beginning of the century, and relations with the kingdom of Granada in the late 1260s and early 1270s, contacts with France now became a central part of the Laras' strategies. Indeed, more continuously aggressive than the Leonese connection had been, and more prolonged than the Laras' contacts with the Nasrids, the association with France lay at the heart of the family's activities. The French relationship that Juan Núñez had begun to cultivate through his presence on Saint Louis' crusade in 1270 reached its peak in an agreement which he made with Philip III of France six years later. The agreement was provoked by the failure of efforts to ensure the succession of Alfonso de la Cerda earlier in the year.[21] It made provision for forty days of annual service to be performed by Juan Núñez for the king of France, with his 300 knights, in any of several territories including Castile.[22] The same month, September 1276, his brother, Nuño González II de Lara, signed a similar contract with Philip III. Here, it was arranged that the younger Nuño's Castilian stipend of 8,000 *livres tournois* would be matched by the French king in return for

106 knights who would serve for an initial period of three months; thereafter he would receive sixty *sous* daily.[23]

Precisely one century earlier, in the mid-1170s, the Laras had enjoyed unrivaled hegemony at the Castilian court; their relationship with the crown—undermined by challenges to the old symbiosis between king and nobility—could not have changed more profoundly in the intervening century. For the next decade, when he was not in Albarracín, Juan Núñez was often in France or in French-controlled Navarre, whose heiress, Juana, was under French tutelage. As early as 1277, he was deployed in French service there, where he defended the castle of Estella and was paid to maintain substantial numbers of troops.[24] He was in Navarre again in 1283, making an incursion with seven thousand men into Treviño, whose castellan had rebelled in the name of Alfonso de la Cerda, before the cooperation of Aragón and Castile forced a withdrawal to Pamplona; and he could be found there once more in 1284.[25] For the French, who had aspirations to the Castilian throne, Juan Núñez was useful as a means of defending interests in Navarre, and in attacking Aragón and Castile.[26]

From 1281, Juan Núñez I had used his estate in Albarracín to launch guerrilla raids into both Castile and Aragón, ostensibly on behalf of young Alfonso de la Cerda and his brother Fernando, who were both imprisoned by Sancho's uncle, Pere III of Aragón (reigned 1276–1285).[27] Pere III, for his part, desperately wanted to defeat the ally of the French and, *en passant*, to annex Albarracín.[28] Following formal embassies sent to Juan Núñez, he declared war against the lord of Albarracín on 14 June 1283, but Juan Núñez immediately took the offensive, attacking the Aragonese lands of Jiloca, Jalón, and Teruel, and the Castilian town of Cuenca.[29] Meanwhile, underestimating the determination of the lord of Lara, the King of Aragón headed to Bordeaux to duel with Charles of Anjou. On his return through the kingdom of Navarre, tracked by Juan Núñez's spies, Pere came dangerously close to capture, in a dramatic series of events recounted by Bernat Desclot. The king was forced to flee in secret through the mountains, accompanied by a solitary knight, while he sent the rest of his company on to the safety of Tarazona.[30] Only in April 1284, keen to secure his western frontier in preparation for an expected French invasion, did he begin a full-scale siege of Albarracín, joined a month later by his nephew Sancho IV. The orders sent by Pere III to the mayors of several

Aragonese towns, instructing them to retain custody of soldiers from Juan Núñez's forces whom they had captured, imply previous raids by Juan Núñez and a new seriousness of purpose on the part of the king of Aragón.[31] The siege itself, Juan Núñez's escape to Navarre, and the sorry plight of the inhabitants—reduced to eating cats and dogs as winter set in and provisions ran out—are all described in detail by Desclot, who may well have been the scribe Bernat who was personally present at Albarracín.[32] The fall of the town was by no means a forgone conclusion: if, on 12 August, Pere III wrote confidently to King Sancho of Castile, a subsequent message was less optimistic.[33] The surrender came only at length, sometime before 18 September 1284.[34]

Following the fall of Albarracín, Juan Núñez fled to France.[35] Indeed, the role of France as a sanctuary was not the least important part of this foreign connection.[36] Sancho, however, made strenuous efforts to close off the route, achieving a gradual improvement in Castilian-French relations after Philip III's death in 1286. Sancho and María de Molina had a variety of reasons for this policy, among them a hope that the French pope would regularize their marriage, but the problems caused by Juan Núñez must have been high on their agenda. In the Treaty of Bayonne, 13 July 1286, Sancho and Philip IV of France went so far as to recognize Juan Núñez's rights to Albarracín.[37] A second Castilian-French alliance, in 1288, probably accelerated his return to Castile the following year.[38] The rapprochement between Castile and France may at first have been favorable to the Laras, as Lope Díaz de Haro had feared in 1286, since the French were sympathetic to the family's cause.[39] Ultimately, however, the improvement in relations between the two kingdoms undermined the importance of the Laras' influence at the French court, since France had been significant largely as a means of confronting Castile.

Juan Núñez's long-awaited return to Sancho IV's court in 1289 was not achieved by any new solution to the succession crisis; nor was he lured by tenancies, as would have been the case in the twelfth century. Instead, he was coaxed back by promises of land. His hopes of recovering Albarracín were raised by its continued de facto independence; curiously, after initial attempts to absorb Albarracín, Pere III had decided to preserve its autonomy by granting it to his illegitimate son Fernando, perhaps in order to defuse resentment from Castile.[40] The first steps toward Juan Núñez's reconciliation with Sancho IV had occurred on 13 July 1286, when his title to Albarracín was recognized in a treaty between Castile and France, but Juan Núñez had been mistrustful, partly because of the hegemony of Lope Díaz de Haro at court at this time.[41] The fall of the Haro family between 1286 and 1288 created a more auspicious climate for his return. Sancho IV now pardoned Juan Núñez and his brother Nuño González II, promised to return their property and indemnify them for damage done to it, and finally confirmed Juan Núñez's right to Albarracín.[42] Juan Núñez was also granted lifetime lordship of the two border strongholds of Moya and Cañete, north from Albarracín on the Aragonese frontier.[43] These twin strongholds, some forty kilometers apart, had each been Moorish bastions until the end of the twelfth century, whereupon they had become Castilian bulwarks against the Aragonese. The castle and town of Moya are set upon a rocky outcrop, and the town is fortified by a strong wall and ditch; the castle at Cañete is primitive, austere, and immense.[44] We may assume that these were hardly the kinds of fortresses that Sancho IV was pleased to place in the hands of Juan Núñez; it is almost certain that the grant was forced upon him as a form of compensation for Juan Núñez's loss of Albarracín. It may also have been designed to ensure Juan Núñez's help against the Aragonese, toward whom the lord of Lara might justifiably have been assumed to have an irreconcilable hatred.

Any such assumption proved unwarranted. Almost immediately, Moya and Cañete assumed the role held by Albarracín six years earlier—that of a military base for the advancement of Juan Núñez's own interests; and he showed not the slightest interest in attacking the Aragonese. In March 1290, instead of going to the Aragonese frontier as Sancho IV had ordered, Juan Núñez left for the province of Burgos to settle old scores with Pedro and Nuño Díaz de Castaneda, allies of the Haros.[45] The testament of Gonzalo Ruiz de Zúñiga, a follower of Juan Núñez, contains a remarkable eyewitness account of an unspecified campaign by Juan Núñez I which may well have occurred during this attack on the Haros. Ruiz enumerates various debts: "When Don Juan was pillaging near Burgos, I had from this pillage up to 120 sheep, which may have been worth, on average, three *maravedís* each. And one ox which may have been worth forty *maravedís*. And I had from this pillage forty pigs, which I ate, I believe, which may have been worth eight *maravedís* on average, and no more."[46]

Meanwhile, a complete volte-face in Aragonese policy toward the Laras was taking place. Aragonese hostility to the family had lasted well beyond Pere III's capture of Albarracín in 1284, because of Juan Núñez's ferocious determination to win it back.[47] But the Castilian rapprochement with the French in the later 1280s was a considerable blow to them. For Juan Núñez himself, overtures from the Aragonese would now have seemed a godsend, opening up the possibilities of recovering Albarracín by peaceful means and of using the threat of military force, backed by Aragón, against Castile. In early August 1290, he met with Alfonso III of Aragón (reigned 1285–1291) before returning to Moya and advancing on the Castilian towns of Cuenca and Alarcón, proceeding to defeat the Castilian army decisively at Chinchilla. We may infer from the fact that, on 22 August, he met again with Alfons III, becoming his vassal and agreeing to hold Moya and Cañete from him as fiefs, that the intervening attacks on Castile were part of an understanding reached earlier that month—perhaps an emphatic statement of good will. Zurita, who recounts these meetings, is full of suspicion toward Juan Núñez, claiming that none of his promises were in earnest.[48] It is certainly plausible that Juan's broad intent was to exploit the strategic value of Moya and Cañete in order to wring concessions from both Castile and Aragón. He may well have remembered Sancho's willingness to come to terms with him during a critical stage of the siege of Albarracín, a flexibility that had contrasted then with the Aragonese determination to crush Juan Núñez's troublemaking.[49]

If Juan Núñez had intended to force concessions from the Castilian monarchy through the threat of force, he enjoyed at least one short-term success. This time, in late 1290, he was won back to court by the arrangement of a marriage between his son, Juan Núñez II, and Isabel, heiress of Molina (see Map 14).[50] The potential of this marriage, in view of his own hopes of recovering Albarracín for the family, was enormous. Had Molina and Albarracín been united in his son's hands, the Laras would have enjoyed vast territorial power on the frontier, and it is possible that attempts would also have been made to absorb the tenancies of Cañete and Moya. It has been suggested that Juan Núñez I aimed at nothing less than the creation of a buffer state on the Castilian-Aragonese border.[51] Whatever the case, the reconciliation remained tense, and the chronicle suggests that Juan Núñez was respon-

14. Juan Núñez II (d. 1315)

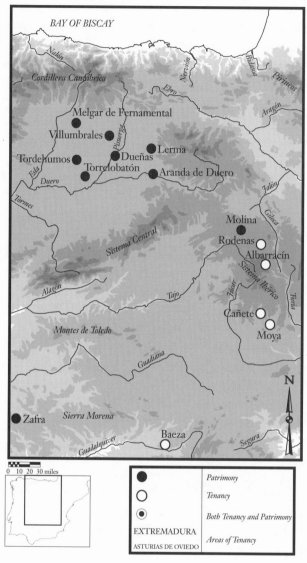

sible for inciting a rebellion by Juan Alfonso de Alburquerque in June
1291.[52] There were desperate efforts to shore up the rapprochement
through the marriage of his daughter Juana *la Palomilla* ("the Little
Dove") to the *infante* Alfonso, the four-year old son of Sancho IV
and María de Molina, but the boy's death prevented this union from
occurring. Finally, in 1291, in a masterpiece of double-dealing, Sancho

confirmed the rights of the Aragonese to Albarracín.[53] The principal modern study of the reign reveals its sympathies when it mysteriously suggests the king did not realize that this reversal of policy might alienate Juan Núñez; but this oversight would have required extraordinary amnesia. In speculating that the frustration of Juan Núñez's aspirations to Albarracín lay behind his renewed rebellion in January 1292, the study is much closer to the mark.[54]

Juan Núñez was destined to remain frustrated. His rebellion failed utterly, forcing him to flee to Navarre. Not only had he proved unable to recapture his great estate of Albarracín, but Sancho IV had recaptured the fortresses of Cañete and Moya.[55] If the Laras still retained any hopes of creating a buffer state, these were finally dashed in February 1293 by the premature death of Isabel de Molina.[56] The couple had no heirs, and it was unacceptable to the monarchy that Molina remain in the hands of Juan Núñez II. Instead, it reverted to Isabel's mother, Blanca de Molina, and it was arranged that the lordship would pass to her sister, Sancho IV's queen, María de Molina, upon Blanca's death. Given that King Sancho had previously imprisoned Blanca for pursuing an independent policy on Molina, there can be no doubt who was calling the shots in this arrangement. Blanca passed away soon afterward, but a further arrangement had already been reached whereby Sancho paid her 300,000 *maravedís* in exchange for Molina.[57] Juan Núñez II now entered into rebellion alongside the *infante* Juan, but the uprising was crushed with a ferocity that had not been shown toward the Laras since the beginning of the century. The town of Castrotorafe, where the younger Juan Núñez took refuge as the royal army approached, was burned to the ground.[58] In May 1293, both he and his father, who had returned from exile in Navarre, put their signatures— surely with enormous regret—to a royal privilege granting Molina, along with Mesa and Zafra, to the queen.[59]

For the remaining months of his life, the aging Juan Núñez I resigned himself to a hollow truce with the crown.[60] By the summer, he was providing lodging to the king, and even assisting him against the rebellious *infante* Juan.[61] One detects a note of wry surprise in a letter sent to Sancho on 20 December by Jaume II of Aragón: "It pleases us greatly that Juan Núñez and his sons are getting along very well in your service."[62] What accounts for Juan Núñez's apparent loyalty at this time? There are two main answers: money and office. Both enhanced the power of the royal court to lure in malcontents and disguise deep rifts. Never in the Middle Ages could a noble lineage expect to prosper for long without proximity to the crown; access to the king would remain lucrative well into the modern age, though after the twelfth century its importance declined relative to patrimonial power. A string of entries in the royal account books for the spring of 1294 testifies to the size of Juan Núñez's stipends: he received 6,000 *maravedís* on 12 April 1294,[63] and no fewer than 50,000 on 20 May.[64] This may be compared with the figure of somewhere near 1,800 which ordinary household officials might hope to receive. There had in fact been a dramatic increase in the size of stipends paid in the later thirteenth century, both because of inflation and because of the need to quell internal unrest. The escalation of Juan Núñez's stipend from 14,000 *maravedís* in 1276 to more than 50,000 in 1294 should be linked to a particular desire to retain the loyalty of the Laras.[65] He was also bought off by reappointment as *adelantado de la frontera*, a position which he had held briefly in the winter of 1291–1292;[66] it was in this capacity that, in early 1294, he was sent on a campaign against the king of Granada, a campaign which would be his last.[67] It has been suggested that the *adelantamientos* were rapidly becoming a bargaining counter in the political game being played between monarchy and nobility in this period.[68] Although we cannot really talk of patrimonialization of office in this period, since the identity of *adelantados* changes rapidly, the thirst of the aristocracy for *adelantamientos* certainly reflects the magnetism of royal office.

JUAN NÚÑEZ II's relationship with the Castilian crown was as checkered as his father's, and likewise followed a frantic dialectic between deep-seated confrontation and superficial reconciliation. If we are to judge from the royal chronicle, he appears at first to have had a working relationship with Sancho IV; in 1287, the king was apparently willing to grant him the tenancies and privileges once held by his elder brother, Álvaro Núñez II.[69] He may well have received a large stipend and fiscal privileges throughout this period, as was certainly the case in 1294, when, according to the royal account books, he was entitled to the quite remarkable sum of 127,000 *maravedís* from the northern ports of Santander, Castro, and Laredo.[70] He was assigned a considerable portion of the taxes on the Jews in four towns;[71] received a stipend of 5,000 *maravedís* on 8 August;[72] and, some time before 13 August,

6,000 *maravedís* for the *tercias* of Plasencia.[73] However, his rebellion
with the *infante* Juan, in the aftermath of the crown's absorption of
Molina the previous year, undoubtedly suggests that these privileges,
far from being a spontaneous expression of largesse, were no more than
the high price paid for his tenuous loyalty.[74] This, of course, is not the
impression that the royal chronicle conveys. We are told that in 1295,
on his deathbed, Sancho IV exhorted him with the words: "Don Juan
Núñez, you know well how you came to me a young beardless man,
and I did you great favors—on the one hand by providing you with a
very good marriage, and on the other by giving you land and money.
And I pray you, since I am very sick, as you see, that if I should die, you
will never forsake the *infante* Fernando, my son, until he has a beard,
and also that you will serve the Queen all her life."[75] Juan Núñez is said
to have reassured the king: "My lord, I know that all this is so, and I
perform homage to you and make an oath that I will do as you ask."[76]
But the chronicler is fully aware of what happens next. He wishes to
provoke outrage at an imminent violation of an oath and act of homage, the deception of a dying lord, the betrayal of a fresh-faced child-
king and his mother, and in general the thoroughly ungrateful action of
a well-favored servant. Again we need to remind ourselves of the deep
tension between monarchy and nobility, a tension which—whether or
not the participants fully understood it—entirely transcended individual character. For the first five years of the reign, the Castilian nobility
was almost uniformly hostile to the new king, Fernando IV.[77]

Of course, there were always specific grievances and aspirations. The
immediate reason for Juan Núñez II's decision to turn his back on the
king was his dream of a territorial power base on the Aragonese frontier. It was this, above all, which accounted for the complex twists and
turns of his diplomatic policy.[78] Juan Núñez's principal objective in the
late 1290s was to court the Aragonese, and to negotiate the return of
Albarracín, which he saw as his rightful patrimonial possession. Alongside the *infante* Juan, he collaborated in an Aragonese incursion in
1296;[79] and a letter which was sent the next year by Jaume II of Aragón
to the "noble and beloved Juan Núñez" acknowledges having met with
a messenger sent by the lord of Lara to discuss Albarracín.[80] A second
letter, sent on 13 March 1298, refers more specifically to a request
made by Juan Núñez for either hereditary lordship of Albarracín or a
ten-year tenure accompanied by an annual payment of 60,000 *sueldos*.

Jaume II accepted the proposal, although he rejected the demand that if any of the stipends were not forthcoming, Albarracín should revert to Juan Núñez.[81] Jaume was clearly eager to draw Juan Núñez into his service.[82] Following swiftly on the heels of the second letter, Juan Núñez became a vassal of the king of Aragón on 7 April 1298, accepting the tenancies of Albarracín and Rodenas, just to the north.[83] In 1299, Juan Núñez made for France and returned with the command of a substantial number of French and Aragonese troops, who ravaged the lands of Juan Alfonso de Haro, a close adviser of the Castilian king.[84] However, his tenancy of Albarracín was revoked the very same year because he had failed to keep his promise to come to the king of Aragón within the year to recognize that Albarracín was held as a fief. Aragonese forces were arrayed against the city, which on this occasion was surrendered quickly by its castellan.[85] On 2 March 1300, the estate was incorporated fully, and finally, into the crown of Aragón.[86] The loss of Albarracín effectively ended the Laras' friendship with the Aragonese. It is true that Fernando IV of Castile appears to have recognized Juan Núñez's familiarity with the court of Aragón, sending him as emissary to Jaume II in 1303, but the developing détente between Castile and Aragón deprived him of his last bargaining counter.[87] During negotiations between Castile and Aragón in 1305, the Aragonese guaranteed that they would refuse to return Albarracín to him.[88]

Faced with such a disaster, it is hardly surprising that as Fernando's reign progressed, Juan Núñez was increasingly lured into the fold by the rewards of royal office.[89] The desirability of closeness to the king may be illustrated by a passage in the royal chronicle, describing events that probably occurred in 1301. Even after his return to court, says the chronicler, Juan Núñez was unhappy, and determined to separate Fernando from the control of his mother, María de Molina. Through a knight who enjoyed the king's trust, he persuaded the adolescent Fernando to go hunting with him while the Queen Mother was preparing to leave to negotiate with the French in Vitoria. He then exhorted the king to stop hiding behind his mother's skirts, to seize the reins of government himself, and to take the counsel of *ricos hombres* like himself.[90] Shortly thereafter, Juan Núñez acquired Cañete and Moya as lifetime lordships, and became *mayordomo mayor*.[91] Even more importantly, he held the office of *adelantado de la frontera* for several years, like his father, and in this role participated actively in the campaigns against

Gibraltar and Algeciras.[92] In 1310, he would be sent as an envoy to Pope Boniface VIII, with the responsibility of seeking assistance in the Algeciras campaign, a mission he performed with considerable success.[93]

Yet every phase of cooperation was fragile, and every period of confrontation revealed a scar only cosmetically disguised by the attraction of the court. Even in periods of ostensible friendship, tension between the Laras and the crown was high. One of the more intriguing motifs in the chronicles of Sancho IV and Fernando IV is the plethora of allegedly false rumors of assassinations planned by the king against the Laras. The chronicler of Sancho IV's reign recounts how, back in April 1290, a letter had been sent to a confidant of the elder Juan Núñez claiming that the king wanted his murder. Juan Núñez, we are told, then fled to San Andrés de Arroyo and only at length was persuaded to return.[94] In a later stage of rapprochement, he had again been alarmed by a report that the king planned to kill him, and attempted to flee at night, only to find the city gates of Toledo closed and his men and horses trapped inside. Sancho IV upbraided the rumormonger, and a semblance of order was reestablished.[95] Finally, in 1308, according to the chronicler of Fernando IV, a brief period in which Juan Núñez II basked in royal grace came to an end when certain unnamed people, jealous of his newfound favor, led him to believe that the king was intending his murder. Juan Núñez left for Torrelobatón and allied himself with the *infante* Juan, who had heard a similar story; they gathered a large force, and the negotiations that were begun soon deteriorated.[96] While the chronicler dismisses these rumors, it is eminently possible that some, or all, were true. Indeed, the chronicle itself relates how three years later Fernando IV would try to enlist Juan Núñez's help in capturing or killing his *ally* the *infante* Juan, with whom the king was furious because he believed he had hampered him in the Algeciras campaign of 1310. Juan Núñez refused, recognizing it would do nothing to strengthen his own position, but Fernando continued to look for ways to capture or kill the *infante*; his plan to do so at the wedding of the *infanta* Isabel in 1311 was foiled only by the intervention of María de Molina.[97]

The failure of this assassination attempt sealed the victory of the noble faction led by the *infante* Juan, which had now become the focal point of opposition to the king.[98] Juan Núñez II had gravitated increasingly toward this camp, and again we do not have to look far to find the immediate source of tension: Albarracín. It is true that Juan Núñez does appear to have gained possession of a number of other places, notably on the border between Castile and León. Among his holdings here were Torrelobatón and Melgar.[99] More briefly, he controlled Amaya, Dueñas, Tordehumos, Villagarcía, Tordesillas, Medina de Rioseco, Ampudia, and Palenzuela; but some of these had been acquired in the course of the 1299 rebellion, and all were surrendered later in the year, along with Lerma and Osma.[100] We know that he was lord of Aranda de Duero, where he was besieged during a later rebellion in 1305;[101] and of Iscar, acquired along with Melgar and Tordehumos (again) in 1305.[102] But quite apart from the instability and ephemeral nature of many of these possessions, none of them would ever have soothed his sense of outrage at his loss of Albarracín. In 1304, a brief rupture with Fernando IV occurred when a peace agreement between Castile and Aragón failed to restore Albarracín to him.[103] A more serious break occurred in 1307 after an explosive meeting with Fernando, when he declared: "I see that I do not have your favor, nor did I receive any honor from you in these Cortes."[104] It is not clear precisely to what type of honor Juan Núñez aspired; he may have been referring either to patrimony or to the stipendiary payments that had often managed to quell patrimonial anxieties in the past. The eventual settlement, following the type of painstaking negotiations which the chronicle narrates in excruciating detail, involved a compromise over territorial control in which Juan Núñez was allowed to keep Tordehumos and Iscar but agreed to surrender Moya and Cañete.[105]

Bitterly aggrieved, Juan Núñez sought to recover lost pride in Portugal. The Portuguese *Livro das Linhagens*, which describes him as a "very good hidalgo," is uniquely sympathetic.[106] The Laras' connections with Portugal had been forged by his elder brother, Álvaro Núñez, who participated in a campaign by the Portuguese *infante* Alfonso against the kings of Portugal and Castile in 1287.[107] Juan Núñez II had begun his own journey down this path in the spring of 1296, when he cooperated with the *infante* Pedro of Portugal, as well as with the Aragonese and Alfonso de la Cerda, in the course of a campaign against Fernando IV.[108] The connection culminated in 1312, when (according to the Castilian royal chronicle) a tax designed to subsidize a campaign against the Moors was paid by everyone other than Juan Núñez, who was now a vassal of the king of Portugal.[109] In a subsequent attempt to persuade Juan Núñez II to accept the *infante* Pedro's tutelage over the young king Alfonso XI, the Aragonese would negotiate through the Portuguese king.[110] It appears to be this strategy which led the nineteenth-century historian Antonio Benavides, in his *Memorias de Fernando IV,* to comment: "We do not wish to narrate the sad deeds of the two brothers [Juan Núñez II and Nuño González III]. In peace and in war they were not worthy emulators of their ancestors."[111] In reality, they were pursuing the same strategy of foreign alliance and military confrontation toward the Castilian crown that had been followed by Álvaro Núñez I and his brothers in 1217 and that had intensified in every succeeding generation. The Laras' attempts to establish themselves on the mountainous border of Aragón had failed; but in the next generation, they would make one last, successful attempt to dominate a huge territorial estate, turning their attention further north to Vizcaya.

6

Ricos Hombres

*T*HE ESCALATING CONFRONTATION between the monarchy and the Laras was not an isolated phenomenon. It was part of a more general process whereby, from the mid-thirteenth century, the Castilian nobility increasingly asserted interests conflicting with those of the crown. The nobles found their most eloquent ideologist in the rebellious Juan Manuel (1282–1348), whose aristocratic self-consciousness and passionate conviction in the exceptional qualities of a *rico hombre* were the natural product of the conflicts of the previous two generations. According to Juan Manuel, a *rico hombre* was not merely a wealthy man, an *hombre rico;* he was a man supremely rich in honor. Nor were all *ricos hombres* created equal, for "there are some who come from the lineage of the kings."[1] This was true both in his own case, as nephew of Alfonso X, and in the case of his brother-in-law, Juan Núñez III de Lara, great-grandson of the Learned King. Juan Manuel and the Laras were close allies, as well as relatives. Their alliance would be steeped in the same aristocratic hauteur that ran through most of Juan Manuel's writings. Beneath it lay a faith that the Castilian *ricos hombres* stood at the peak of a divinely ordained social hierarchy, endowed with responsibilities which had to be performed to save their souls, but also blessed with ethereally elevated status. Don Juan would prove to be the nemesis of Alfonso XI (reigned 1312–1350). The noble *mentalité* that he expressed would stoke the fires set by the Laras' patrimonial accumulation and royal policies of centralization, now vigorously renewed.

A remarkable narrative in the *Gran crónica de Alfonso XI* (written between 1376 and 1379) tells us that in the summer of 1315, while the Cortes were meeting in Burgos, the elderly Juan Núñez II de Lara was approaching death:

> And he made his will; and because he did not have a male heir or daughter who might inherit after his death, he donated Lara, which was his, and everything he had in the world, for the sake of his soul. And the hidalgos of Castile agreed that it was not a good thing for the honorable house of Lara to be without a lord, because it had always been one of the three great lineages of Castile; and with the consent of the king and his advisors and everyone else, they gave a hereditary lord to the house of Lara, and this was Juan Núñez [III]. And so that [he] might inherit the house of Lara, the hidalgos of Castile imposed a tax on themselves and collected a very large sum, so that land and towns and castles were bought for the lordship of Lara.[2]

This narrative raises some perplexing questions. Why should Juan Núñez II, who had fought so hard to expand his territorial strength, have wished to alienate his lands in an era when they were more essential than ever for the future of his lineage? Even more curious, why should everyone else in the Cortes have wished to prevent this from happening? The story is not present in the earlier *Crónica de Alfonso XI*, which often forms the basis for the *Gran crónica* but which here says simply that "Don Juan Núñez died in Burgos, while he was in the Cortes."[3] The more elaborate account may well be fictitious; it has all the color of an apocryphal tale. Yet its views are significant, because the two versions of the event clearly reflect markedly different attitudes toward political power. Whereas in the earlier *Crónica* the motivations of the nobility are selfish and royal authoritarianism is justified, the sympathies of the *Gran Crónica* lie squarely with the nobility.[4] Its perspective was, in fact, widely shared. Now that hostility between the Lara family and the crown had become endemic, the strength of this great lineage was perceived in many quarters as an essential balance to the aspirations of the crown. In this sense, the anecdote is entirely accurate. The Laras would receive conspicuous support from the townsmen and other Castilian nobles, just as they had earlier received support from abroad.

For the Lara family, the promise of foreign connections had finally dissipated. Their relationship with Granada had proved too ephemeral, their relationship with Portugal too weak, and their relationships with France and Aragón too subject to the higher interests of these great kingdoms to serve the long-term purposes of the lineage. For firmer friendships, they would need to look closer to home. None of the great secular powers in Castilian society—monarchy, aristocratic families, or municipalities—operated in isolation; all sought the collaboration of others. The centralizing monarchy of Alfonso X, for instance, relied more heavily than his twelfth-century predecessors on the urban *concejos*, which he used as a counterbalance to the growing power of the nobility.[5] The townspeople in turn might seek either royal patronage or collaboration with an aristocratic lineage; the *concejos* of Extremadura had frequently rallied around the Laras in the late twelfth and early thirteenth centuries.[6] The Laras were typical of all aristocratic families in their fluctuating alliances with the municipalities, other segments of the nobility, and the Castilian monarchy. However, the degree of power they had amassed by the end of the thirteenth century was exceptional, and this gave them a special role in the balance of power in Castile. They were widely perceived as a counterbalance to the monarchy, as an alternative locus of power, and they became representative of a broad segment of society in moments of crisis.

The degree to which this perception had evolved by the middle of the fourteenth century is reflected in another curious passage, this time in the *Crónica geral de Espanha de 1344*. The Portuguese chronicler, Dom Pedro de Barcelos, is describing the early years of the reign of Alfonso VIII of Castile (1158–1214), and recounting how Diego López de Haro advised the king on the best way to raise a contribution from the nobility for a campaign against the Moors. An assembly of the nobility is arranged. Nuño Pérez de Lara, however, leads intense resistance to the proposed contribution, claiming that it is unprecedented. He storms out of the meeting, and, according to the chronicle, three thousand rebels then gather in a field under his leadership, with the proposed contribution of five *maravedís* stuck provocatively to the ends of their lances. They send a message to the king, sardonically explaining where he can pick up the money, and the king quite understandably declines the offer. The situation is defused only by Diego López de Haro's voluntary departure from the kingdom. The hidalgos of Castile then recognize the leadership of Nuño Pérez by deciding to give him and his future descendants the fruits of their lands. Thus, there would always be mutual assistance if the kings did not behave as they should. This, the chronicler concludes, is the origin of the Laras' powerful seigneurial position in Castile.[7]

Quite rightly, Julio González—perhaps the principal historian of the reign—questions the veracity of this tale. He argues that it is not credible in several respects, such as the king's ignorance about methods of tax raising, the extraordinary number of rebels, and the claim that Nuño Pérez (a member of a family known to have enjoyed good relations with Alfonso VIII) organized a rebellion against him. Most conclusively, the actual departure of Diego López de Haro from the kingdom did not come until 1203.[8] However, the chronicler's assumption of a confrontational attitude between the Laras and the monarchy reveals a good deal about Castilian affairs in the fourteenth century, if not the twelfth. It suggests a perception that the Laras in this later period enjoyed considerable support from the other noble families, who required their leadership in order to resist the encroachments and impositions of royal authority. In the late twelfth and early thirteenth centuries, the support that the Laras received from other lineages had actually rested in large part on their proximity to the crown. The control over resources that they enjoyed during their hegemony in Enrique I's reign, for example, had inevitably attracted widespread aristocratic support, since the monarchy was the fulcrum of the patronage system. But the family's new role as a counterbalance was catalyzed by the new adversarial relationship between the Laras and other noble lineages, on the one hand, and the monarchy, on the other. Nuño González's role as spokesman and leader of the rebellious nobles in 1272, expressing a number of widely shared grievances to Alfonso X, had been the first occasion when this role became clear. The depoliticized unrest of the reigns of Sancho IV and Fernando IV, and our reliance on the royal chronicles, makes it hard to trace the evolution of the Laras' role in these decades, but there is at least one important clue. Incorporated in an ordinance of the Cortes of Valladolid, dated 4 April 1312, is an agreement which had been reached on 28 October 1311 between Fernando IV and a group of nobles including Juan Núñez II, acting on their own behalf and for the other *ricos hombres* of the land. The nobles agreed that they would not take *yantar* or *pedido* from lands which were not their own and that any castles built on such lands since the death of

Sancho IV were to be destroyed. In return, they would assist in the administration of justice; royal *merinos* would not demand food and lodging on the patrimonial lands of the *ricos hombres;* and the king would continue to grant the stipends and grants agreed in the ordinance of Burgos, along with their customary *fueros.*[9] We begin to see here the same kind of politicized struggle for position between a centralizing monarchy and an assertive nobility which had been a feature of the reign of Alfonso X, with the Laras at the center of the action.

During the long minority of Alfonso XI, which lasted from 1312 until 1325, the Laras' political leadership was much clearer. It is important to recognize the breadth of popular support that Juan Núñez II enjoyed at the beginning of the minority. After he had outmaneuvered the *infante* Pedro and successfully secured provisional custody of the king (1312–1313), Juan Núñez gained the backing of a number of important towns. Although the bishop-elect of Ávila decided to keep the king under guard in the town, we are told that Juan Núñez successfully persuaded the townspeople of his good intentions and managed to prevent the *infante* Pedro from entering the town until the people had decided what his future should be. He then went to Burgos, making oaths of mutual support with the townspeople there, and gained similar support in Cuellar and Extremadura.[10] At the Cortes held in Palencia in the early summer of 1313, the *infante* Juan, with whom Juan Núñez had allied himself, was duly elected regent.[11] Certainly, his cause did not enjoy universal support. A rival meeting of the Cortes was summoned by Queen María and the *infante* Pedro, and León in particular was bitterly divided.[12] On 1 August 1314, María was granted the custody and tutelage of her grandson, Alfonso XI.[13] Even so, it is clear that Juan Núñez was far from politically isolated. In the first clause of the ordinance issued at the Cortes of Carrión (28 March 1317), Queen María and the *infante* Juan stated that they would give the king the knightly governor that a new *hermandad* of nobles had requested "with the advice of Juan Núñez and other good men."[14] They may have been referring either to counsel given sometime earlier by Juan Núñez II, who had died in 1315,[15] or to that given by his nephew and successor as head of the lineage, Juan Núñez III (d. 1350). Juan Núñez III was still very young; he does not otherwise appear in any active role until 1322.[16] If the reference is to him, it is possible that his role was simply that of a figurehead—that he was championed as the leader of the *hermandad* because the Laras had traditionally assumed this role. In any case, the pivotal role of the family in the expression of broader grievances was evidently well recognized. The otherwise baffling account of how Juan Núñez III had inherited the title to the possessions of the house of Lara as a result of the machinations of the Cortes (the narrative from the *Gran crónica de Alfonso XI*, quoted at the beginning of this chapter) now begins to make more sense. Like the tale of Nuño Pérez's resistance to royal taxation, we should certainly not take the account at face value. The scenario that Salazar depicts—in which the old lord's sister, Juana *la Palomilla*, inherited the family estates and immediately granted them to her eldest son, Juan Núñez III—is more likely; inheritance by a nephew was not unheard of.[17] Yet the basic element in the account is the implication that the Laras, who by diplomacy and patrimony had accumulated immense wealth and influence, enjoyed very widespread support among the nobility of the realm and in the Cortes. Even the relatively sanguine *Crónica de Alfonso XI* states that because of Juan Núñez's inheritance, "many hidalgos of the kingdoms of Castile and León wanted to help him against the king of Castile."[18] The perception of the family as a counterbalance to the Castilian monarchy would persist into the adulthood of Juan Núñez III, the twilight of the Laras.

UNTIL THE END OF THE 1320S, the young Juan Núñez III remained a loyal presence at the royal court. He confirmed a large number of royal diplomas from 1322 onward;[19] and by the late 1320s he even enjoyed the coveted office of *alférez*.[20] Interestingly, between 1328 and 1337, he appears in the documentation as Juan Núñez "de Lara." This is the first series of references in the diplomas to a "lord of Lara" who was not its tenant.[21] Jurisdiction over Lara itself had now been fully absorbed by the town of Burgos, and the appellative "de Lara" had vanished in thirteenth-century diplomas along with the tenancy.[22] At that stage, the family's sense of ancestry had typically been limited to the one preceding generation, and indeed Juan Núñez III himself had initially appeared simply as "son of Don Fernando." True, Nuño González I had been identified as a "Lara" in the *Crónica del rey don Alfonso décimo* and in the *Chronicle of James I*.[23] In diplomas, however, even the belated use of the *apellido* by Juan Núñez II had been isolated, and only now did it became regular practice.[24] Neither Juan Núñez III nor his uncle and namesake enjoyed any rights in their ancestors' tenancy. The reasons for his adoption of the title "de Lara" lie instead in the increasingly general use of *apellidos* among the Castilian nobility, in the emergent sense of ancestry that this reflected, and above all in the aristocratic ethos associated with Don Juan Manuel.[25]

In January 1329, as Juan Manuel was putting the finishing touches to his *Libro de los estados,* he was betrothed to one of Juan Núñez's five sisters, Blanca.[26] He was a man of unusual erudition, and was consciously instrumental in forging new cultural and intellectual standards among the social elite.[27] But he also shared and articulated the spirit of insubordination that had become increasingly typical of the Castilian aristocracy. A man should endure all things except dishonor, rather than go to war, he wrote in the *Libro.*[28] Just over a year earlier, he had been stripped of his royal offices; but by virtue of his territorial power, he (unlike the nobles of the twelfth century) had the option of long-term resistance, and a rebel alliance with the Laras now quickly took shape. Juan Manuel, whom the chronicler perceives as the arch-conspirator, first approached the mother of Juan Núñez to seek her consent for a marriage between her son and María de Haro. He maintained that María, no more than a small child, was the rightful heiress to the lordship of Vizcaya, which he claimed had been taken wrongfully from her father, Juan *el Tuerto,* who had been executed by Alfonso XI. He proposed that the two men should go to war in order to recover this lordship for María and her groom. The marriage was solemnized, and thenceforth, his ally Juan Núñez "complained that the king had disinherited him."[29] Although Juan Manuel seems to have seen war as a necessary evil, rather than as a source of glory, it is entirely probable that he did indeed play the conspiratorial role attributed to him in the chronicle. Certainly, he was the dominant partner in the relationship in the early 1330s.[30] But the seeds of conflict over Vizcaya had been sown long before these machinations. The Laras' new claim to the lordship was merely the latest in a series of attempts by the family to establish control over a number of large territorial estates. These attempts had hitherto focused on the Aragonese frontier, and had revolved around the efforts of Juan Núñez's uncle and great uncle to consolidate a hold on Albarracín and Molina. But Vizcaya was the largest, most coherent, and possibly wealthiest estate in Castile. It was almost inevitable that the Laras would be drawn into the struggle for its possession.

To the extent that we may judge from a letter of 1373 written to

King Enrique II, in which Juan Núñez's sister María would describe the extent of the lordship to which she felt entitled, Juan Núñez III was laying claim to a quite enormous lordship (see Map 15). First and foremost, it included "the land of Vizcaya, with all its monasteries and rights and *divisas*."[31] This would have encompassed a range of thriving towns, such as Bilbao, Lekeitio, and Durango, many of which had been given charters in the late thirteenth and early fourteenth centuries. Urban growth in Vizcaya had been stimulated by the importance of the region as a transit zone for Castilian trade, and over the course of the thirteenth century long-distance trade, the fishing industry, and iron production had all flourished. The period between 1280 and 1350 was characterized by stagnation in the rural economy, yet also by continued urban and mercantile growth.[32] But this was not all. The lordship of Vizcaya also encompassed a wide array of patrimonial and jurisdictional rights elsewhere in Spain:

Beyond the land of Vizcaya, these places—namely, the Encartaciones . . . and the town of Santa Gadea, and Lozoya, Grisaleña, and Fuentebureba, and Berzosa, and Cevico de la Torre, and Cigales, and Paredes de Nava, and Villalón de Campos, and Cuenca de Tamariz [Cuenca de Campos], and Melgar de la Frontera, and El Barzón, and Moral de la Reina, and Aguilar de Campos, and Castroverde de Campos, and Cabreros del Monte, and Belver de los Montes, and Santiago de la Puebla near Salamanca, and Oropesa, and El Campo de Arañuelo. . . . Furthermore, the lord of Vizcaya is *natural* of the *behetrías*, but not so much as the [lord] of Lara.[33]

Not all of these places were part of the lordship of Vizcaya when Juan Núñez first acquired it (Cigales, Villalón, and Moral de la Reina were all granted to him later in a single grant by Alfonso XI).[34] Equally, it is certain that not all remained part of it by the end of Juan Núñez's career; for instance, he alienated Fuentebureba and Berzosa in 1346.[35] Nonetheless, a number of places to which María refers (for instance, Cevico de la Torre, Cigales, Cuenca de Campos, Moral de la Reina, and Aguilar de Campos) would still be patrimonial possessions of the Laras in the middle of the century. Alfonso XI, who was particularly determined to establish his authority in the restless Basque country,

15. Juan Núñez III (d. 1350)

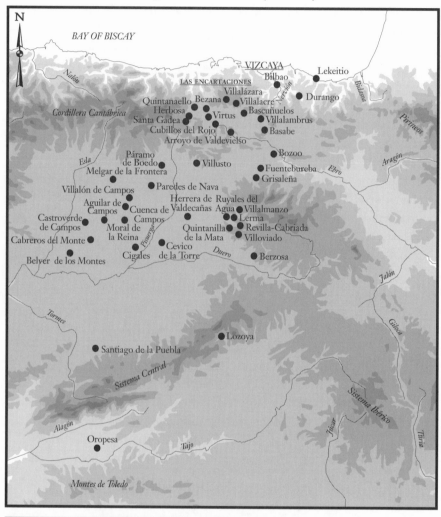

N

BAY OF BISCAY

VIZCAYA

Lekeitio

Bilbao

LAS ENCARTACIONES

Villalázara

Durango

Quintanaello Bezana   Villalacre

Herbosa   Bascuñuelos

Santa Gadea   Virtus   Villalambrus

Cubillos del Rojo   Basabe

Arroyo de Valdevielso

Cordillera Cantábrica

Nalón

Bozoo

Páramo
de Boedo   Villusto   Fuentebureba

Melgar de la Frontera   Grisaleña

Esla

Villalón de Campos   Paredes de Nava

Aguilar de   Herrera de Ruyales del

Campos   Cuenca de Valdecañas Agua Villalmanzo

Castroverde   Campos   Lerma

de Campos   Moral de   Quintanilla   Revilla-Cabriada

Cabreros del Monte   la Reina   de la Mata   Villoviado

Cevico

Belver de los Montes   Cigales   de la Torre   Berzosa

Pisuerga

Duero

Ebro

Aragón

Pirineos

Bidasoa

Nervión

Arlanzón

Jalón

Tormes

Lozoya

Santiago de la Puebla

Sistema Central

Gállego

Sistema Ibérico

Alagón

Oropesa

Tajo

Júcar

Turia

Montes de Toledo

●	Patrimony
○	Tenancy
◉	Both Tenancy and Patrimony
EXTREMADURA ASTURIAS DE OVIEDO	Areas of Tenancy
CASTILLA BUREBA	Areas of Patrimony

0   10   20   30 miles

was not prepared to tolerate the challenge to his possession of this enormous lordship. In 1332, he had finally managed to place the neighboring Basque province of Alava under royal jurisdiction, superseding its old judicial and fiscal autonomy.[36] Two years later, in 1334, he attempted to establish effective control of Vizcaya, over which the crown had enjoyed only nominal authority, and to expel Juan Núñez from the region. After besieging Peña Ventosa, he succeeded in this immediate aim despite meeting stiff resistance near Bermeo.[37] The war now began to escalate, however, spreading to Juan Núñez's stronghold of Herrera de Valdecañas, and Alfonso was soon forced to offer to relinquish his claims to Vizcaya in return for Juan Núñez's loyalty and a number of places granted as surety.[38] But tensions remained severe, and after the rebels secured an alliance with the Portuguese, conflict erupted again. On 14 June 1336, royal forces arrived at the fortress of Lerma, preparing for a long siege.[39]

JUST AS JUAN NÚÑEZ'S MARRIAGE should be seen against the backdrop of a longer patrimonial strategy, Alfonso XI's policy toward Vizcaya was one aspect of a more general affirmation of central authority. As Hilda Grassotti has shown, this strategy involved, for instance, the defense of royal patrimony by limiting the number of grants in *merum imperium* (full jurisdictional lordship), which had begun to flourish in the early part of the century. Grassotti claims that, without using the precise formula, Alfonso XI did continue to make such grants on occasion—to his illegitimate children, to his mistress Leonor de Guzmán, to influential court officials, and to his noble vassals. But with regard to the last of these categories, she rather revealingly adds in a footnote that she has found no examples.[40] It seems clear that in reality Alfonso pursued a fairly successful policy designed to shackle the advance of patrimonial jurisdiction among the aristocracy, and that his absorption of Vizcaya was absolutely central to this policy. Royal centralization also assumed a number of other forms in this reign. In the aftermath of the civil war of 1334–1336, Alfonso XI would begin administrative reforms "designed to make the crown's hard-won victory over the nobility permanent"—the reimposition of the *Fuero Real*, in 1339, being prominent among them.[41] The Ordenamiento of Alcalá (1348) imposed a partly Roman legal system of the type which Alfonso X had attempted to introduce, with less success, almost a century earlier. There is also evidence of such policy from earlier in the reign. During the king's minority, the three positions of *merino mayor* (in Castilla, León, and Galicia) had been dominated by people of high noble status, but from the 1320s the positions were granted more frequently to lesser nobility—usually from the same *merindad*—and for shorter periods of time.[42] Alfonso wanted to raise his favorites, men like Álvar Núñez Osorio and Garcilaso de la Vega, to the level of *ricos hombres* in order to challenge the power of established aristocrats like Juan Núñez III and Juan Manuel. The influence of the *letrados*, professional jurists and administrators who may be considered public officials, also increased markedly under Alfonso XI.[43] Among them was Fernán Sánchez de Valladolid, who was probably the chronicler of the reigns of Alfonso X, Sancho IV, and Fernando IV and author of the thoroughly monarchist *Crónica de Alfonso XI*. This latter chronicle reveals an intimate knowledge of confidential royal documents, and a sympathetic perception of the king as the supreme judge and rightful creator of laws.[44]

The reaffirmation of royal authority ran headlong not only into the Laras' own policy of patrimonial accumulation, but also, more generally, into widespread noble disaffection. For many lords, this was an era of falling real income. Inflation in the price of food was consistently high in the early fourteenth century, and there were intermittent agrarian crises (for instance, in 1331–1333 and 1343–1346). Repeated monetary devaluations (1330, 1343) accentuated inflation and contributed to a vicious circle of economic depression.[45] The role of this inflation in accentuating political unrest and heightening territorial sensitivities in the late thirteenth and early fourteenth centuries has been emphasized in earlier chapters, and it is possible that the economic tension of the early 1330s was associated once again with the escalating political crisis. The Laras' confrontation of the monarchy was far from unique, and there is evidence of extensive support for the Laras before, during, and even after the civil war. Juan Núñez III's support had begun to grow significantly in 1333 as a result of palace defections. To the king's considerable consternation, Juan Martínez de Leiva (who was dissatisfied by the favor shown at court to Alfonso Fernández Coronel), Juan Furtado, his brother Diego Furtado, Sancho Ruiz de Rojas, and Ruy Pérez de Soto all joined the lord of Lara at his stronghold at Lerma.[46] Perhaps even more usefully, Juan Núñez retained influential contacts at court, and, following a royal assault on his mother's castle of

Torrelobatón in 1334, he "sent letters to some friends he had in the king's household, asking that they speak to the king—but not on his behalf, rather with the appearance of giving counsel—and that they tell him that it would be good if there were an agreement between him and Juan Núñez; and they did so."[47]

A little later, when tension had been defused (but not eliminated), and when the king was appointing a mediator between himself and the king of Aragón, he chose the archbishop of Rheims rather than a Castilian noble "because he was not certain that Juan Manuel and Juan Núñez wanted to serve him, and also because he was told that some of the aristocrats of his lordship and other knights wanted to help Juan Manuel and Juan Núñez."[48] This apprehension was borne out by events themselves, once the long siege of Lerma began. The *Gran crónica* recounts that, taking advantage of a brief departure by the king (who had been distracted by Juan Manuel's activities near Peñafiel), Juan Núñez stormed out of the town and attacked the besieging forces "on the advice of some of the king's men."[49] As the tide began to turn decisively at the siege of Lerma and it became clear that Alfonso XI would win, some of the *ricos hombres* and hidalgos in the royal camp—fearing that the king would have Juan Núñez executed—asked Queen María to come from Burgos and have the siege lifted.[50]

The Laras, then, had come to be perceived as a political counterbalance, an alternative focus of power around which opposition to the crown might coalesce. This role was heightened by the absence of a truly powerful representative assembly. The Cortes was not much of a balance to royal authority; it exerted some control over taxation and was frequently the arena for expression of aristocratic discontent, but it was not an institution accustomed to acting against the king and could not function without him. There is some indication, however, that in the first half of the fourteenth century the lord of Lara came to be acknowledged as the respondent in the Cortes for the nobility as a whole. Both Juan Núñez II and Juan Núñez III had been focal points of opposition in the Cortes during the 1310s; María de Lara would claim in 1373 that "the lord of Lara always speaks in the Cortes for the nobles of Castile."[51] Juan Núñez's cooperation with Alfonso XI in the 1340s may have reduced his prominence in the Cortes, and it is unlikely that he was associated with the complaints against the Ordenamiento of Alcalá which were voiced in 1348.[52] Even so, he appears to have retained an active voice in the Cortes. Describing a dispute over primacy between the representatives of Toledo and Burgos in the Cortes of Valladolid in 1351, Ayala refers to a similar dispute at the Cortes held in Alcalá in which Juan Manuel had upheld the rights of Toledo while Juan Núñez had spoken in defense of Burgos. Juan Núñez, here, was acting on behalf of a specific group of urban representatives and not the Castilian nobility as a whole, but his activism within the Cortes is striking.[53]

Juan Núñez III's foreign alliances were varied, but less crucial than internal support. In the summer of 1332, he and Juan Manuel had collaborated with the Nasrid dynasty of Granada in a military campaign against Alfonso XI of Castile; more indirectly, he exploited hostilities between Castile and Granada on more than one occasion in order to force the king to negotiate over Vizcaya.[54] The two rebel leaders also seem likely to have been in contact with the French at this stage, since Alfonso XI was apprehensive that the king of France would assist them in rebellion.[55] Juan Núñez's sister María was raised at the court of Philip VI of France and in 1336 (significantly, the year in which Lerma was besieged) was married to Charles de Valois, count of Alençon and a brother of the French king.[56] The royalist force at Lerma, in contrast, included a large number of English and Gascon soldiers, hailing from regions which were involved in intense hostilities toward the French.[57] Nevertheless, there is no evidence that the rebels received direct assistance from France. Peace overtures between the French and the Castilians, late in 1336, would certainly have prevented any alliance between France and the Laras had it been sought thereafter. Equally, Juan Núñez and Juan Manuel had contacted the king of Aragón, as military conflict with Alfonso XI developed, but they did not (at least at first) receive the direct assistance they sought.[58] An alliance with Portugal, originally secured in 1334, bore more fruit during the siege of Lerma. After requesting in vain that Alfonso XI raise the siege, the king of Portugal first besieged Badajoz and then—after abandoning this action—began a series of invasions across the Galician border.[59]

After Lerma was eventually surrendered, on 4 December 1336, Juan Núñez III and the king were reconciled.[60] The key to the détente was recognition of Juan Núñez's right to the lordship of Vizcaya; from 1338, he proudly dropped the *apellido* "de Lara" in favor of emphasizing his possession of Vizcaya.[61] Juan Núñez was again a frequent presence at the royal court.[62] On the basis that he ultimately spent a greater number of years at court than in opposition, it might appear that cooperation was more fundamental than confrontation. Certainly it was more conspicuous than in the previous generation. His position was strengthened by his closeness to the king's beautiful mistress, Leonor de Guzmán, to whose son, Don Tello, he would marry his daughter Juana.[63] But cooperation was, in the long term, an economic necessity for Castilian noble families, and could mask deep personal suspicions and even deeper structural tensions between crown and nobility. The superficiality of the reconciliation was doubtless palpable when, the siege barely ended, Juan Núñez spent Christmas with the king in Valladolid. His appointment as *alférez* at that time, like the hereditary grant of Villalón, Cigales, and Moral de la Reina, must have been recognized as a mercenary purchase of his loyalty.[64] The tournament arranged in Burgos for Easter Monday, 1338, in which Juan Núñez and other nobles participated, cannot have been—as the chronicler would have us believe—an effort to ensure that the knights did not lose their military skills.[65] After all, the king could hardly have been concerned that Juan Núñez was out of practice. Instead, it should be seen as an effort to harness these military skills in royal service.

For the next dozen years, this effort was very successful. Juan Núñez was present, as *alférez*, in the royal army that attacked Ronda in 1339.[66] The following year, he played a vital role in an assault on Moorish forces at Tarifa, forcing the Muslims to flee.[67] Along with Chaucer's pilgrim-knight, he took part in the siege of Algeciras (1343), and launched a successful frontal assault on the Moorish troops holding the port.[68] By the summer of 1344, he had also acquired the position of *mayordomo mayor*, either as a reward for loyal service or as an inducement to remain at court now that the siege of Algeciras was over. To judge by a letter of 5 July, Juan Núñez pursued his duties with enthusiasm. He complained that his *despensero mayor*, who was supposed to give Juan Sánchez de Arce 6,000 *maravedís* from the treasury so that he could serve in the campaign at Algeciras, had given him only 2,000 and that Juan Sánchez had not used them for the campaign. He now demanded the payment of double this sum, under threat of seizing the *despensero*'s property and selling it to the royal *merinos*.[69] Like the office of *alférez*, Juan Núñez retained the position of *mayordomo* until the end of the reign.[70] To all appearances, he was now the very model of a royal servant.[71] A phase of success in Andalucía had transformed the court into a virtually irresistible political magnet.

Yet the harmony between Juan Núñez and Alfonso XI, after 1336, was illusory. Juan Núñez was present at the siege of Gibraltar in 1350, where the king and many other soldiers perished from the plague, and he loyally accompanied the king's body through Medina Sidonia to Seville, where Alfonso was buried. But his loyalty to the crown lasted little longer than the king himself.[72] The new monarch, Pedro I (reigned 1350–1369), and his mother, María of Portugal, had been ingloriously ostracized by his father, Alfonso XI; Alfonso had favored his mistress, Leonor de Guzmán, and their illegitimate children, Enrique, Fadrique, and Don Tello. Doña Leonor had been a close and active confidante of the king, as well as a devoted mother and lover, and had feared for her future even before Alfonso's death. She had sought to strengthen her position through a marriage alliance between one of her sons, Don Tello, and Doña Juana, daughter of Juan Núñez III. The lord of Lara became her principal ally in the early days of the new reign, and for a moment it must have seemed that her calculations had paid off. Juan Núñez retained the offices of *alférez* and *mayordomo mayor* for a few months, and played an active role in the formation of the new regime.[73] But King Pedro and his mother then took their revenge: Leonor was imprisoned, and enormous influence in administration was granted to a Portuguese nobleman, Juan Alfonso de Alburquerque, who became the archenemy of the Laras.

There was still a ray of hope. In August 1350 Pedro fell gravely ill, having probably contracted the plague, and lay on the point of death. Among the aspirants to succeed the childless king was none other than Juan Núñez himself, basing his claim on his descent from the dispossessed La Cerdas; he was supported by Alfonso Fernández Coronel, Garcilaso de la Vega, and many other Castilian knights. One might perhaps have thought, in the summer of 1350, that the power of the Laras was about to reach a height unequaled in the family's history. Far from it. Juan Núñez's candidacy was now rejected on the grounds that his grandfather, Alfonso de la Cerda, had allegedly renounced his claims to the throne. Efforts by Juan Núñez's party to marry him to Alfonso XI's widow, María, were supported by her father, the king of Portugal. But quite unexpectedly the king regained his health, his relations with the lord of Lara much the worse for the affair. Leaving the royal court at Seville, Juan Núñez returned, enraged and empty-handed, to Castile. His old preeminence at court was now assumed by Alburquerque, whose marriage to Isabel de Meneses had helped catapult him into a position of extraordinary power. Juan Núñez immediately began to drum up opposition; but on Sunday, 28 November 1350, he suddenly died.[74] One recent study suggests: "It is not too far-fetched to suppose, as his contemporary supporters did, that Alburquerque had a hand in his death; in fact, it was rumored that Lara was poisoned by one of Alburquerque's men."[75] The royal chronicle, meanwhile, states that after Juan Núñez's death, to the delight of Juan Alfonso de Alburquerque, many *behetrías* reverted to the king.[76] This was by no means the normal legal procedure, since the *behetrías* were not royal possessions to be granted out or reclaimed; rather, they were places where—at an intermediate level—multiple lords enjoyed a share of the jurisdiction, and where at a superior level a nobleman acted as lord. The inhabitants theoretically enjoyed some degree of freedom in choosing this lord.[77] The reversion of Juan Núñez's *behetrías* reflects, therefore, his essentially poor relationship with King Pedro and, in the long term, the more fundamental interest of the monarchy in limiting the patrimonial power of the Lara family.

PATRIMONIAL AND JURISDICTIONAL authority was, after all, the principal basis of noble power in the mid-fourteenth century. In discussing it, we have an exceptional source, the *Libro becerro de behetrías* (*LBB*). During the Cortes of 1351, King Pedro promised an inquiry into the nature of royal landholding, as the first step toward meeting a request by the nobility to increase the size of his grants in land and money. The driving force seems to have been Juan Alfonso de Alburquerque, who must have hoped to parlay his political prominence into greater territorial power. There soon followed a petition requesting a redistribution of the *behetrías* in the form of *solariegos*—that is to say, villages where the lord was a nobleman. The petition further called for an inquiry into the nature of lordship and the identity of lords in each *behetría*. Pedro agreed, and between the autumn of 1351 and August 1352 an inquiry was conducted into landholding in northern Castile, resulting in the great *Libro becerro*.[78] The *LBB*, if not quite a Spanish *Domesday Book*, is still a fundamental source on the social and economic history of fourteenth-century Castile, and on the Laras. Strictly speaking, the lord of Lara in 1351–1352 was the little infant Nuño de Lara, but in view of the short time that had elapsed since his father's death, we can assume that Juan Núñez III had enjoyed similar interests. Indeed, Juan Núñez's exactions are sometimes mentioned specifically. The shortcomings of the text are admittedly considerable. It does not list all settlements but mentions only those which are a fiscal entity, and therefore ignores a number of dependent villages; its coverage is sketchy in the *merindad* of Santo Domingo de Silos. It completely excludes four *merindades*, in some of which the Laras were powerful, and six smaller areas within the boundaries of those fifteen *merindades* which are included.[79] Finally, throughout the text there are insidious signs of haste: blank entries, the vague statement that the inhabitants of Lerma pay "what it befalls them to pay," or a frustrated remark that the villagers of Quintanilla do not know how much of the payment known as *infurción* is due. Nevertheless, the *LBB* allows a reasonably full quantitative analysis of the Laras' property rights in the north of the peninsula.

The most immediately conspicuous feature of the Laras' profile in the *LBB* is the astonishing number of settlements in which they enjoyed some form of lordship: 320 out of the 2,402 settlements listed, or 13.2 percent of the total. Map 15 includes the places that appear as full *solariegos* (exclusive seigneurial villages) of the Laras in the *LBB*, but not the hundreds of other instances where they hold other forms of property rights. The Laras were a little weaker in western Castile than elsewhere. Four of the five *merindades* where they were lords in fewer than ten settlements lay toward the west;[80] this is also true of Saldaña and Carrión, in which their presence may be described as no better than moderate.[81] Overall, they were more influential in the eastern *merindades* of Castilla la Vieja and Santo Domingo de Silos, and in the central *merindades* of Cerrato, Monzón, Castrojeriz, and Candemuño.[82] The Laras' greatest economic base, within the area covered by the survey, was Castilla la Vieja, the largest and most heavily seigneurialized district. Almost a third (eight out of twenty-nine) of all the family's exclusive *solariegos* were located here. If we add to this the partial *solariegos*, where hereditary seigneurial rights were shared with other nobles, with the church, or with the crown, the proportion rises to over half (thirty-nine out of sixty-four). This is likely to have been by far the most lucrative of the *merindades* for the Lara family.[83] But the family's presence was diffuse: they appear in all but one of the fifteen *merindades menores* (the regional subdistricts) covered by the *LBB*, the solitary exception being Asturias de Santillana. Particularly prominent is the large number of places where they were *diviseros* (or, synonymously, *naturales*)—in other words, villages where they figured among the intermediate ranks of nobles who had a share *(divisa)* in the jurisdictional spoils of a *behetría*. It was this form of lordship that was in fact most ubiquitous, since family members were *naturales* or *diviseros* in all but three districts (Asturias de Santillana again, the *infantazg*o of Valladolid, and Aguilar de Campóo). Superior lordship of *behetrías*, and far more commonly the intermediate function of *diviseros* alone, together comprised exactly four-fifths of their influence as revealed by the *LBB*.[84]

The income which the Laras received was partly monetary and partly in kind. *Yantar*, a form of imposition originally consisting of the right of a noble and his entourage to be fed by those over whom he was lord, is a good example. In a few cases it retained its original character (several entries refer to the lord of Lara "eating" *yantar*), but elsewhere this obligation had been commuted into monetary form.[85] Figures are sometimes given for payment of *yantar* by the whole village;[86] less often, they are given by head.[87] Two other common forms of income—payment given to *diviseros* and *martiniega*—were usually paid in coin. In the case of the Laras, the former is assessed with curious uniformity at either 6 or $6\frac{1}{3}$ *maravedís* (a sum quite frequently higher than that received by other *naturales*), typically payable on Saint John's day.[88] *Martiniega*, whose origins were more recent, seems to have been paid almost invariably in monetary form; the figures are generally high, and this must have been a very desirable form of income.[89] Finally, we may also assume that judicial fines were paid in coin, although explicit references to fines are surprisingly few and far between.[90] These monetary payments were surely collected and processed by private *merinos*. Such payments must have provided essential support for the Laras in periods of alienation from the royal court. The most varied form of income, however, was *infurción*, the form of rent paid to a lord by virtue of his possession of a *solariego* or *behetría*—and only rarely was *infurción* fully monetarized.[91] Far more frequently, it was paid partly in kind—in hens, pigs or bacon, wheat, barley, bread, wine, or unfermented grape juice. With the exception of one case in which a village appears to have provided fifty eggs at Christmas and Easter, this comprised the entire pool of staple products from which payment was made. The impression is of one of a very basic system of production, and a rural population within which economic divisions were limited. The social differentiation of the peasantry, as revealed by this source, appears to rest on possession and nonpossession of a small number of oxen. Means-testing for payment of *infurción* is frequently based on the number of these animals owned by each individual, the highest category of peasantry being defined as those with just two oxen. Occasionally, there are glimpses of extreme, abject rural poverty.[92] There may also be some indications of seigneurial aggression on the part of the Laras. In the *behetría* of Villasilos, the inhabitants complained that it had been the practice of Juan Núñez III to levy *martiniega* by force, and apparently for this reason they had now transferred their loyalties to another noble.[93] In the hamlet of Vadocondes, Nuño is one of a number of *diviseros* who—according to the villagers—"take from them what they have and do them many wrongs." The impotent frustration of the people of Vadocondes in the face of lordly exactions may well have been ubiquitous.[94] None of the evidence relating to the Laras in the *LBB*, however, suggests the profound social and economic upheaval one sees elsewhere in Europe in the aftermath of the Black Death. There is none of the tension regarding labor services which was racking England and France, and in fact such services appear to have had almost negligible importance.[95] It may be that labor services were higher than the *LBB* indicates, but it is hard to avoid the conclusion that they represented a relatively minor part of the Laras' extraordinary seigneurial power.[96]

IRONICALLY, the exceptionally revealing nature of the *LBB* presents us with a profoundly difficult (and equally important) question. To what degree had the Laras' jurisdictional and patrimonial rights in northern Castile already been developed in an earlier period, served less well by the documentary sources? As Claudio Sánchez Albornoz pointed out, the disproportionate prominence of the Laras in the *LBB* clearly reflects a seigneurial offensive at some stage: in his view, this took place in the twelfth and thirteenth centuries but may have been more recent.[97] In fact, it may tentatively be proposed that the family's extensive presence had advanced significantly in the previous few decades. There are indications within the *LBB* itself that the Laras had undertaken a seigneurial offensive of a rather pervasive and insidious

sort. It is interesting that in almost no area was there a correlation between the number of Lara *solariegos* and the number of places in which
they were exclusive lords or part-lords of *behetrías*.[98] We should surely
interpret this as a manifestation of the general process whereby in the
late thirteenth and fourteenth centuries *behetrías* were increasingly
controlled by the aristocracy, becoming particularly important as royal
donations dried up.[99] It was precisely in those *merindades* where the
Laras enjoyed extensive patrimonial strength that they would have
been in the best position to absorb *behetrías*, transforming them into
solariegos.[100] It is highly plausible that Juan Núñez III and his predecessors had absorbed a significant number of *behetrías*, either by purchase
or by less formal means.[101] Certainly, the general seigneurial offensive,
the infiltration of the high nobility into the *behetrías*, and the Laras'
new patrimonial strategy all suggest that this process can be associated
with the late thirteenth and early fourteenth centuries.[102]

The acquisition of Vizcaya was, of course, the most crucial element
in the Laras' strategy. This lordship itself was not included in the *LBB*,
although many of the attendant patrimonies and jurisdictions elsewhere in Castile were. Some of the lordship of Vizcaya had at various
stages been lost. Fuentebureba and Berzosa seem to have been alienated on a permanent basis;[103] and Aguilar de Campos and Castroverde
de Campos had been granted to Alfonso XI as surety for the peace settlement which recognized Juan Núñez's title to Vizcaya, and it is not
clear that he ever regained them.[104] Yet it was through the acquisition of Vizcaya that the Laras had become indisputably the most powerful aristocratic landowners in Castile.[105] It was this territorial power
which allowed the sixteenth-century author of the *Libro de los linages de
Hespaña* to write that the lord of Lara had "gran mayorasgo."[106] The
use of the late-medieval term *mayorazgo* (an entailed estate) to describe
the Laras' patrimony is technically inaccurate, since there is no evidence that any part of it was transmitted as an unalienable unity, and
the patrimony remained distinctly incoherent. But the fact that by the
mid-fourteenth century the Laras possessed landholdings that could be
seen as a *mayorazgo* along late-medieval lines is significant. Their territorial strength, long subordinate to their courtly influence, had by now
evolved to an extent comparable to that of the great noble lineages of
the fifteenth century. The Laras thus experienced a structural change—
the development of great seigneurial estates—that is widely but inaccu-

rately believed to postdate the Trastámara dynastic revolution of 1369. It has correctly been observed that the social and economic autonomy which had already developed among the leading nobles was one of the most important factors behind the emergence of noble lineages in the next century.[107] Any notion of a break between an "old nobility" and a "new nobility" around the mid-fourteenth century is undermined by biological continuity in the great lineages and by continuity in the evolution of power, since the Castilian aristocracy had already begun to accumulate a great deal of *dominio señorial*.[108]

The patrimonial power achieved by the Laras would not, however, ensure their survival into the Trastámara period. The heir to the Lara fortune, little Don Nuño, did briefly inherit his father's offices and principal titles: lord of Lara and Vizcaya, *alférez del rey*, and *mayordomo mayor*.[109] But in 1351, the year in which the matriarch of the family, Juana *la Palomilla*, passed away, an acute political crisis developed.[110] At the instigation of Juan Alfonso de Alburquerque, the king executed one of Juan Núñez's close supporters. The infant Nuño de Lara was immediately spirited away to the safety of his greatest lordship by some people of Vizcaya and his nurse, who had hitherto been raising him at Paredes de Nava. Not resting until they had crossed the Ebro, literally burning the bridge behind them, the young lord of Lara and his nurse escaped the clutches of the king.[111] But the family's reprieve was temporary. Nuño's premature death shortly thereafter, in mid-1352, would usher in a traumatic period in the family's history.[112]

Conclusion

$\mathcal{W}$HEN DID THE HISTORY of the Laras end? A case might be made for a conclusion in 1352, on the death of Nuño de Lara, the last legitimate male heir. Both his sisters, Juana and Isabel, were immediately taken into royal custody, and "all the lands of Lara" and Vizcaya passed temporarily into the hands of Pedro the Cruel.[1] The end might also be said to have come six years later, when King Pedro drove Don Tello, husband of the Lara heiress Juana, into exile. Most dramatically, perhaps, the history of the family would end in 1361, with the death of Juana's younger sister Isabel in a prison in Jérez de la Frontera. Yet this conclusion had long been foreshadowed. Royal policy toward the Laras had been characterized by confrontational behavior since the late thirteenth century; the conflict was accelerated, but not caused, by the accession of a hostile king. The chronicle of Pedro's reign, written under the usurping Trastámara dynasty, vilifies the king and obscures the reality that his policies differed only in degree from those of his father, Alfonso XI.[2] Both sought to centralize the government of Castile and undermine what they saw as the immoderate influence of the nobility; both relied on *letrados* of more humble background.[3] The underlying tension was heightened by Pedro's antipathy to the Laras because of their close association with Leonor de Guzmán; yet beneath individual resentments and the king's much-mythologized personal instability, there were far more deep-seated problems.

The imprisonment of the two Lara sisters was undoubtedly and unforgivably harsh; it was a manifestation of the provocative policies which have led one scholar to dub the king "Pedro the Politically Inept."[4] But in a fourteenth-century context, these policies were not unique; his father had, after all, dispossessed and even executed an earlier lord of Vizcaya. In each case the motivations of the monarch went beyond personal cruelty. For the crown, the vast patrimonial and jurisdictional influence of the Lara family was an unacceptable challenge to royal authority, and both Alfonso XI and Pedro made concerted attempts to combat it. In 1353, Pedro married the imprisoned heiress Juana to his estranged half-brother, Don Tello, who thus acquired the lordships of Lara and Vizcaya; the king clearly hoped thereby to eliminate the challenge, and simultaneously to bind a potential enemy more securely to the crown.[5] But the plan proved singularly unsuccessful: Pedro became convinced, perhaps rightly, that Don Tello was conspiring against him with another half-brother, Enrique de Trastámara (the future Enrique II). As a result, he arranged the marriage of Isabel, the second Lara heiress, to a relative whom he doubtless believed to be more trustworthy, his cousin the *infante* Juan of Aragón. Regretting his earlier decision to marry Juana de Lara to Don Tello, he instructed the *infante* Juan that he would now possess the lordships of Lara and Vizcaya by virtue of his marriage to Isabel, "to whom," he claimed, "the said lands belong."[6]

This royal policy very clearly flouted the rules of inheritance, and hostilities now escalated quickly. The most influential remaining member of the Lara family, Juana Manuel, was among those who gathered in opposition to King Pedro in the castle of Toro in 1355; and when the king forced his opponents to surrender in 1356, she was captured.[7] But military victory was evidently not enough to assuage the king. In June 1358, Pedro arrived at Don Tello's town of Aguilar de Campóo with the express purpose of killing him there. Although he was defeated in his purpose he successfully captured Juana de Lara instead. Don Tello, according to the chronicle, had meanwhile fled to Vizcaya and thence to the English territory of Bayonne.[8] The king was unable to pursue him because of rough seas in the Bay of Biscay, but was now determined to seize personal control of the lordship of Vizcaya. The *infante* Juan—who had married the younger Lara sister, Isabel—not unreasonably took advantage of Don Tello's exile to request Vizcaya, which the king had promised him repeatedly by virtue of his marriage. But Pedro is said to have arranged that the Vizcayanos would declare their refusal to have any lord but the king. The infuriated *infante* was then promptly killed by the king's guards at the royal palace in Bilbao; his body was thrown from the windows and unceremoniously dumped in the river. His mother (Queen Leonor of Aragón) and his wife, Isabel de Lara, were seized almost immediately, and imprisoned in Castrojeriz.[9] It seems likely that, until the outbreak of the civil war in 1366, Pedro managed to retain control of the lordships of Lara and Vizcaya.[10]

The fate of the two young Lara sisters must now have seemed inevitable. In 1359, Juana (to whom the lordship of Vizcaya rightfully belonged) was transferred to the magnificent castle of Almodóvar del Río, and a few days later to Seville where, according to the royal chronicle, she was killed.[11] Two years later, her younger sister Isabel was moved from her own cell in Castrojeriz, and died shortly afterward, allegedly poisoned with herbs administered to her at the behest of King Pedro.[12] The last legitimate heir in the principal line of the Lara family had died, and the lordships of Lara and Vizcaya had been annexed by the crown. In this sense, by 1361 the family was effectively, although not biologically, extinct.[13] But there is a curious postscript to the destruction of the Laras. When, in 1366, the rebellious Enrique de Trastámara, who had recently invaded Castile from his base in Aragón and had been proclaimed king at Calahorra, was holding a Cortes in Burgos, he summoned a lady who claimed to be Juana de Lara. The chronicler tells us that this lady was an impostor. Don Tello, we are told, wished to recover Lara and Vizcaya and initially promoted this lady's claims but soon changed his mind, afraid that she might defect to Pedro's side and that the people of Vizcaya might grant lordship to her independently of him. It was decided that this was not, in fact, the real Juana, and Don Tello proceeded to show the place where his late wife was buried.[14] But given the pro-Trastámara agenda of this chronicle, is surely conceivable that this was the real Juana. King Enrique would have been desperate to retain Lara and Vizcaya; and while his marriage to Juana Manuel gave him some claim to these lordships, his claim was inferior to Don Tello's. Any unscheduled appearance by the original heiress would have been the last straw, and certainly there was persistent tension between Enrique and Don Tello over the two lordships.[15]

We are told that in late 1368 Don Tello was in Vizcaya conspiring against his brother with the king of Navarre.[16] Two years later, he met a mysterious end: "Some said that herbs were given to him; and that they were given to him by a doctor, whom they called Master Romano, who was the doctor of King Enrique; and that they were given to him by order of the said king, for the reason that Don Tello was always dealing with those he knew did not love King Enrique well. But this is not certain, only rumored."[17]

Don Tello's lordships were now granted to the heir to the throne, the *infante* Juan; but wrangling over rightful ownership persisted. Seven years later, when Enrique II (reigned 1369–1379) was safely enthroned, he rejected the claims of a bona fide lady of the lineage, María (sister of Juan Núñez III). María, who had lived in France for most of her life and who by this time must have been well into her fifties, appears to have attempted quite seriously to restore the fortunes of the family. She sent a knight as messenger to the Cortes of Burgos in 1373, stating her right to the lordships of Lara and Vizcaya by virtue of being the aunt of the deceased, heirless children of Juan Núñez III. She claimed in her message that her rights were superior to those of Queen Juana (Manuel), cousin of these children, and even added that Enrique had promised her the inheritances when they met in Paris. In passing, María dismissed the claims of the *soi-disant* Juana de Lara as part of an attempt by Don Tello to recover his lordships.[18]

Enrique took counsel, hearing a variety of opinions from his advisors, none of whom, interestingly, dismissed María's claim as frivolous or untrue. Some recommended that the case be heard in the Audiencia, others that "some beautiful answer" be given to the knightly messenger. At length, Enrique responded cunningly, suggesting that if María sent two of her sons to Castile, he would give the lordship of Lara to one and Vizcaya to the other. The chronicler states that Enrique knew well that María would not accept the offer, since her sons were happily established beyond the Pyrenees: "They had gained great inheritances in France, and lived on lands which were calmer and less turbulent than the kingdom of Castile."[19] The king was determined to retain for the royal family the two lordships he knew to be vital. He had already transferred Lara and Vizcaya to his eldest son and heir, the *infante* Juan; and in 1390, the last year of his eleven-year reign, Juan I would grant the lordship of Lara (along with Peñafiel, Mayorga, and other posses-sions) to his own son, the *infante* Fernando.[20] The Laras had perished, their powers absorbed once and for all by the royal family of Castile and León.

IRONICALLY, it had been as protégés of the royal family of Castile and León that the Laras had first risen to a position of power in the late eleventh century. The weightiest element in the Laras' power, until the second third of the thirteenth century, had been royal tenancies; Pedro González's notorious romantic liaison with Queen Urraca was merely one episode in a long relationship between the Laras and the crown. During the long reigns of Alfonso VII and Alfonso VIII, the family en-joyed remarkable success in heightening their role as royal favorites through personal ability, particularly on the battlefield. Their ascen-dancy in this period did not derive from unique territorial strength; Molina was the only great Iberian estate the Laras held in the twelfth century, and it was repeatedly partitioned. Aristocratic opposition to the Laras was generally limited at this stage; the intimate web of power relations which was spun around the royal court tended to produce a relatively narrow factional pursuit of interests at court and a similarly limited factional type of opposition. But the first quarter of the thir-teenth century, which witnessed the culmination of the family's domi-nation at the court of Castile, also brought the end of it. Their hege-mony had excluded a majority of the nobles from the influence at court to which they felt entitled, so that resentment against the Laras broad-ened rapidly, resulting in a civil war in which the family was roundly defeated. Stripped of their tenancies and their status at court, con-fronted by a hostile crown, they spent much of the next generation at the periphery. The humbling of the Laras by Fernando III marks the end of the first great stage in their history.

By the time the Laras had recovered their status at court, new so-cial and political pressures were conspiring to change the structure of power in Castile and León. From the mid-thirteenth century, the pri-mary quality of the family's relationship with the monarchy was con-frontation. Whereas in the twelfth century their power had rested pri-marily on their close relationship with the crown, in the late thirteenth and fourteenth centuries it began to rest more heavily on autonomous control of land and the people who lived on it. It is true that the king still sought the cooperation of the Laras, who similarly seized any chance to increase their influence over the monarch; and even now, direct stipends and royal office periodically drew the Laras to court. The transformation in the power structures enveloping them was neither total nor sudden. However, the family's relationship with the monarchy was now one of extreme tension, endemic hostility, and frequent military conflict. By the 1270s, the head of the Lara family emerged as the leader of a rebellious aristocratic coalition reacting largely to the expansion, centralization, and professionalization of the royal administrative system. Royal *merindades* gradually replaced the system of tenancies that had played such a large role in the history of the Laras in the twelfth century. Although they were eventually able to establish themselves in important offices such as that of *adelantamiento mayor*, the Laras, like other noble families, deeply and explicitly resented their increasing exclusion from the royal administration.

The bifurcation between the crown and the Laras was both cause and effect of their patrimonial accumulation. Territorial expansion was not a direct consequence of the great mid-century reconquests in Andalucía; the indirect effects were far more important. By intensifying inflation while failing to provide very large lordships for the aristocracy, the Castilian conquests had heightened anxieties concerning the increasing demands of royal finance and the encroachments of monarchical authority. While simultaneously developing a range of diplomatic connections with foreign powers, particularly the French and Aragonese, the Laras responded with a seigneurial offensive in which the acquisition of Vizcaya was the critical element. Despite their failure to establish a permanent power base on the Aragonese frontier, the Laras' territorial authority grew to be comparable to that of the great noble lineages of the fifteenth century. The exceptional degree of power they amassed gave them a distinctive political role. In the absence of a genuinely autonomous representative assembly, they appear to have been perceived as a counterbalance to monarchy, and in times of crisis became politically representative of a broad segment of society. Their eventual destruction at the hands of King Pedro was the inevitable result of deep-rooted structural tensions, accelerated rather than caused by the king's personal instability.

*   *   *

THESE TENSIONS, being larger than the Laras, would also outlast them. There are three main themes in the relationship between crown and nobility after the Trastámara revolution of 1366–1369, each of which had been anticipated by the experience of the Lara family: royal attempts to develop new administrative mechanisms to bypass the high nobility, the emergence of an aristocracy with immense patrimonial and jurisdictional power, and finally civil war. The endless and bewildering conflicts between crown and nobility have been described by Luís Suárez Fernández as the leitmotif of the late Middle Ages in Castile. The great jurists of the day considered the monarchy a morally superior form of government, and popular sentiment saw an increase in royal power as the only effective remedy for the disorder produced by civil wars. However, Suárez concludes that we should not assign all good to the sovereign and all evil to the nobility. While the civil wars of the fifteenth century have often been regarded as a conflict between the monarchical order and a flock of birds of prey, nothing, he maintains, could be further from the truth.[21] This determination to avoid moralistic stereotypes, and to emphasize structural and ideological conflicts, has been valuable in interpreting the history of the Laras in their earlier struggle with the monarchy.

Since the thirteenth century, the crown had attempted a new administrative policy relying less on the aristocracy and more on public officials such as the *adelantados* and *merinos mayores*. As a result of intense aristocratic reaction, this aspiration was not immediately fulfilled (some of the Lara family, for instance, had been granted the new office of *adelantado mayor*), but it continued to be pursued for the rest of the Middle Ages. In stamping his authority on Castile and León, Alfonso XI had deliberately granted a number of important offices to members of the lesser nobility.[22] Equally, after the Trastámara revolution of 1369, Enrique II and Juan I would reform the organs of central government, professionalizing the Chancery and the Royal Court of Appeal, while new positions were developed to circumvent aristocratic domination of the *adelantamientos* and *merindades mayores*.[23] In the late fourteenth and fifteenth centuries, the administrative importance of these posts declined, although they remained useful for honorific purposes and resolving private affairs; their role was now assumed by public officials such as the *regidores*, *alcaldes mayores*, and *corregidores*.[24] The aristocrats of this period saw relatively little of court life, preferring to live on their luxurious country estates, and the Catholic Monarchs, Fernando and Isabel, would prefer to employ royal officials and clerics drawn from the gentry and bourgeoisie. After Isabel's death in 1504, the high nobility made a bid to recover their former influence at court and in administration, but met with only short-term success.[25] Certainly, their relationship with the crown was not structurally antagonistic, because they relied upon the state for the maintenance of the existing social order and continued to invoke the principles of *auxilium* and *consilium* (aid and counsel) in order to legitimize their hegemonic position in Castilian society. However, their retreat from administration was followed by a retreat from the imperial army. There had been a profound and unmistakable change in their role.[26]

As with the Laras of the late thirteenth and fourteenth centuries, the gradual exclusion of the aristocracy from administrative and military influence was accompanied in the late medieval and early modern period by their accumulation of vast patrimonies. The redistribution of lands after the royal acquisition of the lordships of Lara and Vizcaya was an immediate element in this process.[27] The reign of Enrique II has been seen as marking the revenge of the "feudal classes" after decades of royal centralization.[28] Large entailed estates became commonplace; for aristocratic families, these *mayorazgos* provided good insurance against market whims and poor management, and forestalled the rise of any gentrified bourgeoisie.[29] The municipal institutions of small towns, and many of the territorial agents of the monarchy, were effectively taken under the aegis of the lords of these estates;[30] and elaborate clientage systems were developed, catalyzed by competition between noble families.[31] Such lords did not mint their own coinage (although in the late fifteenth century some of them did acquire private mints for the minting of royal currency), and, unlike the Laras, they apparently had no independent foreign policy.[32] However, they did enjoy great de facto independence, as the lordship of Vizcaya had done in the early fourteenth century. The delegation of full jurisdictional authority became widely diffused in the reign of Enrique II, while absorption of royal rents by the nobility and the evolution of *behetrías* into *solariegos* were widespread.[33] By the mid-fifteenth century, some noble families enjoyed extraordinary wealth. A mere 2 or 3 percent of the population owned 97 percent of the land in Castile at the turn of the sixteenth century, and over half this share was owned by a handful of noble families.[34] The other side of the coin was the increase in popular resistance to seigneurial power beginning in the last years of the fourteenth century; but this resistance had relatively little impact.[35] It was hard even for the crown of Castile to challenge an aristocrat such as the Marquis of Villena, who had 150,000 vassals on his lands.[36]

Aristocracy, not monarchy, was the dominant force in Castilian society in the fifteenth century, and it would remain so well into the early modern age. As Perry Anderson has written, "No other Absolutist state in Western Europe was to be so finally noble in character, or so inimical to bourgeois development"; only in Spain did absolutism fail to crush the corporate resistance of the nobility.[37] Royal power remained firmly entrenched within a seigneurial context, and the reforms of the Catholic Monarchs would take place within a fundamentally aristocratic culture.[38] This was the world of *Amadis of Gaul*—of a laborious, stylized, chivalric idealism. In his classic text *The Structure of Spanish History*, the cultural historian Américo Castro pointed to the values of the nobleman as the epitome of an insecure, otherworldly Spanishness: "He had to feel himself a part of magical remoteness, and as if in suspension over the face of the earth."[39] But there were many kinds of structure in this land of magical remoteness—not only the cultural structures to which Castro's title referred. There were changing structures of power, too, enveloping the Lara family, the monarchy, and the rest of Spanish society—not preventing the influence of individual will and character but channeling them toward the creation of a society in which the concept, culture, and authority of nobility were dominant.

Abbreviations

ACL 4	*Colección documental del archivo de la catedral de León, 775–1230, Vol. 4: 1032–1109.* Ed. José Manuel Ruiz Asencio. Fuentes y estudios de historia leonesa, 44. León, 1990.
ACL 5	*Colección documental del archivo de la catedral de León 775–1230, Vol. 5: 1109–1187.* Ed. José María Fernández Catón. Fuentes y estudios de historia leonesa, 45. León, 1990.
ACL 6	*Colección documental del archivo de la catedral de León 775–1230, Vol. 6: 1188–1230.* Ed. José María Fernández Catón. Fuentes y estudios de historia leonesa, 46. León, 1991.
ACL 7	*Colección documental del archivo de la catedral de León 775–1230, Vol. 7: 1230–1269.* Ed. José Manuel Ruiz Asencio. Fuentes y estudios de historia leonesa, 54. León, 1993.
AEM	*Anuario de estudios medievales.* Barcelona, 1964–.
Aguilar de Campóo	María Estela González de Fauve, *La orden premonstratense en España: El monasterio de Santa María de Aguilar de Campóo, siglos XI–XV.* 2 vols. Aguilar de Campóo, 1991.
AHDE	*Anuario de historia del derecho español.* Madrid, 1924–
AHN	Archivo Histórico Nacional, Madrid.
AHPB	Archivo Histórico de la Provincia de Burgos.
Alfons VII	Peter Rassow, "Die Urkunden Kaiser Alfons VII von Spanien." *Archiv für Urkundenforschung* (1928) 327–468, and (1930) 66–137.
Alfonso VIII	Julio González, *El reino de Castilla en la época de Alfonso VIII.* 3 vols. Madrid, 1960.
Alfonso IX	Julio González, *Alfonso IX.* Madrid, 1944.
Anales Toledanos	"Anales Toledanos," in *España sagrada: Theatro geográphico-histórico de la iglesia de España,* vol. 23, 2nd ed., 382–424. Madrid, 1799.
Annales E.S.C.	*Annales: Economies, sociétés, civilisations.* Paris, 1946–.

Arlanza   *Cartulario de San Pedro de Arlanza*. Ed. Luciano Serrano.
                             Madrid, 1925.
Ávila   *Documentación medieval de la catedral de Ávila*. Ed. Ángel
                             Barrios García. Salamanca, 1981.
Benevívere   *Colección diplomática de la abadía Santa María de Benevívere
                             (Palencia), 1020–1561*. Ed. Luís Fernández Martín. Madrid,
                             1967.
C1344   *Crónica de 1344*. Ed. Diego Catalán and María Soledad de
                             Andrés. 2 vols. Madrid, 1970.
CAI   *Chrónica Adefonsi imperatoris*. Ed. Luís Sánchez Belda.
                             Madrid, 1950.
Cardeña   *Becerro gótico de Cardeña* Ed. Luciano Serrano. Valladolid,
                             1910.
Carrión 1   *Documentación del monasterio de San Zoilo de Carrión, 1047–
                             1300*. Ed. J. A. Pérez de Celada. Palencia, 1986.
Cartularios de Toledo   *Los cartularios de Toledo: Catálogo documental*. Ed. Francisco J.
                             Hernández, Madrid, 1985.
Casa de Lara   Luís de Salazar y Castro, *Historia genealógica de la casa de
                             Lara*. Madrid, 1696–1697. Rpt. Bilbao, 1988.
CAX   "Crónica del rey don Alfonso décimo." In *Crónicas de los
                             reyes de Castilla*. Ed. Cayetano Rosell. Biblioteca de Autores
                             Españoles, 68. Madrid, 1875.
CAXI   "Crónica del rey don Alfonso el onceno." In *Crónicas de los
                             reyes de Castilla*. Ed. Cayetano Rosell. Biblioteca de Autores
                             Españoles, 68. Madrid, 1875.
CDAXI   *Colección documental de Alfonso XI*. Ed. Isabel González
                             Crespo. Madrid, 1985.
CEII   "Crónica del rey don Enrique II." In *Crónicas de los reyes de
                             Castilla*. Ed. Cayetano Rosell. Biblioteca de Autores
                             Españoles, 68. Madrid, 1875.
CG1344   *Crónica geral de Espanha de 1344*. Ed. Luís Filipe Lindley
                             Cintra. 4 vols. Lisbon, 1951–1990.
CH   *Cuadernos de historia*. Madrid, 1967–.
CHE   *Cuadernos de historia de España*. Buenos Aires, 1944–.
CL   *Crónica latina de los reyes de Castilla*. Ed. María
                             Desamparados Cabanes Pecourt. Valencia, 1964.
Covarrubias   *Cartulario del infantado de Covarrubias*. Ed. Luciano
                             Serrano. Valladolid, 1907.
CP   "Crónica del rey don Pedro." In *Crónicas de los reyes de
                             Castilla*. Ed. Cayetano Rosell. Biblioteca de Autores
                             Españoles, 68. Madrid, 1875.
CSIV   "Crónica del rey don Sancho el Bravo." In *Crónicas de los
                             reyes de Castilla*. Ed. Cayetano Rosell. Biblioteca de Autores
                             Españoles, 68. Madrid, 1875.
Desclot, *Crònica*   Bernat Desclot, *Crònica*. Ed. Miguel Coll i Alentorn. 5 vols.
                             Barcelona, 1949.
DRH   Rodrigo Jiménez de Rada. "De Rebus Hispaniae." In
                             Jiménez de Rada, *Opera*. Ed. Francisco Lorenzana. Madrid,
                             1793. Rpt. Valencia, 1968.

El Moral	*Colección diplomática de San Salvador de El Moral.* Ed. Luciano Serrano. Valladolid, 1906.
Eslonza	V. Vignau y Ballester, *Cartulario del monasterio de Eslonza.* Madrid, 1884.
Fernando II	Julio González, *Regesta de Fernando II.* Madrid, 1943.
Fernando III	Julio González, *Reinado y diplomas de Fernando III.* 3 vols. Córdoba, 1980–1986.
Fernando IV	Memorias *de D. Fernando IV de Castilla.* Ed. Antonio Benavides. 2 vols. Madrid, 1860.
FMA	*El fuero de Molina de Aragón.* Ed. Miguel Sancho Izquierdo. Madrid, 1916.
GCAXI	*Gran crónica de Alfonso XI.* Ed. Diego Catalán. Madrid, 1977.
Gradefes	Aurelio Calvo, *El monasterio de Gradefes.* León, 1936–1944.
HC	*Historia compostellana.* Ed. Emma Falque Rey. Corpus Christianorum, Continuatio Mediaevalis, 70. Turnhout, Belgium, 1988.
La Cogolla	*Cartulario de San Millán de la Cogolla.* Ed. Luciano Serrano. Madrid, 1930.
La Rioja	*Colección diplomática medieval de la Rioja, 923–1225.* Ed. Ildefonso Rodríguez de Lama. 4 vols. Logroño, 1976–1992.
Las Dueñas	*Catálogo del archivo de San Pedro de las Dueñas.* Ed. José María Fernández Catón. León, 1977.
Las Huelgas 1	*Documentación del monasterio de Las Huelgas de Burgos, 1116–1230.* Ed. José Manuel Lizoain Garrido. Burgos, 1985.
Las Huelgas 3	*Documentación del monasterio de Las Huelgas de Burgos, 1263–1283: Indices, 1116–1283.* Ed. José Manuel Lizoain Garrido. Burgos, 1987.
Las Huelgas 5	*Documentación del monasterio de Las Huelgas de Burgos, 1307–1321.* Ed. Araceli Castro Garrido. Burgos, 1987.
LBB	*Libro becerro de las behetrías: Estudio y texto crítico.* Ed. Gonzalo Martínez Díez. 3 vols. León, 1981.
Liébana	*Cartulario de Santo Toribio de Liébana.* Ed. Luís Sánchez Belda. Madrid, 1948.
Linhagens	"Livro das Linhagens." In *Portugaliae monumenta histórica, I: Scriptores.* Lisbon, 1860.
Loaysa, *Crónica*	Jofré de Loaysa, *Crónica de los reyes de Castilla Fernando III, Alfonso X, Sancho IV y Fernando IV.* Ed. and trans. Antonio García Martínez. Murcia, 1961.
OB	*El obispado de Burgos y Castilla primitiva desde el siglo V al XIII.* Ed. Luciano Serrano. 3 vols. Madrid, 1935.
Oña	*Colección diplomática de San Salvador de Oña, 822–1284.* Ed. Juan de Alamo. 2 vols. Madrid, 1950.
Orden de San Juan	*Libro de privilegios de la orden de San Juan de Jerusalén en Castilla y León, siglos XII–XV.* Ed. Carlos de Ayala Martínez. Madrid, 1995.
Palencia	*Documentación de la catedral de Palencia, 1035–1247.* Ed. Teresa Abajo Martín. Burgos, 1986.

PCG	*Primera crónica general.* Ed. Ramón Menéndez Pidal. Madrid, 1977.
Piasca	*Colección diplomática de Santa María de Piasca, 857–1252.* Ed. Julia Montenegro Valentín. Santander, 1991.
Pruebas	*Pruebas de la historia de la Casa de Lara, sacadas de los instrumentos de diversas iglesias, y monasterios, de los archivos de sus mismos descendientes, de diferentes pleytos que entre sí han seguido, y de los escritores de mayor crédito, y puntualidad.* Ed. Luís de Salazar y Castro. Madrid, 1694.
Puerto	Juan Abad Barrasús, *El monasterio de Santa María de Puerto (Santoña), 863–1210.* Santander, 1985.
RAH	Real Academia de la Historia, Madrid.
RS	Julio González, *Repartimiento de Sevilla.* 2 vols. Madrid, 1951.
Sahagún 2	*Colección diplomática del monasterio de Sahagún, II: 1000– 1073.* Ed. Marta Herrero de la Fuente. Fuentes y estudios de historia leonesa, 36. León, 1988.
Sahagún 3	*Colección diplomática del monasterio de Sahagún, III: 1073– 1109.* Ed. Marta Herrero de la Fuente. Fuentes y estudios de historia leonesa, 37. León, 1988.
Sahagún 4	*Colección diplomática del monasterio de Sahagún, IV: 1110– 1199.* Ed. José Antonio Fernández Flórez. Fuentes y estudios de historia leonesa, 38. León, 1991.
Sahagún 5	*Colección diplomática del monasterio de Sahagún, V: 1200– 1300.* Ed. José Antonio Fernández Flórez. Fuentes y estudios de historia leonesa, 39. León, 1994.
Sancho IV	Mercedes Gaibrois de Ballesteros, *Sancho IV de Castilla.* 3 vols. Madrid, 1922–1928.
Segovia	*Documentación medieval de la catedral de Segovia, 1115–1300.* Ed. Luís-Miguel Villar García. Salamanca, 1990.
Sepúlveda	*Colección diplomática de Sepúlveda.* Ed. Carlos Saez Sánchez. 2 vols. Segovia, 1991.
Silos	*Recueil des chartes de l'abbaye de Silos.* Ed. Marius Férotin. Paris, 1897.
SJB	*Documentación del monasterio de San Juan de Burgos, 1091– 1400.* Ed. F. Javier Peña Pérez. Burgos, 1983.
Sobrado	*Tumbos del monasterio de Sobrado de los Monjes.* Ed. Pilar Loscertales de G. de Valdeavellano. 2 vols. Madrid, 1976.
Valvanera	*Documentación medieval del monasterio de Valvanera, siglos XI a XIII.* Ed. Francisco Javier García Turza. Zaragoza, 1985.
Vega	*Cartulario de monasterio de Vega, con documentos de San Pelayo y Vega de Oviedo.* Ed. Luciano Serrano. Madrid, 1927.
Zurita, *Anales*	Jerónimo Zurita, *Anales de la corona de Aragón.* Ed. Angel Canellas López. 5 vols. Zaragoza, 1967–1985.

Notes

See "Abbreviations" for acronyms, short titles, and abbreviated terms. All translations are my own, unless otherwise noted.

Introduction

1. Antonio Machado, excerpt from "Orillas del Duero," in Machado, *Selected Poems*, trans. Alan S. Trueblood (Cambridge, Mass., 1982), 108–112.

2. Rosa Santos de Campo et al., *Tierra Lara: Estudio antropológico social* (Burgos, 1992), 13, 59–61, 74.

3. Ibid., 32.

4. José Antonio Abasolo and Rosario García Rozas, *Carta arqueológica de la provincia de Burgos: Partido judicial de Salas de los Infantes* (Burgos, 1980), 7–8, 22–23.

5. Santos et al., *Tierra Lara*, 32.

6. Abasolo and García Rozas, *Carta arqueológica*, 60–65; Santos et al., *Tierra Lara*, 32.

7. Carlos Estepa Díez, "El alfoz castellano en los siglos IX al XII," *En la España medieval, IV,* vol. 1: *Estudios dedicados al profesor D. Ángel Ferrari Núñez* (Madrid, 1984), 314–327, explains some elements determining the demarcations of *alfoces*. In Lara, the role of the castle was complemented by the presence of a small river valley.

8. A document purporting to date from 28 January 929 ostensibly indicates that the countess and her children granted the convent of Santa María de Lara and its dependencies to the monastery of Arlanza (*Arlanza*, 18–21). But the authenticity of this charter has been questioned; see Ignacio Álvarez Borge, *Monarquía feudal y organización territorial: Alfoces y merindades en Castilla, siglos X–XIV* (Madrid, 1993), 79, n. 94.

9. The story, set in the tenth century, tells of a feud that develops at the wedding, in Burgos, between one Ruy Velázquez and a lady from the ruling count's

family. A cousin of the bride is infuriated when he is outdone in a contest by one of the groom's seven nephews. The feud escalates rapidly, setting Ruy Velázquez on his new bride's side and against the nephews—the Seven Infantes. He sends the father of the *infantes*, Gonzalo Gustioz, to Córdoba to meet Almanzor (the de facto ruler of the Spanish caliphate from 981 to 1002), using the pretext that the latter helped to pay for the wedding. He entrusts him with a sealed envelope that secretly instructs Almanzor to decapitate Gonzalo Gustioz. When Almanzor reads the letter, he tears it up, but has Gonzalo imprisoned and placed under the guard of a charming Moorish girl, who soon gives birth to a baby boy. Meanwhile, the Seven Infantes are treacherously sent into battle against the Moors; they are decapitated, and their heads are taken to Almanzor. But Almanzor is saddened, and releases his captive. Eventually, Gonzalo Gustioz's son wreaks spectacularly successful revenge on his father's Castilian enemies. *PCG*, 431–442, 446–448.

10. Santos de Campo et al., *Tierra Lara*, 32–33.

11. *Pruebas*. There are, nevertheless, important errors in Salazar's genealogy; two of them (his explanation of the ancestry of Gonzalo Núñez I, and his conflation of two thirteenth-century lords of Lara, Juan Núñez I and II) are colossal.

12. Otto Brunner, *Land and Lordship*, trans. and with an introduction by Howard Kaminsky and James Van Horn Melton (Philadelphia, 1992), 4.

13. Miguel Ángel Ladero Quesada, Los señores de Andalucía: Investigaciones sobre nobles y señoríos en los siglos XIII a XV (Cádiz, 1998), 125–127.

1. The Chains of Love

1. Simon Barton has recently suggested that the poem served a didactic purpose, articulating the bonds of vassalage that held this structure together at a moment when cross-border defections were beginning to challenge the king's authority; but he emphasizes that symbiosis remained the norm. See Barton, "Reinventing the Hero: The Poetic Portrayal of Rodrigo Díaz, the Cid, in its Political Context," in David G. Pattison, ed., *Textos épicos castellanos: Problemas de edición y crítica* (London, 2000), 65–78.

2. Marie-Claude Gerbet, *Les noblesses espagnoles au Moyen Age, XIe–XVe siècle* (Paris, 1994), 5.

3. Georges Duby, *The Early Growth of the European Economy*, trans. Howard B. Clarke (Ithaca, 1978), 52, 140–141.

4. Margarita Torres Sevilla-Quiñones de León, *Linajes nobiliarios en León y Castilla, siglos IX–XIII* (Salamanca, 1999), 416–419.

5. Esther Pascua Echegaray, *Guerra y pacto en el siglo XII: La consolidación de un sistema de reinos en Europa occidental* (Madrid, 1996), 168–172. For a historiographic review of the feudal transformation in France, see Thomas N. Bisson, "The "Feudal Revolution," *Past and Present*, 142 (1994), 6–42.

6. Gerbet, *Les noblesses espagnoles*, 49–51; Claudio Sánchez Albornoz, "La potestad real y los señoríos en Asturias, León y Castilla, siglos VIII al XIII," *Revista de archivos, bibliotecas y museos*, 31 (1914), 283–290. Regarding the control that the crown retained over the mints, see James J. Todesca, "What Touches All: Coinage and Monetary Policy in Leon-Castile to 1230" (Diss., Fordham University, 1996), 444–449, 451–456.

7. Bernard F. Reilly, *The Contest of Christian and Muslim Spain* (Oxford, 1992), 55.

8. Although not quite so much as we might think. Peter Linehan has effectively demonstrated how much our view of Toledo is a legacy of the vision of Rodrigo Jiménez de Rada; see Linehan, *History and the Historians of Medieval Spain* (Oxford, 1993), 313ff.

9. Torres Sevilla-Quiñones, *Linajes nobiliarios*, 419–421.

10. This view of feudalism was most famously expressed by Claudio Sánchez Albornoz; see, for instance, "La potestad real," 263–290, or the more polemical *España y el Islam* (Buenos Aires, 1943). A similar argument was made by Luís G. de Valdeavellano, *El feudalismo hispánico, y otros estudios de historia medieval* (Barcelona, 1984). A corresponding model of aristocratic development was delineated in a number of articles by Salvador de Moxó: "Los señoríos: En torno a una problemática para el estudio del régimen señorial," *Hispania*, 94 (1964), 185–236; "De la nobleza vieja a la nobleza nueva: La transformación nobiliaria castellana en la baja Edad Media," *CH*, 3 (1969), 1–210; "La nobleza castellano-leonesa en la Edad Media," *Hispania*, 114 (1970), 5–68; "La nobleza castellana en el siglo XIV," *AEM*, 7 (1970–1971), 493–511.

11. Reyna Pastor, "Poder y sociedad feudal en León y Castilla, siglos XI–XIV," *Estructuras y formas del poder en la historia* (Salamanca, 1991), 12; idem, "Reflexiones sobre los comienzos de la formación política feudo-vassallática en Castilla y León," in Adeline Rucqoi, ed., *Realidad e imagenes del poder: España a fines de la Edad Media* (Valladolid, 1988), 15–16; idem, "Sur l'articulation des formations économiques-sociales: Communautés villageoises et seigneuries au nord de la péninsule ibérique, X–XIII siècles," *Structures féodales et féodalisme dans l'occident méditerranéen, X–XIII siècles: Bilan et perspectives de recherches* (Rome, 1980), 192–214; idem, "Consenso y violencia en el campesinado feudal," *En la España Medieval, V,* vol. 2, 731–742. For other influential arguments in favor of the existence of feudalism in Castile and León, see Hilda Grassotti, *Las instituciones feudo-vassalláticas en León y Castilla*, 2 vols. (Spoleto, 1969); Carlos Estepa Díez, "Formación y consolidación del feudalismo en Castilla y León," *En torno al feudalismo hispánico: Primero congreso de estudios medievales* (Ávila, 1989); and Pierre Bonnassie, "From the Rhone to Galicia: Origins and Modalities of the Feudal Order," in Bonnassie, *From Slavery to Feudalism in South-Western Europe* (Cambridge, 1991), 122–124.

12. Simon Barton, *The Aristocracy in Twelfth-Century León and Castile* (Cambridge, 1997), 71–99; Sánchez Albornoz, "La potestad real," 275–282.

13. Linehan, *History and the Historians of Medieval Spain*, 194.

14. If feudalism is the delegation of public powers to private lords, for instance, Sánchez Albornoz and Valdeavellano remain substantially correct. See José Ángel García de Cortazar, "La inmadurez del feudalismo español," *Revista de Occidente*, 50 (1985), 49–52.

15. Pastor, "Reflexiones," 15–16. While in most cases we cannot trace biological links between the magnates of the tenth century and those of the eleventh, there is continuity in social structure. See Ignacio Álvarez Borge, "Estructura social y organización territorial en Castilla la Vieja Meridional: Los territorios entre el Arlanzón y el Duero en los siglos X al XIV" (Diss., Universidad de León, 1991), 281–321; and especially Estepa Díez, "Formación y consolidación del feudalismo."

16. For an imaginative portrait of life at this traveling court, see Bernard F. Reilly, *The Kingdom of León-Castilla under King Alfonso VI, 1065–1109* (Princeton, 1988), 157–160.

17. Nilda Guglielmi, "La curia regia en León y Castilla," *CHE*, 23–24 (1955), 116–267; idem, "La curia regia, II," *CHE*, 28 (1958), 43–101; Evelyn Procter, *Curia and Cortes in León and Castile, 1072–1295* (Cambridge, 1980), ch. 1.

18. Richard A. Fletcher, *St. James's Catapult: The Life and Times of Diego Gelmírez of Santiago de Compostela* (Oxford, 1984), 42–52; Barton, *Aristocracy*, 192–194. In *The Episcopate in the Kingdom of León in the Twelfth Century* (Oxford, 1978), 71–72, 84–85, Fletcher suggests that Bishop Manrique of León (who held the see from 1181 to 1205) was a member of the Lara family and thus an exception to the rule of modest social origins; he cites a document of 16 February 1182 in which Elvira Pérez de Lara receives a loan from the bishop as evidence that they are brother and sister, and he states that the bishop was a son of Pedro Manrique. This relationship, however, is not actually stated in the document (*ACL*, 5:526–528); and Salazar, whom Fletcher cites, does not include the bishop among Pedro Manrique's offspring (*Casa de Lara*, 1:154–156).

19. Torres Sevilla-Quiñones, *Linajes nobiliarios*, 439–440.

20. Bernard F. Reilly, *The Kingdom of León-Castilla under King Alfonso VII, 1126-1157* (Philadelphia, 1998), 169.

21. Barton, *Aristocracy*, 30–33.

22. Pascual Martínez Sopena, *La Tierra de Campos occidental: Poblamiento, poder y comunidad del siglo X al XII* (Valladolid, 1985), 520–521. José María Lacarra, "Honores y tenencias en Aragón, siglo XI," *CHE*, 45–46 (1967), 151–190.

23. Nilda Guglielmi, "El *dominus villae* en Castilla y León," *CHE*, 19 (1953), 55–62.

24. Ignacio Álvarez Borge, *Monarquía feudal y organización territorial: Alfoces y merindades en Castilla, siglos X–XIV* (Madrid, 1993), 103–122.

25. Carlos Estepa Díez, "El alfoz castellano en los siglos IX al XII," *En la España medieval, IV,* vol. 1 (1984), 7–26; idem, "El alfoz y las relaciones campo-ciudad en Castilla y León durante los siglos XII y XIII," *Studia histórica: Historia medieval*, 2, no. 2 (1984), 7–26; Álvarez Borge, *Monarquía feudal*, 9–47; Jean Gautier-Dalché, "Châteaux et peuplements dans la péninsule ibérique, X–XIII siècles," in Gautier-Dalché, *Economie et société dans les pays de la couronne de Castille* (London, 1982), 98–104; Carlos de Ayala Martínez, "Las fortalezas castellanas de la Orden de Calatrava en el siglo XII," *En la España medieval*, 16 (1993), 9–35, points out the importance of castles as centers of rent collection. Julio Escalona Monge, "Las prestaciones militares de servicios militares en fortalezas y la organización de la sociedad feudal castellana: Los infanzones de Espeja," *Castillos de España*, 94 (1987), 57–60, shows the long-term administrative importance of the castles of Clunia and Lara.

26. Torres Sevilla-Quiñones, *Linajes nobiliarios*, 440.

27. Reilly, *Alfonso VII*, 170–171, 238; Lacarra, "Honores y tenencias," 176–178.

28. Barton, *Aristocracy*, 69–73.

29. Pascual Martínez Sopena, "Parentesco y poder en León durante el siglo XI: La 'casata' de Alfonso Díaz," *Historia medieval*, 5 (1987), 36–40; and idem, *Tierra de Campos*, 522.

30. Martínez Sopena, "Parentesco y poder," 38–42. María Isabel Loring

García, "Poder económico y relaciones sociales en las Asturias de Santillana en los siglos X y XI," *En la España medieval*, 5 (1986), 603–615, provides a striking example of female power in the eleventh century: Doña Fronilde, patroness of the abbey of Santillana del Mar.

31. Pascual Martínez Sopena, "La nobleza de León y Castilla en los siglos XI y XII: Un estado de la cuestión," *Hispania*, 185 (1993), 810; Isabel Beceiro Pita and Ricardo Córdoba de la Llave, *Parentesco, poder y mentalidad: La nobleza castellana, siglos XII–XV* (Madrid, 1990), 51–52, 57.

32. Álvarez Borge, "Estructura social," 471–472; Reyna Pastor, "Historia de las familias en Castilla y León (siglos X–XIV) y su relación con la formación de los grandes dominios eclesiásticos," *CHE*, 43–44 (1967), 113–118; idem, "Ganadería y precios: Consideraciones sobre la economía de León y Castilla, siglos XI–XIII, *CHE*, 35–36 (1962), 37–48, suggests that the price of land was low in the tenth and eleventh centuries and that cereal production in particular was underdeveloped; this too may have undermined the value of landed possessions, although Todesca, "What Touches All," 128–130, is skeptical about the evidence for price movements in this period.

33. Martínez Sopena, *Tierra de Campos*, 367.

34. The argument is made persuasively by Torres Sevilla-Quiñones, *Linajes nobiliarios*, 217–218.

35. Antonio Sánchez de Mora, "Aproximación al estudio de la nobleza castellana: Los llamados Salvadores-Manzanedo y sus relaciones con el linaje de Lara, siglos XI–XIII," *Medievalismo* (1998); *Sahagún*, 3:280–282, 357–358. Nuño Álvarez, who had married into the Alfonso family, owned the monasteries of San Juan de Santibáñez de Esgueva and San Martín de Marmellar, the second of which Gonzalo Núñez (probably his son-in-law) would inherit. He also had properties in Citores, Itero de la Vega, and Castrillo de la Vega (Álvarez, "Estructura social," 296–297, 304, and 1004, n. 365).

36. During this period, Núñez means "son of Nuño," just as a man or woman named González is the child of Gonzalo, Pérez the child of Pedro, Rodríguez the child of Rodrigo, Sánchez the child of Sancho, Fernández the child of Fernando, and Álvarez the child of Álvaro. Only from the thirteenth century does this pattern break down, as families with stronger pride in lineage give their sons the full names of illustrious fathers, grandfathers, and uncles.

37. The argument was originally expressed by María del Carmen Carlé, in "Gran propiedad y grandes propietarios," *CHE*, 57–58 (1973), 1–224. See also Martínez Sopena, "Parentesco y poder," 57, 73, 77–78; Álvarez Borge, *Monarquía feudal*, 125–126.

38. On the Salvadores family, see Félix Sagredo Fernández, "Los condes de Bureba en la documentación de la segunda mitad del siglo XI," *CH*, 6 (1975), 94, n. 6.

39. Torres Sevilla-Quiñones, *Linajes nobiliarios*, is entirely convincing on Gonzalo's marriage, but offers no documentary evidence for her claim (219) that he was the son of Nuño Salvadores, brother of Count Gonzalo Salvadores; and in the genealogical tables (220, 395), he has mysteriously become a son of Munio González, Gonzalo Salvadores' uncle. In his recent article, Antonio Sánchez de Mora traces the interaction between the two families, and indicates one other possible connection with the Salvadores clan, by means of Gonzalo's marriage into the Álvarez family. Elvira, daughter of Diego Álvarez (brother of Nuño Álvarez) mar-

ried Gonzalo Salvadores; see Sánchez de Mora, "Los Salvadores-Manzanedo," *Medievalismo* (1998), 43, 46–59.

40. *Casa de Lara*, 1:87; but there is no evidence that Gonzalo Núñez's wife Godo (or Goto) was the daughter of Gonzalo Salvadores, who was also named Godo (Álvarez Borge, "Estructura social," 1005, n. 369).

41. The claim in the thirteenth-century *Primera Crónica General* that "Count Nuño of Lara" was the progenitor of the Lara family is two hundred years distant from the events it describes (*PCG*, 617–619). The full but probably fictitious line of descent from Count Fernán González is traced in *Casa de Lara*, 1:1–83 passim, and dismissed by Álvarez Borge, "Estructura social," 305.

42. *Sahagún*, 3:280–282. Two years later, an almost identical donation was made by Urraca Núñez, probably his sister-in-law (*Sahagún*, 3:357–358).

43. *Arlanza*, 164.

44. *La Cogolla*, 287–288.

45. The monastery of San Martín de Marmellar (north of Burgos), in 1087, and that of San Millán de Revenga, in 1089. See *La Cogolla*, 320–321.

46. Barton, *Aristocracy*, 185–191.

47. His first certain subscription is from 12 May 1075 (*Oña*, 109).

48. Richard Fletcher, "Reconquest and Crusade in Spain, circa 1050–1150," *Transactions of the Royal Historical Society*, 5th series, 37 (1987), 31–47.

49. *Casa de Lara*, 1:87.

50. Reilly, *Contest*, 112–115; idem, *Alfonso VI*, 285.

51. *La Cogolla*, 291 (7 April 1098). Gonzalo Núñez is less prominent after the turn of the century, but his donation to Oña in 1103 is not the last record we have of him, as *Casa de Lara* (1:87) states: he appears in documents of 13 November 1103 (*Covarrubias*, 49–51), 22 September 1105 (*OB*, 3:123–124), and 12 December 1105 (*Oña*, 157).

52. Fletcher, *St. James's Catapult*, 16–20. See also Simon Barton, "Two Catalan Magnates in the Courts of the Kings of León-Castile: The Careers of Ponce de Cabrera and Ponce de Minerva Re-examined," *Journal of Medieval History*, 18 (1992), 236. Barton comments: "It was characteristic of many a medieval ruler struggling to establish his authority that he should seek to raise up 'new men': nobles whose families enjoyed no substantial cushion of wealth and privilege and whose fortunes were therefore inextricably linked to those of the royal dynasty that had favored them."

53. María del Carmen Pallares and Ermelindo Portela, "Aristocracia y sistema de parentesco en la Galicia de los siglos centrales de la Edad Media: El grupo de los Traba," *Hispania*, 185 (1993), 831–838; Fletcher, *St. James's Catapult*, 32–42.

54. J. Mattoso, *Ricos-homens, infançoes e cavaleiros: A nobreza medieval portuguesa nos séculos XI e XII* (Lisbon, 1985), 245–249. The nascent Portuguese monarchy was considerably weaker, however, so the importance of the royal court is likely to have been secondary to possession of land; unlike their Castilian counterparts, the high nobility often managed to remain independent of the king and royal military campaigns, and some noble families remained in control of tenancies despite not having a preeminent role at court.

55. During this reign, Pedro González appears as *alférez* in documents of 27 December 1088 (Reilly, *Alfonso VI*, 226); between 7 February 1090 (*Sahagún*, 3:164–166) and 16 September 1090 (ibid., 3:178–179); 24 September 1091 (ibid.,

3:197–198); 3 November 1091 (*SJB*, 5); 10 November 1091 (*Sahagún*, 3:198–200); 30 September 1107 (Reilly, *Alfonso VI*, 354 n.); and 1 October 1107 (AHN Códices 267B, 272r). A man named Rodrigo González possesses the *alferecía* on 29 January 1078 (*Sahagún*, 3:40–42); 1 March 1078 (ibid., 3:45–46); 20 March 1078 (ibid., 3:50–52); 10 August 1079 (ibid., 3:59–61); 3 December 1080 (ibid., 3:76–79); 31 March 1081 (ibid., 3:82–83); 9 June 1081 (*ACL*, 4:494–496); 2 April 1083 (*Sahagún*, 3:99–101); 1 March 1084 (AHN Códices 989B, 5r–v); 8 May 1086 (ibid., 1v–2r, 3v–4r); 3 December 1100 (ibid., 22v–23r). But in view of the very long lifespan this would imply—Rodrigo González de Lara would live until circa 1143—I share Barton's doubts (*Aristocracy*, 292, n. 1) as to whether this is our man.

56. Sometime before November 1127, Pedro González married Eva, whom Salazar y Castro believed to have come from the influential Traba family of Galicia (*Casa de Lara*, 1:99, 101); Pedro's own daughter Elvira would eventually marry García Pérez de Traba. Simon Barton (*Aristocracy*, 229) points out, however, that there is no documentary evidence for Salazar's claim, and it is possible that Eva was in fact French. Meanwhile, Gonzalo Núñez's two daughters each made important marriages: María to the lord of Cameros, who was influential in La Rioja, and Godo to Rodrigo Núñez de Guzmán, which consolidated the influence of the Laras between the Arlanza and the Duero (*Alfonso VIII*, 1:259).

57. His tenure may have been even longer, since the last tenant of Lara other than Gonzalo Núñez in the eleventh century, Gonzalo Salvadores, appears with it for the final time in 1074, and the earliest other tenant in the twelfth century, Pedro González, appears with it first in 1107.

58. In a document of 1074 (*La Cogolla*, 221–222), Gonzalo Salvadores is referred to as lord of Lara, and there are also a few references to the presence of the Salvadores brothers in the area in the 1060s and the early 1070s; but this may simply have reflected tenancy.

59. Álvarez Borge, *Monarquía feudal*, 135.

60. Beceiro Pita, *Parentesco, poder y mentalidad*, 58–59.

61. Álvarez Borge, *Monarquía feudal*, 80–81. Escalona Monge, "Las prestaciones militares," 59, shows how Carazo was generally tied to the *alfoz* of Lara in the twelfth century.

62. *Arlanza*, xv–xvi, 31–34.

63. Álvarez Borge, *Monarquía feudal*, 79–80. Even if the diploma were not a forgery, it would be very inadequate evidence for the dimensions of the tenancy of Lara two hundred years later; and indeed, the very specificity of the territorial borders in the document is suspect. Early tenth-century diplomas normally reveal a somewhat imprecise sense of territorial lordship, not least because Christian possession of the region was still tenuous.

64. The *fueros* of Lerma delineated a border with the *alfoz* of Lara which passed near Nebreda, as alleged by the diploma (*Arlanza*, 32, n. 9).

65. *HC*; Fletcher, *St. James's Catapult*, 129–162.

66. Bonnassie, "From the Rhone to Galicia," esp. 122–124, argues that this was a period in which a public and monarchical order was destroyed; thus, what had occurred almost a century earlier in Catalonia (1020–1060) now developed, belatedly, in Castile. He claims that there was a power vacuum for at least fifteen years, giving rise to conflictive alliances between nobles and a crescendo of homages. Reyna Pastor similarly argues that feudalization was accelerated by the turbu-

lent reign of Urraca, before its definitive consolidation under Alfonso VII ("Poder y sociedad feudal," 12–20; idem, "Reflexiones," 16–22).

67. Bernard F. Reilly, *The Kingdom of León-Castilla under Queen Urraca, 1109-1126* (Princeton, 1982), esp. 46, 361–362; Grassotti, *Instituciones feudo-vassalláticas*, 953–987. Most recent Spanish historians of feudal structures, in fact, tend to deny the rapidity of feudal change that is suggested by Bonnassie. For example, Pascual Martínez Sopena, "La nobleza de León y Castilla en los siglos XI y XII: Un estado de la cuestión," *Hispania*, 185 (1993), 806–807, queries the emphasis which Bonnassie places on one short period of unrest.

68. *HC*, 234 (book II, ch. 8).

69. DRH, 145–146, 148.

70. Ibid., 149.

71. He holds this office in diplomas of 22 July 1109 (*ACL*, 5:3–7) and 10 September 1109 (ibid., 7–9). He witnesses royal diplomas up to 21 July 1125 (*Silos*, 50).

72. Elvira Pérez, daughter of Pedro González and Urraca, makes her first appearance in the documents as early as 1117 (Reilly, *Urraca*, 217). A document of 5 November 1123 is witnessed by one "Fernandus Petri minor filius," who may be Pedro González's son by the queen (Reilly, *Urraca*, 176). *HC*, 458, book III, ch. 24, seems to suggest that there must have been more children: "Cum matre ipsius regis adulterine concubuerat et ex ipsa regina adulterinos filios et filias genuerat" ("He slept with the king's mother, and with this queen he had sons and daughters out of wedlock").

73. 6 May 1107 (José Manuel Garrido Garrido, *Documentación de la catedral de Burgos, 804–1183* [Burgos, 1983], 154–155).

74. José García Pelegrín, *Studien zum Hochadel der Königreiche León und Kastilien im Hochmittelalter* (Munster, 1991), 122, points out the patrimonial implications in the phrases "comes de Lara" or "comes Lara."

75. Reilly, *Urraca*, 127, 137.

76. DRH, 149.

77. *PCG*, 648.

78. *HC*, 234 (book II, ch. 8).

79. *Sahagún*, 3:299–300; *Casa de Lara*, 1:98; Álvarez Borge, "Estructura social," 743–744. Finally, on 2 September 1125 he would grant properties in Uranau and Ranedo (near Frías) to the monastery of Santo Domingo de Silos, in return for two properties which the monks had in San Pedro de Arlanza and Tordueles (*Silos*, 51–52).

80. For instance, the land in Abia which he granted to his new wife, Doña Estefanía, on 5 September 1135 (*Pruebas*, 655). This dower also included the property in Huérmeces "which the lord emperor Alfonso Raimúndez has granted me by hereditary right" (*Arlanza*, 187–189; *Pruebas*, 8). Estefanía was the daughter of Armengol V, Count of Urgell, and María Pérez, daughter of Pedro Ansúrez. Julio González suggests that the marriage may have been political because Estefanía had been highly favored by Urraca (*Alfonso VIII*, 1:261).

81. *Pruebas*, 653. See also Barton, *Aristocracy*, 292 (Arce) and *Piasca* 132–134 (San Mamés).

82. The land was located in Castil de Peones, just southwest of Brivisieca, and in nearby Carrias.

83. Rodrigo witnessed diplomas issued by Queen Urraca from 22 March 1115 (*Casa de Lara*, 1:94) to 1 November 1125 (*Liébana*, 128–129), appearing with the comital title from 1121 (*Silos*, 43–45).

84. Sancha was the daughter of Alfonso VI by his first wife, Isabel; Rodrigo had married her sometime before July 1122 (Barton, *Aristocracy*, 292). By 10 May 1125, three daughters had been born of the marriage (*Vega*, 46–48).

85. Reilly, *Alfonso VII*, 13, 171, 279.

86. Pedro González had confirmed diplomas issued by Alfonso on 13 May 1124 (*Segovia*, 54–56) and 12 July 1124 (*Casa de Lara*, 1:97); the latter was also witnessed by Rodrigo González de Lara.

87. See, for instance, Grassotti, *Instituciones feudo-vassalláticas*, 953–961, taking its cues from the royal chronicle. Reilly's *Urraca* and *Alfonso VII* are, in contrast, refreshingly levelheaded.

88. *CAI*, 7.

89. Ibid., 8–10.

90. *Casa de Lara*, 1:5.

91. Ibid., 1:506.

92. AHN Ordenes Militares, Calatrava, carp. 455 2P.

93. Anselm Biggs, *Diego Gelmírez, First Archbishop of Compostela* (Washington, D.C., 1949), 175–176.

94. Reilly, *Urraca*, 127, 137, 305; Barton, *Aristocracy*, 113.

95. Reilly, *Contest*, 170.

96. Both brothers had been in the royal retinue as early as 3 May 1126 (*Sahagún*, 4:98–102); remarkably, Pedro appears as "nutritor regis" on 18 June that year (*Documentos del monasterio de Santo Domingo de Silos*, 954–1254, ed. Miguel C. Vivancos Gómez [Burgos, 1988], 54–55, 57–59). They also confirm royal diplomas of 1 May 1127 and 26 March 1128 (*Alfons VII*, 69, 70).

97. *CAI*, 12; Reilly, *Alfonso VII*, 17–22.

98. *CAI*, 16; Reilly, *Alfonso VII*, 26–27.

99. Ibid., 19. The immediate cause of Pedro's discontent may well have been the birth of a male heir to Alfonso VII (Barton, *Aristocracy*, 113).

100. *Arlanza*, 176–181. Five years later, in 1135, a revised *fuero* was granted to Lara, effectively affirming royal authority over the *alfoz* (ibid., 176–180). Álvarez (*Monarquía feudal*, 131–132) claims that despite the absence of documentary evidence, it is likely that Pedro's son Manrique was tenant of Lara between 1139 (when Ordoño Gustios died) and 1164 (when Manrique himself died). This may conceivably be true; but it would be peculiar for a twenty-five-year tenancy to be completely invisible in the royal diplomas, especially in view of the delicate recent history of the tenancy of Lara. The silence in the diplomas surely reflects the determination of Alfonso VII to keep the tenancy out of the hands of the aristocracy in general and the Laras in particular.

101. *CAI*, 19–20.

102. Ibid., 20. An obituary in the Burgos cathedral archives states that Pedro died on 16 October 1130 (*OB*, 3:390).

103. Barton, "Two Catalan Magnates," 235.

104. Barton, *Aristocracy*, 35–38.

105. *CAI*, 22.

106. Ibid., 23.

2. The Revels of War

1. Richard Fletcher, *St. James's Catapult: The Life and Times of Diego Gelmírez of Santiago de Compostela* (Oxford, 1984), 292–300; idem, "Reconquest and Crusade in Spain, circa 1050–1150," *Transactions of the Royal Historical Society*, 5th series, 37 (1987), 37–42. But scholarly debate continues on the concept of reconquest; Peter Linehan describes it as "a Serbonian bog in which to stay afloat you have to be metaphysically literate" (*History and the Historians of Medieval Spain* [Oxford, 1993], 207).

2. Simon Barton, *The Aristocracy in Twelfth-Century León and Castile* (Cambridge, 1997), 173–184.

3. Esther Pascua Echegaray, *Guerra y pacto en el siglo XII: La consolidación de un sistema de reinos en Europa occidental* (Madrid, 1996), esp. 347–355.

4. James F. Powers, *A Society Organized for War: The Iberian Municipal Militias in the Central Middle Ages, 1000–1284* (Berkeley, 1988).

5. *CAI*, 23. Count Rodrigo González witnessed royal diplomas again beginning 1 February 1132 (*Alfons VII*, 72), and very frequently between 8 March 1132 (*Sahagún*, 4:142–143) and February 1137 (*Alfons VII*, 75; *Sahagún*, 4:157–58).

6. Theresa Vann, "Castilian Royal Government of the Kingdom of Toledo, 1085–1252" (Diss., Fordham University, 1992), 95–96, also suggests that a desire to distance Rodrigo González from his erstwhile power base in Asturias and even an awareness of the high mortality rate among frontier governors may have been equally important considerations.

7. *CAI*, 92–93; Anales Toledanos, 389.

8. The grant included properties in Vallegera, Cisneros, Antigüedad, Baltanás, and Huérmeces, July 1135 (*Pruebas*, 654; *Casa de Lara*, 4:251).

9. Margaret M. Cullinan, "Imperator Hispaniae: The Genesis of 'Spain'" (Diss., City University of New York, 1975).

10. The diminution of the flow of Muslim gold to Barcelona in the eleventh century had catalyzed patrimonial accumulation in Catalonia, as magnates sought new forms of peasant-generated wealth at home (John C. Shideler, *A Medieval Catalan Noble Family: The Montcadas, 1000–1230* [Berkeley, 1983], 42–43). Peasant servitude and patrimonial accumulation were both much less developed in Castile.

11. Bernard F. Reilly, *The Kingdom of León-Castilla under King Alfonso VII, 1126–1157* (Philadelphia, 1998), 57.

12. In 1139, he held the lordship of Huesca in Aragón (Barton, *Aristocracy*, 116).

13. *CAI*, 39–40. The impression given by the chronicle is that Rodrigo had never, in fact, returned to Castile. However, it appears that on 8 February 1141 he and other family members made a donation of property to the monastery of Arlanza; the list of relatives leaves little doubt that this is our Count Rodrigo (*Arlanza*, 187–189). The same year, he appears in a list of subscribers to a privilege of Alfonso VII (*Cartulario de San Millán de la Cogolla, 1076–1200*, ed. María Luisa Ledesma Rubio [Zaragoza, 1989], 263). Simon Barton (*Aristocracy*, 116) considers that he may be the count Rodrigo who witnesses a will in Urgell on 24 March 1143. He may, however, have died before 15 February 1143, when Countess Estefanía and her children—but not her husband—founded the monastery of Valbuena (*Pruebas*, 656; *Casa de Lara*, 4:256).

14. *CAI*, 183.

15. See Margarita Torres Sevilla-Quiñones de León, *Linajes nobiliarios en León y Castilla, siglos IX–XIII* (Salamanca, 1999), 421–423 and 451–480. But the tendency is perhaps not as strong as she claims: her own evidence shows, to take a random example, that León continued to be juggled between several of the leading families of the realm.

16. He was *alférez* between 10 November 1134 (*La Cogolla*, 308) and 2 June 1137 (*Silos*, 72).

17. José García Pelegrín, *Studien zum Hochadel der Königreiche León und Kastilien im Hochmittelalter* (Munster, 1991), 125, suggests that the reason for the lacuna may lie in Manrique's efforts to consolidate his new lordship of Molina. In this period, he witnessed a plethora of royal diplomas, from September 1142 (*Alfons VII*, 72) through 13 April 1157 (*Vega*, 172); he increasingly appears at or near the top of witness lists. He was closely associated with the *infante* Sancho, appearing as his tutor in a document of 1 March 1149 (Barton, *Aristocracy*, 264); he witnesses a number of diplomas issued by Sancho, first as *infante* and then as king, sporadically from 1149 (*Alfonso VIII*, 2:10–13) to 23 July 1153 (ibid., 2:24–25), and with great frequency between 4 January 1154 and, the last in Sancho's reign, 30 July 1158 (*Alfonso VIII*, 2:26–91 passim).

18. Manrique was made a count on 21 August 1145 (Barton, *Aristocracy*, 264, n. 4). Regarding the annexation of Baeza and Calatrava, see Anales Toledanos, 390; *Casa de Lara*, 1:112–113. Salazar y Castro suggests that Manrique may also have been present at the capture of Andújar, Pedroche, and Santa Eufemia in 1155 (ibid., 1:118).

19. *CAI*, 183.

20. Barton, *Aristocracy*, 58–63; Luís Sánchez Belda, "En torno a 3 diplomas de Alfonso VII," *Hispania*, 11 (1951), 47–61. He also had an *alcalde* in Molina, in 1153 (Toribio Mingüella y Arnedo, *Historia de la diócesis de Sigüenza y de sus obispos*, 3 vols. [Madrid, 1910], 1:390–391). Hilda Grassotti, "Sobre la retenencia de castillos en la Castilla medieval," in *Estudios medievales españoles* (Madrid, 1981), 261–281, discusses the granting of *retenencias*, sums given to the tenant of a fortress by the monarch or a private lord; the term originated in the early thirteenth century, but Grassotti suggests the practice has a much longer history, and we may imagine that Manrique's *alcaldes* also received grants of this nature.

21. Anselmo Arenas López, *Orígen del Muy Ilustre Señorío de Molina: El Cid y Don Manrique* (Madrid, 1928), 171, 201.

22. María Concepción Quintanilla Raso, "El protagonismo nobiliario en la Castilla bajo medieval: Una revisión historiográfica," *Medievalismo*, 7 (1997), 199–200.

23. Álvaro Pérez confirms royal charters of 2 May 1148 (*Oña*, 245); 15 March 1149 (*Alfons VII*, 103); 26 March 1149 (*Oña*, 247); 14 May 1149 (*Alfons VII*, 106; 8 October 1153 (ibid., 120); and a large number of royal charters from 30 April 1152 onward (*Alfonso VIII*, 18ff.). Although, as always, it is dangerous to argue from silence, the silence regarding Don Álvaro's property is almost total; we have only a confirmation by "Domnus Aluari" of a donation of houses in Toledo, 9 November 1148, by people including Manrique "and all our relatives" (AHN Ordenes Militares, Calatrava, carp. 455, 2P).

24. Álvaro Pérez first appears as count on 19 November 1166 (*Alfonso VIII*,

159–160), later than each of his brothers and even his nephew Pedro Manrique. He confirms a large number of royal diplomas until 10 May 1172 (ibid., 2:93–290 passim).

25. March 1145 (*Sahagún*, 4:256–258) until 2 July 1155 (*Palencia*, 118–120); he also served as a *submayordomo* in June 1144 (*Sahagún*, 4:185–186). In Alfonso VII's reign, he continues to witness diplomas through 4 February 1157 (*OB*, 3:201–202) and diplomas issued by Sancho, already styling himself Sancho III, on 8 August 1151 (*Arlanza*, 199–200) and 30 April 1152 (*El Moral*, 60–62). He first appears with the title of count on 9 December 1155 (*Aguilar de Campóo*, 2:184), narrowly in advance of the date that Salazar claimed to be the first occasion, 4 March 1156 (*Casa de Lara*, 4:7). However, he would not use it regularly until his power had been consolidated at the court of Alfonso VIII (beginning in 1162).

26. He was in prison on 22 October 1148; see Aurelio Calvo, *El monasterio de Gradefes* (León, 1936–1944), 306–307.

27. *ACL*, 5:254–255.

28. *OB*, 3:274–275.

29. *Casa de Lara*, 1:114.

30. AHN Códices 1046B, 219–220; *Alfonso VIII*, 1:273.

31. RAH F-40, 90v–91v; *Pruebas*, 10. In February 1152, he also redistributed his lands in the villages of Cedillo and Balaguera, which are hard to identify with certainty (Barton, *Aristocracy*, 313–314).

32. *FMA*, 63.

33. The editor of the *fuero* comes to the curious conclusion that, in this clause, *desierto* must mean "abandoned by Christians" (ibid., 22–24), but it surely makes more sense to speculate that the word implies that the Aragonese advance on Zaragoza (taken in 1119) and the surrounding area had led to an almost total depopulation of the town. It may be for this very reason that the recapture of Molina does not appear in either Castilian or Aragonese chronicles.

34. *Alfonso VIII*, 1:272.

35. *FMA*, 22. Zurita, *Anales*, 1:276, explicitly follows Count Pedro's account.

36. Ibid., 65.

37. AHN Ordenes Militares, Calatrava, carp. 455, 15P. García Pérez Manrique was the son of Pedro Manrique and his first wife, the *infanta* Sancha of Navarre (see *Alfonso VIII*, 1:280, which states that they were married by 1165, correcting the chronology of *Casa de Lara*, 1:154).

38. *FMA*, 37–40.

39. Ibid., 84, 177.

40. Pascua Echegaray, *Guerra y pacto*, 176–180; Simon Barton, "Reinventing the Hero: The Poetic Portrayal of Rodrigo Díaz, the Cid, in Its Political Context," in David G. Pattison, ed., *Textos épicos castellanos: Problemas de edición y crítica* (London, 2000), 65–78.

41. DRH, 160.

42. Manrique could not have disinterred his archenemy, since he himself had died two years earlier (*Alfonso VIII*, 1:56–57). For a highly idiosyncratic but intriguing study of political instability in the early stages of this reign, based on mathematical analysis of variations in the lists of subscribers of royal charters, see Lorle Ann Porter, "Social Status at the Court of Alfonso VIII of Castile (Diss., University of New Mexico, 1965), 16–36.

43. DRH, 159–160.

44. *Fernando II*, 44, n. 77; DRH, 160; *Alfonso VIII*, 1:158–159; Anales Toledanos, 391.

45. DRH, 161.

46. *Alfonso VIII*, 1:160–161.

47. Manrique witnessed various diplomas issued by Fernando II between 26 October 1162 (*Fernando II*, 58, 371) and 4 October 1163 (ibid., 376). Nuño Pérez does so from 30 October 1162 (ibid., 251–252) to 4 October 1163, as well as the much later diplomas of August 1173 (ibid., 430), December 1174 (*ACL*, 5:447–448), and September 1175 (*Fernando II*, 289; *Sahagún*, 4:354–355). "Comes Aluarus" witnesses Leonese royal diplomas between 6 July 1161 (*Fernando II*, 250) and 14 April 1165 (ibid., 258).

48. Ibid., 162.

49. "Manente super negocia regni," 1158 (*Sahagún*, 4:277–279); "nutritius regis," March 1161 (*Segovia*, 109–110).

50. "Procurantibus negocia regis Adefonsi," 15 February 1163 (*Sahagún*, 4:297–300).

51. 10 February 1164 (*Sahagún*, 4:304–305). In fact, he subscribed every single royal charter from November 1159 to 10 February 1164 (*Alfonso VIII*, 2:93–108).

52. According to the Anales Toledanos, 392, Manrique died on 9 July 1164; *Aguilar de Campóo*, 2:186–187, suggests 3 June.

53. *CG1344*, 4:275–276.

54. A point raised by García Pelegrín, *Hochadel*, 133.

55. *Alfonso VIII*, 1:370.

56. Ibid., 2:93–470 passim. He first appears as count in a royal donation of 11 March 1162 (*Alfonso VIII*, 2:100).

57. The first use of *fideliter* is 14 January 1168 (ibid., no. 17; *Sahagún*, 4:319–321); the last occasion on which he appears as "manente super negocia regis" is in 1176 (*Vega*, 102). By 1173, he had assumed Manrique's earlier status as the king's advisor: "Comite dom Nugno, amo del rei Alfons," June 1173 (*Carrión*, 1:67).

58. "Tenente curia regis et eius imperio," 18 February 1174 (*Sahagún*, 4:343–344); "tenent [sic] curia regis Aldefonsi," 5 July 1175 (ibid., 4:352–354).

59. *CL*, 25.

60. New aquisitions included Amaya, Carrión, Castilla, Nájera, and San Román de Entrepeñas. Fernando Núñez confirmed Castilian royal diplomas from 27 January 1173 (*Alfonso VIII*, 2:295)—a document in which he already has the comital title—through his father's death in 1177 (ibid., 470); he would continue to do so almost uninterruptedly until the end of 1190, and frequently thereafter. The middle son, Álvaro Núñez, also received the tenancy of Aguilar, in 1167 (*Alfonso VIII*, 1:176).

61. Granted to Nuño Pérez by Alfonso VII on 1 May 1146 (*Pruebas*, 619–620).

62. *Arlanza*, 221–223.

63. *Cartularios de Toledo*, 180–181 (Alcabón); AHN Ordenes Militares, Calatrava, carp. 455, 9P (Aceca).

64. In 1176, the archbishop of Toledo granted Nuño Pérez and his wife the right to live in the houses there which had belonged to Sancha, the sister of Alfonso VII (*Orden de San Juan*, 172). The following year, in July 1177, the couple endowed a chapel dedicated to St. Thomas à Becket in the cathedral of Toledo with their

properties next to the city's Alcázar, as well as those in Alcabón (ibid., 180–181; Barton, *Aristocracy*, 328).

65. He and his wife granted the rights to the *diezmo* (tithe) of the hospital to Burgos cathedral in April 1174 (*OB*, 3:250–251).

66. On 29 January 1160, he and his wife founded the Cistercian convent of Santa María de Perales, granting it land in these two villages (*Alfonso VIII*, 1:178–179, 521); I suspect that Zorita may be Zorita de la Loma. Along with his sons Álvaro and Gonzalo, he granted the convent to Santa María de Aguilar in 1169 (ibid., 1:284–285). He evidently retained other holdings in Perales, since he granted a further property there to the cathedral of Toledo in 1174 (ibid., 1:284–285) and again in 1176 (AHN Códices 996B, 46v).

67. Count Nuño and one Pedro Martínez are described as "herederos in Cisneros et Villella" in a document of 15 February 1163 (AHN Clero, carp. 900, no. 6).

68. Santiago, Vega Mayor, and Lobroyo. See Carlos Manuel Reglero de la Fuente, *Los señoríos de los Montes de Torozos* (Valladolid, 1993), 126–127.

69. 27 March 1168 (*Pruebas*, 620). He had also been responsible for the repopulation of Castronuño, southwest of Tordesillas; see José Luís Martín Martín et al., ed., *Documentos de los archivos catedralicio y diocesano de Salamanca, siglos XII–XIII* (Salamanca, 1977), 104–105.

70. Pedro Rodríguez witnessed many royal diplomas between 1165 and 1180 (*Alfonso VIII*, 2:114–559).

71. Namely, in Vedia, Elechas, Ambojo, Muslera, Pontejos, and Gajano, all in the *alfoz* of Cudeyo; his father, Rodrigo González, had owned Arce, west of the bay. These properties were granted to the bishopric of Burgos on 23 February 1168 (*OB*, 3:230–231; *Covarrubias*, 61, n. 16).

72. He pawned these places to the bishop of Burgos for 200 *maravedís* in 1166. They were Zorita, Encinillas, Visjueces, La Riba, Villalázara, "Triova" (perhaps Trueba, a depopulated village 400 meters from Loma de Montija), "Campdonad" (conceivably Campillo de Mena), and Lezana de Mena (*OB*, 3:223–225; cf. *LBB*, 2:538, n. 40).

73. *OB*, 3:225–226. His sister, Elvira Rodríguez, does appear to have had more southerly possessions, making a donation of property in Talavera to the Order of Calatrava in 1172 (*Alfonso VIII*, 1:342).

74. Granted to the cathedral on 23 April (*OB*, 3:275–276).

75. He and his sister María pledge these possessions to the abbey of La Vid in 1183 (Barton, *Aristocracy*, 329).

76. *Cartularios de Toledo*, 181–182 (Carabanchel, alienated on 1 January 1181); *Pruebas*, 16 (Cogolludo and Carabanchel); *Cartularios de Toledo*, 174–175 (Barciles and Añover de Tajo, sold to the archbishop of Toledo on 19 August 1177).

77. Julio González (*Alfonso VIII*, 1:277) draws this conclusion from the decision made by Pedro Manrique's wife to pledge the town of Carabanchel to his servant Gonzalo Díaz for 100 *maravedís* on 1 January 1181 (AHN Códices 996B, 84v–85r); while Hilda Grassotti ("El sitio de Cuenca en la mecánica vasallático-señorial de Castilla," in *Estudios Medievales Españoles* [Madrid, 1981], 238–241) sees the sale of Añover and Barcilés as symptomatic of administrative carelessness by the Laras.

78. In this frontier region Pedro Manrique had and sold the village of Valtablado, just southeast of Cifuentes (AHN Códices 1046B, 42–43; AHN

Ordenes Militares, Santiago, carp. 98, no. 1); salt mines in Bonilla (AHN Códices 104B, 26r), granted to the monastery of Sacramenia; Beteta, half of which he acquired from the see of Sigüenza in return for the monastery of Santa María de Molina (Barton, *Aristocracy,* 282); and Anquela—either Anquela del Ducado or Anquela del Pedregal—which may have lain within the lordship of Molina (*Pruebas,* 14–15).

79. Pedro Manrique confirmed royal privileges as early as March 1161, and continued to do so frequently between 1165 to 1201; he acquired comital status in 1164, and was typically listed second among secular witnesses, after Nuño Pérez, in the early 1170s (*Alfonso VIII,* 2:96–97, 2:117–3:257 passim). With the solitary exception of a diploma of 16 April 1164 (*Sahagún,* 4:306–307), he first begins to appear as count on 1 September 1166 (*Alfonso VIII,* 2:144).

80. Anales Toledanos, 392.

81. August 1173 (*Fernando II,* 430); December 1174 (*ACL,* 5:447–448); September 1175 (*Fernando II,* 289; *Sahagún,* 4:354–355). He had also made a donation to the cathedral of León, on 22 September 1170, with his wife and children; perhaps this was intended as an olive branch (*Fernando II,* 120). The Anales Toledanos, 393, give the date of his death as June 1177, but since he is known to have made a grant to the cathedral of Toledo in July, the correct date is more likely to be late July or August (*Cartularios de Toledo,* 180–81).

82. *Fernando II,* 121, 457. Teresa Fernández, whom Nuño had probably married by 18 March 1154, was the illegitimate daughter of Fernando Pérez de Traba (Barton, *Aristocracy,* 269, n. 3).

83. *CG1344,* 4:306–307; Linhagens, 263; *Casa de Lara,* 4:83; *Alfonso VIII,* 1:289.

3. A Zenith and a Nadir

1. Faustino Menéndez Pidal, "Los sellos de los señores de Molina," *AEM,* 14 (1984), 117.

2. The *infanta,* whom Pedro Manrique had married by 1165, was the daughter of King García Ramírez of Navarre (reigned 1134–1150). See Simon Barton, *The Aristocracy in Twelfth-Century León and Castile* (Cambridge, 1997), 282.

3. María Eugenia Lacarra, *El Poema de Mio Cid: Realidad histórica e ideología* (Madrid, 1980). Martín de Riquer, *Los cantares de gesta franceses: Sus problemas, su relación con España* (Madrid, 1952), points to the Laras' exposure to the French epic tradition, and particularly the *cantar* of Aymeri de Narbonne, as the reason for the emergence of the legend of the Siete Infantes of Lara in this period. Note that Angelo Monteverdi, "Il cantare degli Infanti di Salas," *Studi medievali,* 7 (1934), 113–150, persuasively demonstrates that, contrary to the opinion of Menéndez Pidal, the *cantar* of the seven *infantes* cannot have been composed before the late twelfth century.

4. Simon Barton, "Reinventing the Hero: The Poetic Portrayal of Rodrigo Díaz, the Cid, in its Political Context," in David G. Pattison, ed., *Textos épicos castellanos: Problemas de edición y crítica* (London, 2000), 65–78.

5. Teresa appears frequently alongside the king in donations made between 7 October 1178 (*Fernando II,* 1:124, 460) and February 1180 (ibid., 1:129, 465–456), shortly before her death. Salazar argued that this Teresa was more likely to have

been Nuño Pérez's daughter than his widow, because marriage to the widow implies a large age difference (*Casa de Lara*, 4:13, 15–16). However, Fernando II may have been pursuing a policy of marriage alliances with Castilian noble houses (his next marriage was to Urraca López de Haro) in which considerations of age were secondary. There does not seem to be any indication that Nuño Pérez and his wife, Teresa, had a daughter of the same name, and Fernando II's grant of the churches of Pallares for the services performed by Teresa and her husband is virtually conclusive.

6. José García Pelegrín, *Studien zum Hochadel der Königreiche León und Kastilien im Hochmittelalter* (Munster, 1991), 138.

7. Esther Pascua Echegaray, *Guerra y pacto en el siglo XII: La consolidación de un sistema de reinos en Europa occidental* (Madrid, 1996), 185–191.

8. Cristina Jular Pérez-Alfaro, "'Alfoz' y 'Tierra' a través de documentación castellana y leonesa de 1157 a 1230: Contribución al estudio del 'dominio señorial,'" *Studia Histórica: Historia Medieval*, 9 (1991), 40–41.

9. It is true that there were some cases of patrimonialization—Astorga, for instance, fell to various members of the Froilaz clan for a period of around sixty years—but this was exceptional. For example, Asturias had twenty-six successive tenants in a thirty-nine-year period, 1188–1227 (*Alfonso IX*, 1:349). Margarita Torres Sevilla-Quiñones de León, *Linajes nobiliarios en León y Castilla, siglos IX–XIII* (Salamanca, 1999), 451–480, perhaps exaggerates the tendency toward long-term delegation of tenancies; for instance, the mid-century dominance of the Froilaz clan in Ulver was subsequently challenged by the *concejo* of Bembibre, the Templars, and others.

10. Cristina Jular Pérez-Alfaro, *Los adelantados y merinos mayores de León, siglos XIII–XV* (León, 1990), 54–104.

11. Many of the Lara brothers' patrimonies in León may have been inherited from their mother; they may have belonged to Teresa Fernández either through her marriage to Fernando II or, more likely, through her affiliation to the Traba family. In this category we might place their property in Sarantes, near La Coruña (*Sobrado*, 2:335, 350–352). The properties that the brothers exchanged with Alfonso IX for Tines and a constellation of royal properties on the small peninsula between La Coruña and Ferrol in February 1210 may also have been part of the maternal inheritance (*ACL*, 6:211–212).

12. *Alfonso VIII*, 1:692. He confirms a donation by Fernando II to the monastery of Lorenzana in March 1180 (*Fernando II*, 130, 467). On 23 May 1180, he confirmed a donation by the king to the monastery of Vega (*Vega*, 105). In an undated document, probably from 1180 or 1181, the king notified his "faithful vassal Gonzalo Núñez" that Teresa had given the four churches in Pallares to Lugo (*Fernando II*, 516). He was again in the company of Fernando II on 10 and 21 March 1186 (ibid., 333, 506).

13. Pedro Manrique was at the Leonese court on 27 January 1185 (*Fernando II*, 499), enjoying the status of *mayordomo* on 11 February (ibid.); by 4 March 1186, he was styled "vassallo regis Fernandi" (ibid.).

14. There is just one hiatus, in 1209, which may have been connected with his brother's hostilities against Leonese forces in that year. In 1212, he traveled south to take part in the campaign which culminated in Las Navas de Tolosa, but two years later he was back again: he appeared with Alfonso IX in the city of León on 28 April 1214 (*Alfonso VIII*, 1:750).

15. In addition to holding tenancies granted by the king of León, Gonzalo Núñez also held the tenancy of Aveancos from the archbishop of Compostela, in 1214 (*Alfonso IX*, 1:155; *Fernando III*, 1:148). Note, though, that even his tenancies characteristically lasted for periods of two years or less.

16. Pedro Rodríguez remained among witness lists until 13 January 1180 (*Alfonso VIII*, 2:559), although this does not indicate that he died in 1180, as *Casa de Lara*, 4:254 suggests: he confirms a Leonese diploma dated 2 April 1183 (*Fernando II*, 488). Pedro Manrique was a witness on a very frequent basis until 11 December 1201, shortly before his death (*Alfonso VIII*, 2:117–3:257 passim). From 1 April 1191 onward, he was often the only lay lord in a first column otherwise consisting exclusively of bishops (ibid., 3:10). He died in January 1202 (Anales Toledanos, 395).

17. Salvador de Moxó, "De la nobleza vieja a la nobleza nueva: La transformación nobiliaria castellana en la baja edad media," *CH*, 3 (1969), 147; *Oña*, 379 (8 January 1196); ibid., 381 (2 December 1196). There is no evidence of the presence at court of the elder son, Gonzalo Pérez Manrique.

18. Of the diplomas published in *Alfonso VIII*, he confirms as follows: 27 January 1173 to 15 December 1190 (2:295–967 passim); 26 June 1193 (3:98); 13 January 1195 to 11 April 1198 (ibid., 130–175 passim); 12 September 1201 (ibid., 253); 29 April 1206 to 3 July 1206 (ibid., 375–388 passim); 27 May 1209 to 17 May 1217 (ibid., 476–747 passim). He was also present at the Castilian court at least once in 1199 (AHN Códices 996B, 64r–v), in a role other than *alférez* in the year 1202 (1 July 1202; AHN Códices 987B, 62v), and in September 1208 (*Aguilar de Campóo*, 2:251–252).

19. In the diplomas published in *Alfonso VIII*, he appears with this office on the following occasions: 16 January 1186 (2:770); 8 July 1187 to 28 July 1188 (2:833–872 passim); 11 December 1201 to 23 October 1205 (3:257–363 passim); 8 March 1207 (3:399). The following diplomas, not published by González, fall outside these time frames: 29 October 1188 (*OB*, 3:307–308); 22 October 1201 (Barton, *Aristocracy*, 239; 11 November 1201 (*Casa de Lara*, 4:153); 1208 (*Liébana*, 162).

20. 2 April 1182 (*Carrión*, 1:82); 13 May 1183 (*Alfonso VIII*, 2:701); 8 December 1195 to 18 August 1197 (ibid., 3:150–172 passim); 9 December 1212 (ibid., 2:578).

21. According to Salazar y Castro, the first record of Álvaro Núñez dates from 1194 (*Casa de Lara*, 1:151, 4:51). In fact, he was a witness of a grant made by the abbot of Oña two years earlier, on 11 September 1192 (*Oña*, 365; *Casa de Lara*, 4:51–52). He witnessed royal charters from 7 January 1196 to 6 May 1199 (*Alfonso VIII*, 3:152–201 passim); 2 June 1202 (AHN Códices 105B, 250r–251r); 1 July 1202 (AHN Códices 987B, 62v); 18 August 1202 (*Casa de Lara*, 4:52); and 24 December 1202 to 29 May 1208 (*Alfonso VIII*, 3:286–443 passim). He is listed as *alférez* in diplomas from 1 March 1199 (*Aguilar de Campóo*, 2:219) to 12 September 1201 (*Alfonso VIII*, 3:253); and 23 September 1208 to 6 May 1217 (ibid., 447–744 passim).

22. The brothers, for instance, shared possession of a number of properties in the region of the upper Ebro; they jointly donated properties in Zangandez, Bárcena, Santotis, Quintana, Villamezán, and Baranda to the abbey of Oña, in 1183 (*Oña*, 320–321). Likewise, three years earlier, on 20 March 1180, they had joined in granting their property in Hortigüela, near Lara, to the monastery of Arlanza (*Arlanza*, 192, n. 2); and in 1195 Count Fernando and his unnamed brothers ap-

pear as joint lords in Tamariz de Campos, just north of Medina de Rioseco (*Sahagún*, 4:530–531; also Luís Fernández Martín, ed., "Colección diplomática del monasterio de Villanueva de San Mancio," *Archivos Leoneses*, 26 [1972], 13).

23. 3 March 1203 (*Pruebas*, 622).

24. *Las Huelgas*, 1:196–197.

25. In August 1202 he and his wife gave to Count Gonzalo de Bureba their property in Belorado (and, curiously, a scarlet cloak) in exchange for Valdivielso, "Los Butrones," Moradillo de Sedano, the *alfoz* of Sedano, and the *alfoz* of Ubierna; and in 1205 he granted to the monastery of Aguilar a property in Castrillo de Riopisuerga (*Alfonso VIII*, 1:287, n. 135).

26. In May 1242, for instance, they sold to the bishop of Burgos the lordship of Tardajos, just west of the city. This included property in Rabé de las Calzadas, Mazariegos, Barruelo, and Páramo (Luciano Serrano, "El canciller de Fernando III de Castilla," *Hispania*, 1, no. 5 [1941], 3–40). In the autumn, they added their further-flung possessions in Belorado (*Pruebas*, 624–625). This was followed (on 21 May 1243) by the sale of properties in Sasamón and Mazorrero (RAH M-8, fols. 71v–72r). Other properties near the city, mainly to its northwest, which they transmitted to the bishopric included Tordomar, Las Balbeses, Quintanilla de Pedro Abarca, Las Hormazas, the convent of Palacios de Benaver, the monastery of San Salvador de los Palacios de Daniel, Buitrones, Bureba, and Villafruela. See Demetrio Mansilla Reoyo, ed., *Catálogo documental del Archivo Catedral de Burgos, 804–1416* (Burgos, 1971), 162–168; *Pruebas*, 625; Ignacio Álvarez Borge, "Estructura social y organización territorial en Castilla la Vieja meridional: Los territorios entre el Arlanzón y el Duero en los siglos X al XIV" (Diss., Universidad de León, 1991), 370; Jesús Domínguez Aparicio, "Donación señorial de los Condes de Lara a la cofradía palentina de Santa María de Esperina, siglo XIII, *Hidalguía: La revista de genealogía, nobleza y armas*, 236 (1993), 130.

27. In 1221, she granted to the cathedral all her possessions in Buniel, Villavela, Albillos, and Cayuela (Álvarez Borge, "Estructura social," 369).

28. *Palencia*, 349–350; Álvarez Borge, "Estructura social," 370.

29. *Oña*, 447 (13 April 1208).

30. Don Álvaro granted property there in 1213 to his aunt Urraca López de Haro, so that she might establish a convent there (AHN Códices 1168B).

31. *Alfonso IX*, 1:168–169.

32. *Alfonso VIII*, 3:745; *Fernando III*, 1:234 (Grañón); *Fernando III*, 1:148 (Santibáñez de Ecla); AHN Códices 1046B, 237–238 (Osorno, granted to the Order of Santiago on 20 February 1201); AHN Clero, carp. 1692 no. 13 (Cisneros).

33. *Casa de Lara*, 4:22. Salazar states that Nuño Sánchez clashed with Jaume I over possession of these counties but remained in control of them until his death in 1247, when they reverted to the crown. He argues that this is evidence that Don Nuño died childless, but it is also possible that this reversion was stipulated in the settlement reached as a result of judicial arbitration in 1235.

34. Ibid., 1:149–151. Aimerico in turn granted Montpesat and Lac, in Narbonnese territory, to his younger brother Rodrigo Pérez Manrique in 1208.

35. AHN Ordenes Militares, Calatrava, carp. 456, 27P.

36. A similar lack of concern may have influenced the decision made by his widow and son, on 3 February 1202, to sell Tragacete to the *concejo* of Cuenca (*Alfonso VIII*, 1:273 n. 57).

37. Hilda Grassotti, "Don Rodrigo Ximénez de Rada, gran señor y hombre de negocios en la Castilla del siglo XIII," *CHE*, 55–56 (1972), 1–302.

38. Ignacio Álvarez Borge, *Monarquía feudal y organización territorial: Alfoces y merindades en Castilla, siglos X–XIV* (Madrid, 1993), 135.

39. The only two tenancies which Álvaro Núñez held in successive years, Bureba and Castilla la Vieja, were held almost by default, a result of Diego López de Haro's absence from Castile.

40. *Alfonso VIII*, 3:574–576.

41. Arguably, the military importance of the municipal *concejos* at Las Navas suggests that the crown was already beginning to seek the support of groups other than the nobility, as it would in later centuries; see Hilda Grassotti, *Las instituciones feudo-vassalláticas en León y Castilla*, 2 vols. (Spoleto, 1969), 2:961–969. But the real transformation in the role of the *concejos* would not occur until the reign of Alfonso X, by which time relations between king and nobility had deteriorated; see Teófilo Ruiz, "The Transformation of the Castilian Municipalities: The Case of Burgos, 1248–1350," *Past and Present*, 77 (1977), 3–33.

42. Miriam Teresa Shadis, "Motherhood, Lineage and Royal Power in Medieval Castile: Berenguela de Leon and Blanche de Castille" (Diss., Duke University, 1994).

43. *CL*, 64.

44. *Alfonso VIII*, 2:693–695.

45. *CL*, 65. Gonzalo appears with the comital title on 15 January 1216 (*Alfonso VIII*, 2:711–713).

46. Peter Linehan, *History and the Historians of Medieval Spain* (Oxford, 1993), 383.

47. Elsewhere, Linehan uses soccer imagery to express the animosity between Toledo and its rivals; see "On Further Thought: Lucas of Tuy, Rodrigo of Toledo and the Alfonsine Histories," *AEM*, 27 (1997), 415–436, esp. 425–426. Bernard Reilly examines the positive depiction of the original conqueror of Toledo (Alfonso VI) in "Rodrigo Jiménez de Rada's Portrait of Alfonso VI of Leon-Castile in the *De Rebus Hispaniae*: Historical Methodology in the Thirteenth Century," *Estudios en homenaje a Don Claudio Sánchez Albornoz en sus 90 años*, vol. 3 (Buenos Aires, 1985), esp. 94–96.

48. Grassotti, "Don Rodrigo Ximénez de Rada," 8–18.

49. *PCG*, 192–193 (following DRH, 192–193).

50. *Alfonso VIII*, 1:235, n. 331. Note that Jiménez de Rada emphasizes a journey made by Álvaro Núñez and his followers to drum up support in Extremadura in 1216; his intent is to show that this support was specific and artificial (DRH, 194; *PCG*, 711).

51. *PCG*, 709 (following DRH, 192–193).

52. *PCG*, 709 (following DRH, 193).

53. DRH, 193; *PCG*, 710.

54. *Cartularios de Toledo*, 331.

55. *CG1344*, 4:343–344; *Fernando III*, 1:118, 156.

56. *CG1344*, 4:343–344.

57. DRH, 193; *PCG*, 710. "Albaro Nunnez totam terram sub eo regente," 19 April 1216 (*Sahagún*, 5:99–101). He had become *mayordomo* of the royal curia the previous winter (6 December 1215; *Sahagún*, 5:98–99).

58. "Procuratore regis et regni" (11 March 1217; *Sahagún*, 5:105–106); "procurator regis" (31 March 1217; *El Moral*, 95–97).

59. DRH, 194–195; *PCG*, 712.

60. The exchange of properties with Alfonso IX in 1210 has a nonformulaic terseness to it: "Et ipse domnus Gonzaluus Nuniz debet inducere pro posse suo predictos fratres suos et sororem et nepotem illorum bona fide et sine malo ingenio quod concedant cambium istud." *ACL*, 6:211–212.

61. *Alfonso VIII*, 2:299–301. Álvaro Núñez had earlier received a temporary grant of Alhambra from the Master of the Order of Santiago, confirmed by Enrique I on 1 May 1215 (RAH leg. B, carp. 10, no. 19).

62. DRH, 195; *PCG*, 712; Anales Toledanos, 400–401; Lucas, bishop of Tuy, *Crónica de España*, ed. Julio Puyol (Madrid, 1926), 417.

63. DRH, 195; *PCG*, 712.

64. DRH, 194; *PCG*, 711. The *PCG*, although not Jiménez de Rada, claims that when Álvaro Núñez discovered the spy, he responded first by imprisoning him and then by hanging him. If this account is accurate, these would appear to be either the actions of the psychopathic villain the chronicler would have us imagine, or those of a man with legitimate cause for alarm. It is not transparently obvious why Berenguela would have needed to send a spy simply to check on the condition of her brother, nor even why she would have had a particular concern for Enrique's welfare (since the Laras' continued success rested entirely on his well-being).

65. *CG1344*, 4:354–355; *Alfonso VIII*, 1:755–756; *Alfonso IX*, 1:168–169. This was the second occasion on which Don Álvaro had attempted to orchestrate a marriage for Enrique. He at first had sought a marriage alliance with Portugal (DRH, 194; *PCG*, 711).

66. This appears to have been a somewhat honorific gesture. Álvaro Núñez remained in the entourage of Enrique I and delegated one Pedro Merino to hold the Leonese *mayordomía* (*Alfonso VIII*, 1:759).

67. *CG1344*, 4:350–351.

68. *Alfonso VIII*, 1:237, n. 335, citing Biblioteca Nacional, MS 431, fol. 93.

69. 3 February 1217 (ibid., 3:738–740); 17 February 1217 (ibid., 740–741); 31 March 1217 (ibid., 741–743); 6 May 1217 (ibid., 743–744); 17 May 1217 (ibid., 746–747).

70. Joseph O'Callaghan, *The Learned King: The Reign of Alfonso X of Castile* (Philadelphia, 1993), 70.

71. Manuel Torres López, "Sobre la muerte de Enrique I de Castilla," in *Estudios en homenaje a Don Claudio Sánchez Albornoz en sus 90 años*, 4 vols. (Buenos Aires, 1983), 2:469–487.

72. This chronicle is also adamant, for instance, in claiming that Berenguela was younger than Blanca (Blanche, Queen of France, mother of Saint Louis) and that this was one rationale for the Laras' armed opposition to the new king (*CG1344*, 4:316, 354–355). The same claim is also made by the great Aragonese chronicler Jerónimo de Zurita, who describes Blanca as "la legítima sucesora" and states that it was only a desire to avoid union with the French crown that led many people to affirm that Berenguela was the elder sister (Zurita, *Anales*, 1:385, book II, ch. 75). But Salazar y Castro is persuasive in dismissing the idea, arguing that the first mention of a royal child in the diplomas is of Berenguela (in 1180), followed by Sancho (1181), Urraca several years later, Fernando (1189), and only in 1193 by

Blanca; see *Casa de Lara*, 4:58–61. The dates are modified slightly by Miriam Shadis, who states that the first mention of Berenguela dates from 1 May 1181, and the first mention of Blanca from 1190 ("Motherhood, Lineage and Royal Power," 37–41).

73. DRH, 196; *PCG*, 714.

74. DRH, 197; *PCG*, 715.

75. Cañete, Alarcón, Amaya, Tariego, Cerezo, Villafranca de Montes de Oca, Belorado, and Nájera (DRH, 197–199; *PCG*, 715–716; *CL*, 68–76; Amparo Hernández Segura, ed., *Crónica de la población de Ávila* [Valencia, 1966], 40). *Alfonso IX*, 1:183–184, citing BN 10652, fol. 14r, claims that Álvaro Núñez was mistreated in prison to accelerated the surrender of his castles; Berenguela adds that it was retaliation for Don Álvaro's mistreatment of Gonzalo Rodríguez Girón, who was also being held.

76. Álvaro was among those who swore, on the Leonese side, to uphold the peace with Castile in the early summer of 1218 (*Fernando III*, 1:245); and he was *mayordomo* in León on 8 July of that year (*Alfonso IX*, 1:324).

77. DRH, 199; *PCG*, 717; *CL*, 70.

78. DRH, 199; *PCG*, 717.

79. *CG1344*, 4:360. The chroniclers are agreed on what little remained for Don Álvaro; having joined the Order of Santiago in his final days, he died shortly afterward at Toro and was buried at Uclés (DRH, 199; *PCG*, 717; *CG1344*, 4:361). His relationship with the order was not an entirely thirteenth-hour affair; it had granted him Alhambra, in 1215, as a temporal *encomienda*, and he had granted it Castroverde in June 1217.

80. Along with Álvaro, Gonzalo Núñez confirmed a privilege of Alfonso IX of León on 14 March 1218, styling himself *regis vassalo* (AHN Códices 323B, 60v–61v); and having served in the Leonese army in an early summer campaign against Castile, he reappeared as a vassal of the king on 8 July (*Alfonso IX*, 1:184–185).

81. *Alfonso IX*, 1:186.

82. 13 February 1219 (ibid., 1:187, 192).

83. 16 June 1219 (ibid., 1:193).

84. *Fernando III*, 1:146, states that his sole male heir, Fernando Fernández, also died very shortly afterward.

85. DRH, 199. The decision to serve in Morocco rather than León is curious. *Fernando III*, 1:288, comments that there had been other groups of Christian knights serving there, but this seems an inadequate explanation; it is possible that Fernando III reached an agreement with his father, Alfonso IX, which excluded Fernando Núñez from León. A similar agreement might also explain the even more striking decision by Gonzalo Núñez, long a favorite of Alfonso IX, to enter Almohad service in 1221.

86. DRH, 201, explicitly charges him with responsibility for the rebellion. The *Crónica Latina* is more vague, stating that Gonzalo Pérez Manrique was "led by less wise counsel" (*CL*, 79). On 28 June 1221, Gonzalo Pérez Manrique agreed with the archbishop of Toledo that he would hold Molina and the surrounding area as a hereditary fief of the archbishop (RAH N-10, 179r–180v [60r–61v in modern pagination]). This linkage of vassalic service to the holding of property was unusual in Castile; Claudio Sánchez Albornoz, "Un feudo castellano del siglo XIII," *AHDE*, 1 (1924), 388, argues that it was the only authentic fief in medieval Castile.

87. DRH, 201; *Fernando III*, 1:148. As González points out, he was either still in Castile, or had come back temporarily, in the spring of 1225, when he and his wife María sold a property in Cisneros (AHN Clero, carp. 1692, no. 13; 27 April 1225) and granted the castle of Santibáñez de Ecla to the monastery of San Andrés de Arroyo, to which his wife retired after his death.

4. The Road to Rebellion

1. *Las siete partidas*, trans. and ed. Samuel Parsons Scott (New York, 1931), IV, 25, x (p. 995). This massive code of the 1260s, which drew heavily upon the principles of Roman law, met intense resistance from municipalities and the nobility, and was only belatedly incorporated into legal practice in the Ordenamiento de Alcalá (1348).

2. Otto Brunner, *Land and Lordship*, trans. and with an introduction by Howard Kaminsky and James Van Horn Melton (Philadelphia, 1992), 3–4.

3. *Casa de Lara*, 4:117–118. Salazar's opinion that it was a son of Juan Núñez I, also called Juan Núñez, who married Teresa Álvarez was persuasively dismissed by Mercedes Gaibrois (*Sancho IV*, 2:83–84).

4. Esther Pascua Echegaray, *Guerra y pacto en el siglo XII: La consolidación de un sistema de reinos en Europa occidental* (Madrid, 1996), 361–362.

5. J. C. Holt, *Magna Carta* (Cambridge, 1965); idem, "The Origins of the Constitutional Tradition in England," in Holt, *Magna Carta and Medieval Government* (London, 1985).

6. Ana Rodríguez López, "Fernando III el Santo, 1217–1252: Evolución historiográfica, canonización y utilización política," in *Miscellània en homenatge al P. Agustí Altisent* (Tarragona, 1991), 573–588.

7. Ana Rodríguez López, *La consolidación territorial de la monarquía feudal castellana: Expansión y fronteras durante el reinado de Fernando III* (Madrid, 1994), 313–316. Cristina Jular Pérez-Alfaro, *Los adelantados y merinos mayores de León, siglos XIII–XV* (León, 1990), 163–174.

8. Ana Rodríguez López, "Linajes nobiliarios y monarquía castellano-leonesa en la primera mitad del siglo XIII," *Hispania*, 185 (September–December 1993), 856.

9. Ana Rodríguez López, "'Quod alienus regnet et heredes expelatur': L'offre du trône de Castille au roi Louis VIII de France," *Le Moyen Age*, 105 (1999).

10. Lope Díaz de Haro temporarily lost his tenancies as a result of resistance in 1233, and eight years later Diego López de Haro likewise forfeited his tenancies in the wake of a rebellion, regaining possession of them only in 1243 (Rodríguez López, "Linajes nobiliarios," 850–855).

11. He appears as lord of Molina on 6 April 1238 (*Casa de Lara*, 1:239; *Pruebas*, 30).

12. *Casa de Lara*, 1:238, states that Mafalda was Gonzalo Pérez's daughter rather than granddaughter, but *Fernando III*, 1:87–88, is insistent that Mafalda was the daughter of his son Pedro González.

13. Rodríguez López, *Consolidación territorial*, 248.

14. Mafalda and Alfonso granted a confirmation of privileges to the monastery of Buenafuente on 31 August 1241 (*Fernando III*, 1:89). Alfonso, whose marriage to Mafalda was his first, was later wed to Teresa González de Lara (sister of Nuño

González), and his third wife was Mayor Alfonso de Meneses (*Alfonso IX*, 1:313). The marriage to Teresa seems to have occurred some time after September 1244, when she and her brother made a sale of property to the bishop of Burgos with no mention of a marriage to the *infante* Alfonso (RAH M-8, fols. 72v–73r; *Casa de Lara*, 4:85–86). The couple had a daughter, Juana Alfonso, who was married to Lope Díaz de Haro in 1269 in order to shore up an alliance with the Haros (*Casa de Lara*, 4:86–87).

15. A second effect of this disinheritance was that the Manriques no longer remained close or important allies of the Laras. The disinherited male line of Gonzalo Pérez Manrique came into possession of Úbeda, but otherwise disappear completely from the record. See Salvador de Moxó, "De la nobleza vieja a la nobleza nueva: La transformación nobiliaria castellana en la baja edad media," *CH*, 3 (1969), 45.

16. Joseph O'Callaghan, *The Learned King: The Reign of Alfonso X of Castile* (Philadelphia, 1993), 72–73.

17. CAX, 25.

18. *Fernando III*, 1:141, n. 77, 1:146; Aurembiaix was granddaughter of Manrique de Lara, and daughter of his child Elvira, who had married Armengol VIII of Urgell. In July 1228 she made a donation to her cousin Nuño Pérez II, a younger son of her uncle Pedro Manrique (AHN Sellos, armario 2 caj. 31, no. 26).

19. There is a donation of 1225 made by the two brothers (Diego González and Nuño González) and their parents to the abbess of San Andrés de Arroyo (*Fernando III*, 1:148, n. 133).

20. Zurita, *Anales* 1:394 (bk. II, ch. 78); *Fernando III*, 1:147.

21. RAH M-8, fol. 71; *Casa de Lara*, 4:45.

22. In 1231 he joined his mother, Mayor, and his sisters, Sancha and Teresa, in confirming a sale made by the monastery of Palacios to the Hospital del Emperador in Burgos (*Alfonso VIII*, 1:288). Later, in 1240, he sold property in San Torcuato de Bobadilla del Camino to the bishop of Palencia (*Palencia*, 347–349).

23. 22 April 1235 to 17 September 1240. Julio González quite rightly points out that Álvaro Fernández occupied a lowly position in the list of subscribers, although one might add that by late 1238 he had risen to a middling rank (*Fernando III*, 1:147; ibid., 3:69–199).

24. *CL*, 117.

25. 22 April 1235 to 22 December 1239 (*Fernando III*, 3:69–204); *CL*, 117.

26. *PCG*, 750; Lucas, bishop of Tuy, *Crónica de España*, ed. Julio Puyol (Madrid, 1926), 433–434, 442.

27. His sons Fernán Rodríguez and Sancho Rodríguez became the second and third lords of Alcalá de Guadaira (Moxó, "De la nobleza vieja," 38). As Salazar argues, this probably suggests that Fernán Rodríguez, who had inherited Alcalá by 1270, had no heirs (*Casa de Lara*, 4:69).

28. Nuño González had been present in the royal host at Andújar when Fernando was leading a campaign in Andalucía in 1225. "And then he ordered Nuño González and Don Rodrigo, son of the countess, to make for Arjona and fight strongly everywhere, and to lay siege there so that they would have it surrounded; and he sent most of the people there with them. And when they arrived, they did as the king ordered them, for they began to attack and combat the town very forcefully, so that they caused it great suffering" (*PCG*, 743). *CG1344*, 4:431–

432, also refers to Nuño's role at Arjona. However, his heroism did not ensure him a place at the Castilian court in subsequent years.

29. He did have properties in Sasamón, Abia, and Herrera which, particularly in the first case, may have been inherited. RAH M-8, fols. 72v–73r; and Demetrio Mansilla Reoyo, ed., *Catálogo documental de Archivo Catedral de Burgos, 804–1416* (Burgos, 1971), no. 654 (re: Sasamón). The fact that in 1244, jointly with his sister, he sold property in Sasamón to the bishop of Burgos suggests it was a mutual inheritance. According to *Casa de Lara*, 4:94, and *Pruebas*, 635, a similar sale was made on 7 July 1246; *Fernando III*, 1:149–150.

30. *RS*, 1:149.

31. *Fernando III*, 3:259–431.

32. In a document of 6 January 1251, he appears first among the lay nobility (*Casa de Lara*, 4:96).

33. CAX, 25; *Casa de Lara*, 4:94

34. *Casa de Lara*, 4:94.

35. Ibid.; *CG1344*, 239–241.

36. CAX, 16, 25.

37. Manuel González Jiménez, "Población y repartimiento de Écija," in *Homenaje al profesor Juan Torres Fontes*, 2 vols. (Murcia, 1987), 1:691–692.

38. *Fernando III*, 1:149, suggests that he may also have enjoyed the support of the Girones, but I have found no evidence for this, and indeed such support would seem unlikely in view of the mutual hostility between the Laras and Girones in the previous generation.

39. CAX, 25, and *Casa de Lara*, 4:109, suggest that Teresa Alfonso was the granddaughter (not the daughter) of Alfonso IX—that she was instead the daughter of Pedro Alfonso, illegitimate child of Alfonso IX. However, Linhagens, 263, claims that she was an illegitimate daughter of Alfonso IX and Aldonza Martínez da Silva; the view that she was his daughter is also expressed firmly in *Sancho IV*, 1:197, and *Fernando III*, 1:94. Aldonza Martínez was the lover of Alfonso IX between 1214 and 1218 (*Alfonso IX*, 1:315).

40. Lucas, bishop of Tuy, *Crónica de España*, ed. Julio Puyol (Madrid, 1926), 442; *PCG*, 770.

41. This consisted of approximately 480 acres of land and 30,000 olive and fig trees. He was also granted a smaller parcel of 20 *yugadas* (yokes of land) in the district of Aznalcázar (*RS*, 2:19–20, 229, 267).

42. Ignacio Álvarez Borge, "Estructura social y organización territorial en Castilla la Vieja meridional: Los territorios entre el Arlanzón y el Duero en los siglos X al XIV" (Diss., Universidad de León, 1991), 725–731.

43. Teófilo Ruiz, "Fronteras: De la comunidad a la nación en la Castilla bajo-medieval," *AEM*, 27 (1997), 23–41.

44. Reyna Pastor, "Reflexiones sobre los comienzos de la formación política feudo-vassallática en Castilla y León," *Realidad e imágenes del poder: España a fines de la Edad Media* (Valladolid, 1988), 22.

45. Isabel Beceiro Pita and Ricardo Córdoba de la Llave, *Parentesco, poder y mentalidad: La nobleza castellana, siglos XII–XV* (Madrid, 1990), 62–63, 67.

46. Carlos Estepa Díez, "Propiedad y señorío en Castilla, siglos XIII–XIV," in Esteban Saras Sánchez and Eliseo Serrano Martín, eds., *Señorío y feudalismo en la península ibérica, siglos XXII–XIX*, 4 vols. (Zaragoza, 1993), 1:373–425.

47. Carlos Estepa Díez, "Formación y consolidación del feudalismo en Castilla y León," *En torno al feudalismo hispánico: I° congreso de estudios medievales* (Ávila, 1989), 241.

48. Beceiro Pita, *Parentesco, poder y mentalidad*, 66.

49. Hilda Grassotti, "Novedad y tradición en las donaciones 'con mero y mixto imperio' en León y Castilla," *Homenaje al profesor Juan Torres Fontes*, 2 vols. (Murcia, 1987), 1:723–727.

50. See, for instance, Salvador de Moxó, "La nobleza castellana en el siglo XIV," *AEM*, 7 (1970–1971), 494–496. One can still find echoes of this assumption—for example, in Teófilo Ruiz's claim that "the conquest of Córdoba and Seville and the large donations, grants, and booty which this expansion generated provided the high nobility of Castile with the economic wherewithal to play a greater role in the affairs of the realm" (*Crisis and Continuity: Land and town in late medieval Castile* [Philadelphia, 1994], 298).

51. Beceiro Pita, *Parentesco, poder y mentalidad*, 63–65. The text actually says "la década de 1370," but this is surely a typographical error.

52. Antonio Collantes de Terán Sánchez, "Los señoríos andaluces: Análisis de su evolución territorial en la Edad Media," *Historia, instituciones, documentos*, 6 (1979), 89–112.

53. Miguel Ángel Ladero Quesada, "Sociedad feudal y señoríos en Andalucía," *En torno al feudalismo hispánico*, 438–448.

54. E. Cabrera, "The Medieval Origins of the Great Landed Estates of the Guadalquivir Valley," *Economic History Review*, 2nd series, 42, no. 4 (1989), 469–471.

55. Rodríguez López, "Linajes nobiliarios," 847.

56. Nuño González is a frequent subscriber of royal diplomas from 8 August 1252 (AHN Ordenes Militares, Santiago, carp. 214, no. 11) to 13 September 1256 (Ángel Barrios García, ed., *Documentación medieval de la catedral de Ávila* [Salamanca, 1981], 71), and more infrequently until 14 January 1272 (AHN Códices 833B, 123r–125r). This may be interpreted as a sign of status more than of physical attendance: Evelyn Procter argues that by this reign the subscribers of royal diplomas were not necessarily present as witnesses, but "might be looked on as forming the king's court." See Procter, "The Castilian Chancery during the reign of Alfonso X, 1252–1284," in *Oxford Essays Presented to Herbert Edward Salter* (1934; rpt., New York, 1968), 106.

57. CAX, 7; *CG1344*, 4:506.

58. CAX, 5–6 (Jérez), 9–10 (Matrera); *CG1344*, 4:503–504 (Jérez); *RS*, 1:57 (Écija); Zurita, *Anales*, 1:615–617 (Matrera).

59. CAX, 25.

60. After the capitulation of Jérez to Alfonso X in 1261, the king entrusted its fortress to Nuño González de Lara, who in turn delegated responsibility to one García Gómez Carrillo (CAX, 5–6).

61. González, "Población y repartimiento de Écija," 1: 691–692. The tenancy of Écija was briefly appropriated in 1255 by supporters of the rebellious *infante* Enrique, and in 1262 or 1263 it was transferred to Queen Violante, although he was able to retain command of its fortifications (ibid., 1:692–694).

62. CAX, 25; RAH C-12, 196r; *Fernando III*, 1:150. A lease granted by the abbey of Oña on 24 December 1268 refers to "Don Nunno Gonzalez tenient

Burueba et Rioia et Castiella Vieia" (*Oña*, 694). In a document in the cartulary of the monastery of Vileña, dated 10 October 1274, he appears as "prestamero de Bvrueua et de Rioja" (AHN Códices 1168B, 97–98).

63. 7 June 1258 (*RS*, 2:307).

64. At some point before 15 November 1259 (ibid., 1:262).

65. AHN Sellos, caj. 65, no. 27 (original); AHN Ordenes Militares, Santiago, carp. 313, no. 12 (notarial copy).

66. *Casa de Lara*, 4:98 suggests that by 1263 he already possessed a *bodega* and a district known as La Bastida de Don Nuño. On 22 November 1288, Vela Ladrón de Guevara gave to the Order of Calatrava the property which he had bought in Écija from Nuño González II and which had earlier belonged to Nuño González I (*RS*, 1:63; *Sancho IV*, 3:134). Three years later, the Order received from one Juan Arias de Cadre a *bodega*, in the parish precinct of Santa María de Écija, which had previously belonged to the elder Don Nuño (*RS*, 1:63).

67. Nuño González was just one of nineteen nobles who received property in the district of Aznalcázar, and just one of five receiving twenty *yugadas* there (*RS*, 2:267).

68. RAH C-12, 196r.

69. Ishmael García Rámila, "'Ordenamientos de posturas y otros capítulos' otorgados a la ciudad de Burgos por el rey Alfonso X," *Hispania*, 19 (1945), 179–235; 20 (1945) 385–439; and 21 (1945) 605–650. See also Elena Lourie, "A Society Organized for War: Medieval Spain," *Past and Present*, 35 (1966), 72.

70. Teófilo Ruiz, "Expansion et changement: La conquête de Séville et la société castillane," *Annales E.S.C. 34* (1979), 552–553.

71. Teófilo Ruiz, *Crisis and Continuity*, 297–298.

72. James J. Todesca, "What Touches All: Coinage and Monetary Policy in Leon-Castile to 1230" (Diss., Fordham University, 1996), 334–363, 437–438.

73. María del Carmen Carlé, "El precio de la vida en Castilla del Rey Sabio al Emplazado," *CHE*, 14 (1950), 139–141.

74. Hilda Grassotti, *Las instituciones feudo-vassalláticas en León y Castilla*, 2 vols. (Spoleto, 1969), 788–844.

75. Reyna Pastor, "Ganadería y precios: Consideraciones sobre la economía de León y Castilla, siglos XI–XIII, *CHE*, 35–36 (1962), 48–55.

76. "Súplica hecha al papa (Juan XXII) para que absolviese al rey de Castilla, D. Alfonso X, del juramento de no acuñar otra moneda de los dineros prietos," *Revista de archivos, bibliotecas y museos*, 2 (1872), 58–60.

77. Brunner, *Land and Lordship*, 1–138.

78. *Siete partidas*, II, 1, v (p. 271); O'Callaghan, *The Learned King*, 17–29; Robert A. Macdonald, "Law and Politics: Alfonso's Program of Political Reform," in Robert I. Burns, ed., *The Worlds of Alfonso the Learned and James the Conqueror: Intellect and Force in the Middle Ages* (Princeton, 1985), pp. 150–199.

79. Robert A. Macdonald, "Kingship in Medieval Spain: Alfonso X of Castile" (Diss., University of Wisconsin, 1957), 59–100.

80. Teófilo F. Ruiz, "Expansion et changement," 557–558; idem, "The Transformation of the Castilian Municipalities: The Case of Burgos, 1248–1350," *Past and Present*, 77 (November 1977), 6–7.

81. Ruiz, "Transformation of the Castilian Municipalities," 42–43.

82. Joseph O'Callaghan, *A History of Medieval Spain* (Ithaca, 1975), 452–453.

83. Marie-Claude Gerbet, *Les noblesses espagnoles au Moyen Age, XIe–XVe siècle* (Paris, 1994), 74.

84. See for instance *Siete partidas*, II, 9, vi (p. 314), and II, 9, xvi (pp. 320–321): the *alférez* should be a man of noble lineage "so that he will be ashamed to do anything which may discredit him."

85. *Siete partidas*, II, 9, ii (p. 311).

86. Rogelio Pérez Bustamante, *El gobierno y la administración territorial de Castilla, 1230–1474*, 2 vols. (Madrid, 1976). The first reference to an *adelantado de la frontera* is in 1253; from 1258 we may trace the appearance of *adelantados mayores* of Castile, León, and Murcia, followed in 1263 by one for Galicia, and in 1272 the first *adelantado* of the provinces of Álava and Guipúzcoa.

87. Pérez Bustamante, *El gobierno*, 1:97–148.

88. Jular Pérez-Alfaro, *Adelantados y merinos mayores*, 186–188, 539–541. Jular also argues that Pérez Bustamante (*El gobierno*, 63–95) is mistaken in suggesting that the two offices were substantially different; she argues that the difference is simply semantic, representing a new legal formulation of a de facto evolution (*Adelantados y merinos mayores*, 180–183). In her article "Dominios señoriales y relaciones clientelares en Castilla: Velasco, Porres y Cárcamo, siglos XIII–XIV," *Hispania*, 192 (1996), 137–171, Jular shows how royal offices could be valuable to the nobility in developing networks of clientage.

89. Ignacio Álvarez Borge, *Monarquía feudal y organización territorial: Alfoces y merindades en Castilla, siglos X–XIV* (Madrid, 1993), 141–144.

90. On this process in the case of the tenancies of the city and fortress of León, see William Clyde Fagan, "Municipal Institutions in León, 1100–1400" (Diss., Columbia University, 1983), 112–153.

91. O'Callaghan, *The Learned King*, 182–183, 187–188.

92. One reads, for example, about how Nuño González's two sons, Juan Núñez I and Nuño González II, treacherously negotiated with the king of Granada in the summer of 1268 and alleged that Alfonso X "had committed some offenses and wrongs" against the lord of Lara (CAX, 12).

93. Ibid., 15.

94. O'Callaghan, *The Learned King*, 214. Many of these figures are explicitly mentioned as part of the alliance at a slightly later stage, in 1272 (CAX, 17).

95. Zurita, *Anales*, 1:681, bk. III, ch. 76.

96. See Gaines Post, "Roman Law and Early Representation in Spain and Italy, 1150–1250," in Post, *Studies in Medieval Legal Thought* (Princeton, 1964), 61–90, which argues the case for the slow emergence of corporate ideology and the persistence of the Cortes as a feudal assembly.

97. This might be compared with the claim that in thirteenth-century England rebellion was a normal feature of national political life, one which did not carry any great social stigma (the reign of Edward I being the first to be relatively unaffected by civil war) and one which was increasingly transcending issues of individual discontent to focus on more abstract questions of principle. See J. C. Holt, "The Origins of Magna Carta," in Holt, *Magna Carta and Medieval Government* (London, 1985).

98. CAX, 18.

99. Cf. Joseph O'Callaghan, "Paths to Ruin: The Economic and Financial Policies of Alfonso the Learned," in Burns, ed., *The Worlds of Alfonso the Learned and James the Conqueror* (Princeton, 1985), 41–62.

100. Ibid., 25. This incident must have occurred in 1267, when Nuño González had been sent to negotiate with the Banu Ashqilula, a powerful clan to which the governors of Málaga, Guadix, and Comares all belonged (ibid., 11).

101. O'Callaghan, *The Learned King*, 75–76.

102. CAX, 19–20.

103. Ruiz, *Crisis and Continuity*, 301–310.

104. CAX, 19–20.

105. O'Callaghan, *The Learned King*, 80, 214.

106. Jular Pérez-Alfaro, *Adelantados y merinos mayores*, 186–188.

107. CAX, 21.

108. Ibid., 20–21.

109. Ibid., 22. The king did insist, however, on the necessity of maintaining the import duties.

110. Ibid., 30–31. The complaint regarding salt mines probably arose from a decision by Alfonso X to lease the mines (which the crown owned and monopolized) en masse to the entrepreneur Zag de la Maleha, at the expense of the interests of Nuño González in the mines (O'Callaghan, *The Learned King*, 224).

111. The wedding took place sometime before 23 July 1260. See Jaime Caruana Gómez de Barreda, ed., *Catálogo del archivo de la ciudad de Albarracín* (Teruel, 1955), 28–29: this records a privilege granted by Teresa Álvarez confirming the *fueros* and customs established by her grandfather and father, subscribed by Juan Núñez.

112. Martín Almagro Basch, *Historia de Albarracín y su sierra*, 4 vols. (Teruel, 1959–1964), 4:7–8.

113. Cristóbal Guitart, "Cañete y Moya: Dos plazas fuertes de la serranía conquense ante la frontera del Reino de Aragón," *Castillos de España: Boletín de la Asociación de Amigos de los Castillos*, 57 (1967), 161–162.

114. *Sancho IV*, 2:59.

115. Teresa Álvarez's use of this self-styling in 1260 was a recent case in point; but if Salazar is correct, the tradition was much older. Pedro Ruiz de Azagra referred to himself as "vassal of Saint Mary" in 1176 (*Casa de Lara*, 4:144), as had his brother Fernán Ruiz in 1193 (ibid., 4:146) and Pedro Fernández de Azagra in 1224 and on 18 August 1226 (ibid., 4:147).

116. Desclot, *Cronica*, 4:28.

117. Nuño González's marriage to an illegitimate daughter of Alfonso IX of León may have reflected the strength of family ties there, but it hardly had the same significance, since it was expedited by the *infante* Alfonso of Castile. Alfonso also closed another promising avenue, establishing close relations with Afonso III of Portugal in 1267 and granting him exemption from the knight service that had been claimed. The rebellious barons' aspirations to assistance from the Portuguese appear to have been in vain (O'Callaghan, *The Learned King*, 215).

118. DRH, 184; Zurita, *Anales*, 1:334 (bk. II, ch. 61), 356 (bk. II, ch. 66), 429 (bk. III, ch. 1), 435–460 (bk. III, chs. 3–10), 495–497 (bk. III, chs. 19–20), 502 (bk. III, ch. 23), 508 (bk. III, 26), 1:528–530 (bk. III, ch. 33).

119. *The Chronicle of James I, King of Aragón, Surnamed the Conqueror (Written by Himself)*, trans. John Forster, 2 vols. (London, 1883; rpt., 1968), 614–615; Ferran

Soldevila, ed., *Les quatre grans cròniques*, 2nd ed. (Barcelona, 1983), 172. Events in Burgos may also have provided the occasion for the development of contacts between the Laras and the French royal family. The dauphin Philip, later Philip III of France, whose service Juan Núñez I would enter in 1286, accompanied his sister Blanche to the wedding (CAX, 12–13).

120. 26 January 1273 (Menéndez Pidal de Navasqués, "Los sellos de los señores de Molina," *AEM*, 14 (1984), 116). CAX, 21, claims Henry had aspirations to Castilian territory. In 1271, Juan Núñez I had met the king at Guadalajara, where Alfonso X instructed him to tell the rebels under no circumstances to ally with Henri of Navarre, a condition which was turned down (ibid., 19). As for the origins of the alliance, it may be significant that Juan Núñez I had been on Saint Louis' crusade alongside the king of Navarre in 1270 (ibid., 26).

121. CAX, 12.

122. Ibid., 15, 18–19. We may assume that Nuño González was active in developing a range of Islamic connections; the letter addressed to him from Morocco by Abu Yusuf, the leader of the Marinid empire, who was anxious to extend control over al-Andalus, went so far as to offer that if Don Nuño sent one of his sons to Morocco, preferably Juan Núñez, he would place him in charge of the Christian population (of Morocco) and the army (ibid., 18).

123. Ibid., 30.

124. Loaysa, *Crónica*, 72, specifies the presence of the two sons as part of a contingent of 1,200 barons, *infantes*, and other nobles who leave for Granada.

125. CAX, 33–34. Interestingly, he was subsequently employed as an envoy by the pope, who in 1275 strove to persuade the king to cease making claims to the imperial title (Zurita, *Anales*, 1:742, bk. III, ch. 93).

126. O'Callaghan, *The Learned King*, 226–228.

127. CAX, 41.

128. Ibid., 41.

129. Ibid., 46–49. Mercedes Gaibrois refers to Nuño González as "that brave *caudillo* who met a glorious death fighting the infidel on Andalusian soil"—a striking example of the survival of military mystique into the modern age, and a turn of phrase which would not have seemed out of place in the royal chronicle itself (*Sancho IV*, 2:59).

5. Revolt, Rapprochement, and Rumor

1. CAX, 51, states that his death occurred in August 1275; Loaysa, *Crónica*, 78, gives the date as 24 July.

2. Joseph O'Callaghan, *The Learned King: The Reign of Alfonso X of Castile* (Philadelphia, 1993), 236–238, provides a good discussion of the validity of these conflicting claims. It appears that Alfonso de la Cerda was the legally legitimate heir, but that there was a consensus that the extremity of the crisis of 1275 would be best solved by Sancho's succession.

3. CAX, 51; Loaysa, *Crónica*, 78; Zurita, *Anales*, 1:761 (bk. III, ch. 98).

4. César González Mínguez, *Fernando IV, 1295–1312* (Palencia, 1995), 274–275.

5. Anthony Tuck, *Crown and Nobility, 1272–1461: Political Conflict in Late Medieval England* (Totowa, N.J., 1986), esp. 9–11.

6. María del Carmen Carlé, "El precio de la vida en Castilla del Rey Sabio al Emplazado," *CHE*, 14 (1950), 139. The intense economic pressure which characterized this era has been examined by Jean Gautier Dalché, who, in the context of a discussion of Sancho's rebellion in 1281–1284, has referred to the fiscal oppression caused by both the crown's need to retain the nobility and the nobility's wish to extort maximum financial profit ("L'histoire castillane dans la première moitié du XIVe siècle," *AEM*, 7 [1970–1971], 240).

7. For a 1259 seal, see *Pruebas*, 636; and Faustino Menéndez Pidal, "Los sellos de los señores de Molina," *AEM*, 14 (1984), 116.

8. Isabel Beceiro Pita and Ricardo Córdoba de la Llave, *Parentesco, poder y mentalidad: La nobleza castellana, siglos XII–XV* (Madrid, 1990), 68–79, is a useful general discussion of the significance of changes in naming patterns.

9. *Casa de Lara*, 4:112. After the summer of 1287, Nuño González II was slightly more consistently present than his elder brother, Juan Núñez I, at the court of Sancho IV; he subscribes royal diplomas from 3 July 1287 (*Sancho IV*, 3:100, doc. 164) to 11 January 1291 (ibid., 210, doc. 329), and remained in royal service during Juan Núñez's break with the king late in 1290.

10. Ignacio Álvarez Borge, "Estructura social y organización territorial en Castilla la Vieja meridional: Los territorios entre el Arlanzón y el Duero en los siglos X al XIV" (Diss., Universidad de León, May 1991), 730. His testament refers solely to his *heredamiento*, which in the event of his death was to pass to his wife, Juana Gómez, and thence to any children they might have (*Pruebas*, 640–642); one suspects that this document is the sole basis for Salazar's assertion, and since the term *heredamiento* connotes heritable rather than inherited property, one cannot be sure whether Nuño González II inherited anything at all substantial from his father.

11. *Casa de Lara*, 4:187. After the premature death of the eldest brother, Álvaro Núñez II, in 1287, the weight of primogeniture fell on the middle brother, Juan Núñez II, who was to inherit Torrelobatón and would marry the heiress of Molina. After Juan Núñez II had broken his bonds of vassalage with the king in 1296, Nuño González III received a grant of land from María de Molina which was surely intended to preempt any temptation he might have had to follow a similar path; it succeeded in perpetuating his loyalty until his death later that year (*Sancho IV*, 2:379; Loaysa, *Crónica*, 148; *Fernando IV*, 1:2–3, 22, 30–31; he was the *alférez* of the new king on 3 August 1295 [*Casa de Lara*, 4:186]).

12. Julio Valdeón Baruque, "Reflexiones sobre la crisis bajomedieval en Castilla," *En la España medieval, IV: Estudios dedicados a D. Angel Ferrari* (Madrid, 1984), 1047–1060.

13. Ignacio Álvarez Borge, *Monarquía feudal y organización territorial: Alfoces y merindades en Castilla, siglos X–XIV* (Madrid, 1993), 141–144, 770–779. Claudio Sánchez Albornoz likewise argues that the juridical privileges of the *behetrías* were gradually eroded by the accentuation of aristocratic power in the second half of the thirteenth century and the first half of the fourteenth century, basing his claim on the stipulation in the Ordenamiento de Alcalá (1348) that hidalgos could not become lords of *behetrías* where they were not *diviseros* ("Las Behetrías: La encomendación en Asturias, León y Castilla," *AHDE*, 1 [1924], 302–309). He also argues that the Laras' inordinate power in the *behetrías* by the time of the *Libro becerro de las behetrías* (1352) must date from their great power in the twelfth and thirteenth centuries—a plausible hypothesis but one lacking evidence (ibid., 284–285).

14. Álvarez Borge, "Estructura social," 730.

15. *Oña*, 760.

16. George Daumet, *Mémoire sur les relations de la France et de la Castille, de 1255 à 1320* (Paris, 1914), 30–33.

17. Hilda Grassotti, *Las instituciones feudo-vassalláticas en León y Castilla*, 2 vols. (Spoleto, 1969), 758, illustrates the rising size of private aristocratic armies in the thirteenth century by pointing out that in the middle of the eleventh century the count of Cea had been able to muster just three *infanzones*.

18. Simon Barton, *The Aristocracy in Twelfth-Century León and Castile* (Cambridge, 1997), 165, cites the existence of royal armies with 266–700 knights, and a force with only 400 knights shortly before the siege of Almería. He suggests that when the towns of Ávila and Segovia mustered 1,000 knights in 1132, this was wholly exceptional.

19. The confirmation by "Juan Núñez de Lara" (Juan Núñez II) of a royal diploma dated 20 April 1312 is wholly exceptional (*Fernando IV*, 2:849).

20. Zurita, *Anales*, II, 125, bk. IV, ch. 34. Equally, the only value of Granada for his son, Juan Núñez II, was that his resistance to Fernando IV happened to coincide with military action by the Nasrids (*Fernando IV*, 1:81).

21. Loaysa, *Crónica*, 90.

22. This was probably not the total number of soldiers in his retinue, because the agreement with Philip III specifies that the Castilian stipend of 14,000 *livres tournois* was granted "on account of that part of [Juan Núñez's] armed retinue" which he had provided for royal service in Castile. Since he was now requesting an identical stipend, it seems probable that he was again providing only a part of his armed retinue, and indeed it seems implausible that he would have left his Castilian interests completely undefended at this time.

23. Daumet, *Mémoire sur les relations de la France*, 30–33. On 19 April 1277, he was in Estella, in Navarre, receiving one-third of the 8,000 *livres*: 2,666 *livres*, 13 *sous*, and 6 *deniers* (Charles V. Langlois, *Le règne de Philippe III le Hardi* [Paris, 1887; rpt. Geneva, 1979], 398).

24. Daumet, *Mémoire*, 33; Langlois, *Philip III*, docs. 68, 72, 75, 101).

25. Daumet, *Mémoire*, 82; Zurita, *Anales*, 2:120 (bk. IV, ch. 32); CAX, 63–64. There survives an inventory of clothing and other objects placed on deposit in Albarracín by certain citizens of the towns when they accompanied Juan Núñez to Navarre; it is dated 21 August 1283 (César Tomás Laguia, ed., *Catálogo de la sección de pergaminos del archivo de la S.I. Catedral de Albarracín* [Teruel, 1955], 45). In 1284, Juan Núñez and his men again made incursions into Aragón and Castile (Langlois, *Philippe III*, 368).

26. *Sancho IV*, 1:213.

27. CSIV, 69.

28. His instructions of 15 June 1283 to the royal officials of Teruel, Segorbe, Daroca, Ariza, and Calatayud tell them to prepare for action against Juan Núñez because "he is a vassal of the king of France, who is at war against us" (Martín Almagro Basch, *Historia de Albarracín y su sierra*, 4 vols. [Teruel, 1959–1964], 4:108–109, 111).

29. CSIV, 4:27, 32, 110.

30. Desclot, *Crònica*, 3:170.

31. Almagro, *Historia de Albarracín*, 4:39–40, 119.

32. Desclot, *Crònica*, 4:27–38.

166 Notes to Pages 87–89

33. *Sancho IV,* 1:14–16.

34. Daumet, *Mémoire,* 86–87, suggests 29 September, but various logistical orders issued by Pedro III on 18 September seem to indicate that Albarracín had already been taken (Almagro Basch, *Historia de Albarracín,* 4:127–128).

35. *Sancho IV,* 2:62–63.

36. In 1291, after a brief reconciliation with Sancho IV of Castile, Juan Núñez would again flee north (ibid., 2:154).

37. Two Lara supporters had been involved in the negotiations leading up to the treaty: Martín García, the Navarrese bishop of Calahorra, and Gómez García, a close adviser of Sancho IV (Almagro Basch, *Historia de Albarracín,* 4:66–67).

38. Ibid., 4:74.

39. CSIV, 72–73; *Sancho IV,* 1:96.

40. Almagro Basch, *Historia de Albarracín,* 4:62–64.

41. *Sancho IV,* 1:96; Almagro Basch, *Historia de Albarracín,* 4:69–74; Daumet, *Mémoire,* 104–105, 184–198. Zurita, *Anales,* 2:348, bk. IV, ch. 100, confirms that Juan Núñez and his brothers were in France in 1288 and that their Castilian property had been seized.

42. *Sancho IV,* 2:20–21. Juan Núñez I appears as subscriber of royal diplomas from 20 December 1289 (*Sancho IV,* 3:167) to 14 May 1290 (ibid., 3:192, doc. 303; *Liébana,* 229).

43. CSIV, 82; *Sancho IV,* 2:20–21.

44. Cristóbal Guitart, "Cañete y Moya: Dos plazas fuertes de la serranía conquense ante la frontera del Reino de Aragón," *Castillos de España: Boletín de la Asociación de Amigos de los Castillos,* 57 (1967), 166, 170.

45. CSIV, 82.

46. *Sancho IV,* 3, doc. 508.

47. In the late spring of 1285, Juan Núñez had made incursions into Teruel and Albarracín itself, and in October he was still attacking the Aragonese near Cuenca (Zurita, *Anales,* 2:211, bk. IV, ch. 59). From Barcelona, on 20 October, Pere III wrote to Sancho IV in response to a complaint by the king of Castile alleging that Aragonese troops which had been attacking Juan Núñez near Cuenca had ravaged Castilian lands on their return (*Sancho IV,* 3:58–59, doc. 90).

48. Zurita, *Anales,* 2:405 (bk. IV, ch. 119).

49. *Sancho IV,* 1:16.

50. CSIV, 84; Zurita, *Anales,* 2:411, bk. IV, ch. 120. Juan Núñez I subscribes royal diplomas dated 8 December 1290, 11 January 1291 (*Sancho IV,* 3:209, doc. 327; ibid., 210, doc. 329), and—alongside his two surviving sons, Juan Núñez II and Nuño González III—22 June 1291 (*El Moral,* 128–132). Isabel was the daughter of Alfonso de la Cerda and Blanca de Molina (Blanca Alfonso, daughter of the infante Alfonso and Mafalda Manrique) and was therefore a niece of Sancho IV. The marriage occurred before 27 December 1290 (*Sancho IV,* 2:77, n. 3). More generally, Sancho wished to keep Molina within a Castilian orbit; Blanca de Molina had in 1286 been attempting to marry Isabel to Alfonso of Aragón, a prospect to which Sancho responded by locking Blanca up in the *alcázar* in Segovia until a more satisfactory arrangement was reached; in March 1287, Blanca agreed from her prison cell that any marriage match for her daughter would be made with the advice and consent of the king (CSIV, 74–75; *Sancho IV,* 1:124–125).

51. Salvador de Moxó, "De la nobleza vieja a la nobleza nueva: La transformación nobiliaria castellana en la baja Edad Media," *CH,* 3 (1969), 40.

52. CSIV, 85; *Sancho IV,* 2:105–107.

53. *Sancho IV,* 2:117–119, 143–144; CSIV, 85. It was also agreed that neither party would make any alliances without the consent of the other (Almagro Basch, *Historia de Albarracín,* 4:84–86).

54. *Sancho IV,* 2:153.

55. In 1293, the tenancy of Cañete was held by one Roy Pérez Sangarrer, presumably a trustworthy nonentity (ibid., 2:215, n. 2).

56. *Casa de Lara,* 1:247, claims that Isabel died in 1292 but does not provide evidence for this, and *Sancho IV,* 2:204, n. 3, correctly argues that it seems safer to follow the date of February 1293 given in CSIV.

57. CSIV, 87; *Pruebas,* 32–35. Gaibrois does not raise an eyebrow with regard to this forceful royal policy, but it was surely related to the rebellious activities of Juan Núñez I and II. Moxó, rather more attuned to the nature of Sancho IV's actions, comments that the extinction of Blanca de Molina's line lent some legitimacy to Sancho's occupation of the lordship (Moxó, "De la nobleza vieja," 46). However, even this is generous to Sancho, since it is incorrect to state that the line was biologically extinct: Blanca de Molina's will, dated 10 May 1293, refers to "my daughter Doña Mafalda" (*Sancho IV,* 2:470).

58. CSIV, 87; *Sancho IV,* 2:204–208. The *infante* Juan aspired to be heir to the throne (*CG1344,* 4:515; *Sancho IV,* 2:119).

59. 23 May 1293 (*Sancho IV,* 3:329, doc. 484). Note that Sancho IV had almost certainly been instrumental in a decision by Philip IV, early in 1292, to expel Castilian exiles from Navarre, but Juan Núñez remained there until the spring of 1293 (CSIV, 86; *Sancho IV,* 2:156–157, 164.

60. As Mercedes Gaibrois pointed out, his death cannot have been in April, as Salazar suggested. He continues to appear in royal diplomas until the end of June, and in the royal accounts until August. The king receives news of his death sometime after 10 July, making early July the probable date of his death (*Sancho IV,* 1:42, 2:313, 330). Nuño González III had duly traipsed after his rebellious father, Juan Núñez I, and returned to service at the royal court only very shortly before him. He subscribed a document on 2 May 1293, while Juan Núñez did not do so until 18 May (*Sancho IV,* 2:215); his last subscription is dated 24 April 1295 (*Sancho IV,* 3:408–409, doc. 594).

61. CSIV, 87–88; Linhagens, 264; *Sancho IV,* 1:101, 2:230–231.

62. *Sancho IV,* 3:346.

63. Ibid., 1:68.

64. Ibid., 1:l.

65. Grassotti, *Instituciones feudo-vassalláticas,* 788–844. After Juan Núñez returned in 1293, he received two very generous stipendiary payments from the king, totaling some 50,000 *maravedís,* to cover the year he had missed (*Sancho IV,* 1:51, 54). He remained in royal service from this point on: he joined his brother in accompanying the king to his meeting with the Aragonese in 1293, and took part in a campaign against Granada in early 1294 alongside both his father and his brother (CSIV, 87–88).

66. *Adelantado mayor* on 16 January 1292 (*Sancho IV,* 3:265, doc. 395); as Gaibrois points out, he must have acquired the office after 15 September 1291, when he was *mayordomo mayor* (ibid., 2:153, n. 1)

67. CSIV, 88; *Sancho IV,* 2:277; Zurita, *Anales,* II, 458 (bk. V, ch. 9).

68. Cristina Jular Pérez-Alfaro, *Los adelantados y merinos mayores de León, siglos*

XIII–XV (León, 1990), 239–243; Rogelio Pérez Bustamante, *El gobierno y la administración territorial de Castilla, 1230–1474,* 2 vols. (Madrid, 1976), 97–148.

69. CSIV, 84; *Sancho IV,* 2:77, n. 3.

70. *Sancho IV,* 1:41–42.

71. Berlanga (3,400 *maravedís*), Pedraza (2,170), Ávila (1,761) and Aellón (1,380). Ibid., 2:77, n. 3.

72. Ibid., 1:72.

73. Ibid., 1:70.

74. Juan Núñez II appears as a subscriber in royal diplomas of 20 December 1289 (*Sancho IV,* 3:167, doc. 274); 5 February 1290 (ibid., 180, doc. 291); 11 January 1291 (ibid., 210, doc. 329); 16 January 1292 (ibid., 3:265, doc. 395); 24 April 1295 (ibid., 408, doc. 594).

75. CSIV, 89.

76. Ibid.

77. González Mínguez, *Fernando IV,* 65–66.

78. A new phase of confrontation began sometime after his confirmation of a diploma of Fernando IV dated 3 August 1295 (*Fernando IV,* 2:48) and was interrupted briefly in 1297, when he appears as a subscriber of a diploma dated 20 July (ibid., 2:134). It ended with his capture during defeat by the Castilian army at Alfaro on 7 May 1299.

79. *Fernando IV,* 1:28–29; Zurita, *Anales,* 2:497 (bk. V, ch. 20).

80. *Fernando IV,* 2:118–119.

81. Ibid., 2:159–160.

82. AHN Div. Concejos y Ciudades, leg. 1, exp. 5–6, fol. 17.

83. *Fernando IV,* 2:161–163. His tenancy of Albarracín is mentioned in a donation from Alfonso de la Cerda to Jaume II dated 13 May 1298 (ibid., 2:165).

84. *CG1344,* 4:516; Linhagens, 264; Loaysa, *Crónica,* 182.

85. Zurita, *Anales,* 2:572–573, bk. V, ch. 40. AHN Div. Concejos y Ciudades, leg. 1, exp. 5–6, fol. 17, tells a rather different story, suggesting that the problem is Juan Núñez's decision to reach agreement with María de Molina and to recognize Fernando IV as king of Castile.

86. AHN Div. Concejos y Ciudades, leg. 1, exp. 5–6, fol. 17. On 22 July 1300, in an obvious effort to consolidate this annexation, Jaume II issued a privilege of tax exemption to the citizens of Albarracín (AHN Diversos Comunidades, leg. 11, no. 1). Perhaps because of his eventual failure to recover Albarracín, Juan Núñez made two later alienations of property in the region: Monteagudo in 1306 (Jaime Caruana Gómez de Barreda, ed., *Catálogo del archivo de la ciudad de Albarracín* [Teruel, 1955], 126–127) and La Dehesa de Toyuela in 1311 (ibid., 133).

87. Zurita, *Anales,* 2:642–644. Antonio de Vargas-Zúñiga y Monteros de Espinosa and Baltasar Cuastero y Huerta, *Índice de la colección de don Luís de Salazar y Castro* (Madrid, 1949–1964), 1:180, refers to a letter, now apparently illegible, sent to Jaume II of Aragón with news of this embassy (A-2, fol. 141); the letter was published in *Fernando IV,* 2:383.

88. Loaysa, *Crónica,* 212. With the accession of the young Alfonso XI in 1312, the Laras' Aragonese connection would deteriorate even further. Much against the wishes of Juan Núñez, Jaume II promoted the claims of his son-in-law, the *infante* Pedro, to tutelage over Alfonso (Zurita, *Anales,* 2:775–776).

89. 2 March 1300 (AHN Códices 833B, 129r–132r) to 28 August 1307

(*Fernando IV,* 2:582); 23 June 1308 (ibid., 2:610) to 23 July 1308 (ibid., 28); 20 February 1309 (ibid., 2:638, 641) to 17 March 1312 (ibid., 834).

90. *Fernando IV,* 1:84–88.

91. *Fernando IV,* 1:103 (regarding Cañete and Moya). Loaysa, *Crónica,* 194, presents this as the fruit of flattery. Under Fernando IV, he was *mayordomo* on 15 February 1302 (AHN Códices 104B, 14r–v); 3 June 1302 (*Las cortes de los antiguos reinos de León y Castilla,* 5 vols. (Madrid, 1861–1902), 1:161); 27 July 1302 (*Casa de Lara,* 4:164); 2 November 1302 (ibid., 4:165); 15 June 1307 (*Fernando IV,* 2:565); 4 August 1307 (*Casa de Lara,* 4:173). He would also be *mayordomo* in 1315, shortly before his death: 25 June 1315 (*CDAXI,* 60–61); 25 August 1315 (ibid., 71–75); 16 September 1315 (*Las cortes de los antiguos reinos,* 1:293).

92. 4 October 1303 (*Fernando IV,* 2:371) to 15 September 1305 (ibid., 2:513); 29 June 1307 (*Las cortes de los antiguos reinos,* 1:184); 20 February 1311 (*Fernando IV,* 2:786).

93. *Fernando IV,* 1:219–226; *Acta Aragonensia,* 2:778; Zurita, *Anales,* 2:736, bk. V, ch. 87.

94. CSIV, 83–84.

95. Ibid., 84.

96. *Fernando IV,* 1:197–198.

97. Ibid., 1:228, 231–233.

98. González Mínguez, *Fernando IV,* 276–277.

99. He held Torrelobatón, which he inherited from his father, Juan Núñez I, throughout the reign of Fernando IV (*Fernando IV,* 1:48–49, 197–198; Carlos Manuel Reglero de la Fuente, *Los señoríos de los Montes de Torozos: De la repoblación al Becerro de las Behetrías* [Valladolid, 1993], 127–129). Melgar was acquired as a result of his 1305 treaty with Diego López de Haro (*Fernando IV,* 1:161–178).

100. Reglero, *Los señoríos de los Montes de Torozos,* 127; *Fernando IV,* 1:70–71; Loaysa, *Crónica,* 160, 188. Juan Núñez recovered Tordehumos through his treaty with Diego López de Haro in 1305, with the condition that if he did not have any children it would revert to Diego López (*Fernando IV,* 1:161–178, 186–187; Reglero, *Los señoríos de los Montes de Torozos,* 127–129). Properties not captured in the rebellion included Dueñas, granted by Alfonso de la Cerda, and Amaya, which he had captured in 1297 along with Osma (*Fernando IV,* 1:43, 70–71).

101. *Fernando IV,* 1:159–161.

102. Ibid., 1:161–178.

103. Ibid., 1:148–151.

104. Ibid., 1:182–183.

105. Ibid., 1:188–196.

106. Linhagens, 264.

107. Moxó, "De la nobleza vieja," 41; CSIV, 75–77; *Sancho IV,* 1:154–158. Peace was reached in December 1287, but Álvaro Núñez died almost immediately afterward (*Sancho IV,* 1:166). For the first three years of Sancho IV's reign, he had been the most loyal of the Laras (*Casa de Lara,* 4:124). He subscribed royal diplomas from 10 August 1284 (ibid., 4:126–127) until 2 January 1287 (*Sancho IV,* 3:97, doc. 158).

108. *Fernando IV,* 1:28–29.

109. Ibid., 1:240.

110. Zurita, *Anales,* 2:775–776.

111. *Fernando IV,* 1:102. Nuño González III married Doña Constanza of Portugal, daughter of the *infante* Don Alfonso of Portugal and Doña Violante Manuel (*Casa de Lara,* 4:187; *Sancho IV,* 2:215).

6. Ricos Hombres

1. Don Juan Manuel, *Libro de los estados,* ed. R. B. Tate and I. R. Macpherson (Oxford, 1974), 183.
2. *GCAXI,* 1:295.
3. CAXI, 179.
4. Purificación Martínez, "El contraste ideológico en la representación del reinado de Alfonso XI en la *Crónica* y la *Gran crónica* de Alfonso XI" (Diss., S.U.N.Y. Stony Brook, 1996), esp. 191–206.
5. Teófilo Ruiz, "The Transformation of the Castilian Municipalities: The Case of Burgos, 1248–1350," *Past and Present,* 77 (1977), 3–33.
6. Note also that some of the towns which appeared in the Cortes may have been under seigneurial control. See Hilda Grassotti, "¿Concejos de señorío en las cortes de Castilla?" in *Estudios Medievales Españoles* (Madrid, 1981), 329–346.
7. *CG1344,* 4:301–306.
8. *Alfonso VIII,* 1:42–44.
9. *Las cortes de los antiguos reinos de León y Castilla,* 5 vols. (Madrid, 1861–1902), 1:197–221.
10. CAXI, 173–175; *GCAXI,* 1:275–282; Zurita, *Anales,* 2:774, bk. V, ch. 102.
11. *Las cortes de los antiguos reinos,* 1:221–233.
12. Ibid., 1:233–247; CAXI, 176; *GCAXI,* 1:285.
13. *Pruebas,* 647.
14. *Las cortes de los antiguos reinos,* 1:300.
15. Apart from the statement in the royal chronicle that Juan Núñez II died in the Cortes at Burgos, a statement by four of his executors, dated 10 November 1315, is still extant (AHN Clero, carp. 1033, no. 3). He confirms royal diplomas as *mayordomo mayor* on 25 June 1315 (*CDAXI,* 60–61), 25 August 1315 (ibid., 71–75), and 16 September 1315 (ibid., 78–83), and must therefore have died in the early autumn.
16. AHN Clero, carp. 186, no. 1 (20 April 1322).
17. *Casa de Lara,* 4:190. Juana *la Palomilla* retained Torrelobatón, which she had indeed acquired from Juan Núñez II, until her death in 1351. *CAXI* claims that Juan Núñez III inherited the lordship "through his lineage" (ibid., 233: "por su abolengo").
18. CAXI, 233.
19. In the period before the siege of Lerma, he confirmed diplomas from 20 April 1322 (AHN Clero, carp. 186, no. 1) to 8 May 1335 (*CDAXI,* 400).
20. He held this office from 16 February 1328 (*Casa de Lara,* 4:194) to September 1332 (*CDAXI,* 363).
21. The series begins 3 January 1328 (*CDAXI,* 236) and ends 26 March 1337 (ibid., 419).
22. CAXI, 233; RAH 0-15, fols. 250r–251r; RAH O-7, 66r–v and 70r; RAH 0-13, 5v–6r, 24v–28, and 94v–95v; RAH 0-17, 532r–533v; RAH 0-18, 156r–v, 162r–v, and 173r–174r; RAH 0-22, 137v; *OB,* 3:26–28; *Fernando IV,* 2:179–180.

23. CAX, 5–6; *The Chronicle of James I, King of Aragón, Surnamed the Conqueror (Written by Himself)*, trans. John Forster, 2 vols. (1883; rpt. Farnborough, Hants., 1968), 614–615; Ferran Soldevila, ed., *Les quatre grans cròniques*, 2nd ed. (Barcelona, 1983), 172.

24. *Fernando IV*, 2:849 (20 April 1312).

25. The same developing sense of ancestry was also reflected in the design of his own tomb, and those of his father and grandfather in San Pablo de Burgos. All of these appear to have been adorned with the arms of the House of Lara—cauldrons with serpents' heads—on a white background (AHN Códices 57B, 46r).

26. Blanca had two children with Juan Manuel: Juana Manuel and Fernando Manuel. Fernando married Juana, daughter of the *infante* Ramón Berenguer of Aragón, on 24 January 1346, and died in 1350 leaving a daughter also named Blanca (*Casa de Lara*, 4:220; CP, 410).

27. Isabel Beceiro Pita, "Entre el ámbito privado y las competencias públicas: La educación en el reino de Castilla, siglos XIII–XV," in *Pensamiento Medieval Hispano: Homenaje a Horacio Santiago-Otero* (Madrid, 1998), 861–885.

28. *Libro de los estados*, section 38, 132.

29. CAXI, 223; GCAXI, 1:470, 495.

30. When open war with the king had broken out and an early truce had been reached, Juan Manuel promised that he would follow loyally in royal service and would make sure that Juan Núñez did the same (*GCAXI*, 2:18; CAXI, 240). On one subsequent occasion he informed the king, with delightful irony, that Juan Núñez's suspicion of Alfonso was due partly to the fact that Juan Núñez was young and therefore easily swayed by wicked counselors (*GCAXI*, 2:19–20; CAXI, 240–241).

31. CEII, 20. The transcription in *Pruebas*, 707, is very inaccurate.

32. Fernando García de Cortázar and Manuel Montero, *Historia de Vizcaya, I: Los orígenes, la Edad Media, el antiguo régimen* (San Sebastián, 1983), 27–60.

33. CEII, 20.

34. *GCAXI*, 2:164.

35. RAH 0–17, 738v–740r; *Pruebas*, 649. Aguilar and Castroverde would be granted to Alfonso XI as surety early in the civil war of the 1330s (CAXI, 264; GCAXI, 2:92).

36. Marie-Claude Gerbet, *Les noblesses espagnoles au Moyen Age, XIe–XVe siècle* (Paris, 1994), 87.

37. CAXI, 262; GCAXI, 2:85.

38. Castroverde de Campos, Aguilar de Campos, and Aguilar de Monteagudo (CAXI, 264; GCAXI, 2:92).

39. CAXI, 274; GCAXI, 2:131.

40. Hilda Grassotti, "Novedad y tradición en las donaciones 'con mero y mixto imperio' in León y Castilla," in *Homenaje al Profesor Juan Torres Fontes*, 2 vols. (Murcia, 1987), 1:723–727; the qualification is made in footnote 10. A recent study suggests that the seigneurialization of Andalucía in this reign corresponded specifically to the substantial donations which Alfonso XI made to Doña Leonor and members of his own family; see Antonio Collantes de Terán Sánchez, "Los señoríos andaluces: Analisis de su evolución territorial en la Edad Media," *Historia, instituciones, documentos*, 6 (1979), 94.

41. Jocelyn Hillgarth, *The Spanish Kingdoms, 1250–1516*, 2 vols. (Oxford, 1976), 1:345.

42. Cristina Jular Pérez-Alfaro, *Los adelantados y merinos mayores de León, siglos XIII–XV* (León, 1990), 281–283.

43. Salvador de Moxó, "La promoción política y social de los 'letrados' en la corte de Alfonso XI," *Hispania*, 129 (1975), 5–26.

44. Martínez, "El contraste ideológico," 43–44, 52–58, 62–66, 82–132. See also Gerald Lee Gingras, "The Medieval Castilian Historiographical Tradition and Pero López de Ayala's *Crónica del rey don Pedro*" (Diss., Indiana University, 1982), 59–107 and 199–219. Gingras offers a useful corrective in pointing out that Fernán Sánchez was also suffused with a "chivalric world view"; but to place the chronicle purely in the context of aristocratic culture is to overlook the intense disdain which the text shows toward the high nobility.

45. Julio Valdeón Baruque, "Aspectos de la crisis castellana en la primera mitad del siglo XIV," *Hispania*, 111 (1969), 18–21, 23; idem, "La crisis del siglo XIV en Castilla: Revisión del problema," *Revista de la Universidad de Madrid*, 20, no. 79 (1979), 170–184.

46. CAXI, 235–236; *GCAXI*, 2:12–13.

47. *GCAXI*, 2:91.

48. Ibid., 2:117.

49. CAXI, 279; *GCAXI*, 2:143–145.

50. CAXI, 281–282; *GCAXI*, 2:158–159.

51. CEII, 20; Joseph O'Callaghan, *The Cortes of Castile-León, 1188–1350* (Philadelphia, 1989), 70–71. The claim is repeated by the sixteenth-century author of the "Libro de los linages de Hespaña" (RAH C-12, 114r).

52. *Las cortes de los antiguos reinos*, 1:492–595.

53. CP, 419. There was a Cortes in Alcalá in 1345, in addition to the more famous gathering of 1348.

54. CAXI, 233, 240, 244; *GCAXI*, 1:505, 2:18, 28–29.

55. CAXI, 271; *GCAXI*, 2:117.

56. María was the daughter of Fernando de la Cerda and Juana *la Palomilla*. She had married Charles d'Evreux in April 1335; he died just over a year later, on 24 August 1336, leaving her two sons, Louis and Jean. She then married Charles de Valois, count of Alençon, in December of the same year; this rapid remarriage may suggest an urgent desire to shore up the French alliance. Charles de Valois, in turn, died at the battle of Crécy in 1346. María had four children from this marriage: Charles III, count of Alençon, who became archbishop of Lyon in 1365 and died in 1375; Philippe, bishop of Beauvais, who died in 1397; Robert, who died in 1377; and finally Isabelle, who joined the monastery of Poissy (CP, 417, 426, n. 3; CEII 18; *Pruebas*, 705; *Casa de Lara*, 4:235–239).

57. CAXI, 279; *GCAXI*, 2:146.

58. According to CAXI, 254–255, and *GCAXI*, 2:58–60, this assistance was not forthcoming after the rebels first contacted the king of Aragón; but a letter of 18 October 1336 from Pedro IV to Juana *la Palomilla* (in Torrelobatón) announced that he was sending archers and mounted soldiers to relieve the siege of Lerma. See Antonio de Vargas-Zúñiga y Monteros de Espinosa and Baltasar Cuastero y Huerta, *Indice de la colección de Don Luís de Salazar y Castro* (Madrid, 1949–1979), 1:447 (A-3, fol. 86).

59. CAXI, 272, 280–282; *GCAXI*, 2:120–121, 149–157.

60. CAXI, 282–283; *GCAXI*, 2:162–163.

61. From 10 May 1338 to the end of the reign, he appears in the diplomas not as lord of Lara but as *alférez* and lord of Vizcaya.

62. After the siege of Lerma, Juan Núñez III subscribed the following diplomas of Alfonso XI as *alférez:* 21 March 1337 (*CDAXI*, 418); 26 March 1337 (ibid., 419); 10 March 1338 (ibid., 428); 28 April 1339 (ibid., 457); 10 February 1342 (ibid., 483); 4 April 1342 (ibid., 487 and 491–492); 27 February 1343 (*Casa de Lara*, 4:203); 6 October 1344 (ibid., 205); 20 March 1345 (*CDAXI*, 509); 10 January 1347 (ibid., 549); 10 March 1348 (584); 15 March 1348 (ibid., 591). We know that he also enjoyed the office of *alférez* on 5 July 1344 (*Pruebas*, 705) and as late as 21 September 1350 (ibid., 648–649; *Indice de la colección de Don Luís de Salazar y Castro*, IL 78.386). He also confirmed diplomas of Alfonso XI dated 24 January 1342 (AHN Códices 833B, 106v–110v); 25 May 1344 (*Casa de Lara*, 4:205); and 20 July 1350 (ibid., 206).

63. CP, 405.

64. *GCAXI*, 2:164.

65. CAXI, 293; *GCAXI*, 2:197.

66. CAXI, 297; *GCAXI*, 2:260–261.

67. CAXI, 326; *GCAXI*, 2:428.

68. *CAXI*, 353.

69. *Pruebas*, 705.

70. Juan Núñez was also *mayordomo* from 6 October 1344 (*Casa de Lara*, 4:205) to 21 September 1350 (*Pruebas*, 648–649).

71. His nephew Fernando Manuel (son of his sister Blanca) also seems to have benefited from the reconciliation, acquiring the office of *adelantado* of Murcia as early as 1339, when he must have been less than ten years old (*Casa de Lara*, 4:219). This followed the peacemaking of Juana *la Palomilla*, who had engineered a pact between the king and Juan Manuel (hitherto exiled in Aragón) after the civil war (*GCAXI*, 2:175, 249).

72. CP, 403–405; CAXI, 390–392.

73. Clara Estow, *Pedro the Cruel of Castile, 1350–1369* (Leiden, 1995), 21–35.

74. CP, 409–410.

75. Estow, *Pedro the Cruel*, 38.

76. CP, 417.

77. Ignacio Álvarez Borge, "Lordship and Landownership in the South of Old Castile in the Middle of the Fourteenth Century," *Journal of Medieval History*, 23, no. 1 (1997), 77–78.

78. *Las cortes de León y Castilla*, 2:133–138; *LBB*, 1:18–22.

79. The four excluded *merindades* are Bureba, Rioja-Montes de Oca, Logroño, and Allende Ebro. See *LBB*, 1:73–78; Ignacio Álvarez Borge, "Estructura social y organización territorial en Castilla la Vieja meridional: Los territorios entre el Arlanzón y el Duero en los siglos X al XIV" (Diss., Universidad de León, 1991), 691–693. According to a letter written by María de Lara in 1373, the lord of Lara owned four places in the Montes de Oca and Bureba regions: Villafranca de Montes de Oca, Ameyugo, Busto, and Valluércanes. Busto and Villafranca had been lost temporarily in the civil war (*CEII*, 20).

80. These *merindades* were Infantazgo de Valladolid (3 settlements), Campos (8), Liébana-Pernia (1), and Asturias de Santillana (0). Aguilar de Campóo (6) was the only exception.

81. Here, they were lords in 12 and 23 places respectively, and held no *solariegos*.

82. In Castilla la Vieja they were lords in 49 settlements; in Santo Domingo de Silos, 31; in Cerrato, 36; in Monzón 36; in Castrojeriz, 55; and in Candemuño, 29.

83. We may assume that, in general, possession of a *solariego* consisting of the entire village provided a much higher income than *naturaleza*. In the one case where the text does give a total figure for Nuño's income as *natural*—in Hontoria de la Cantera, in Castrojeriz—he received a total of 250 *maravedís*. This is substantially lower than monetary figures for *solariegos*. Monetary totals from *solariegos* often run into four figures, as is the case, for instance, in the Laras' two *solariegos* in the *infantazgo* of Valladolid. The *merindades* of Candemuño, Monzón, Cerrato, and Castrojeriz were substantially inferior in this sense. In Candemuño, the Laras had 6 full *solariegos* and 23 places in which they had *naturaleza*; in Monzón, they had 1 full *solariego*, 4 partial *solariegos*, and 24 places of *naturaleza*; in Cerrato, they had 2 *solariegos* (1 full and 1 partial) and 31 places of *naturaleza*; and in Castrojeriz, they had no *solariegos* but 5 *behetrías* and 50 places of *naturaleza*.

84. Lordship of *behetrías*, 6.6 percent; *naturaleza* or *divisa*, 73.4 percent; partial *solariego*, 11.6 percent; *solariego*, 8.4 percent.

85. Valle de Cerrato (Cerrato), Villamediano (Cerrato), Piedrahita de Muñó (Santo Domingo de Silos).

86. Cevico de la Torre (Cerrato), 220 *maravedís*; Aguilar de Campos (Infantazgo de Valladolid), 600 *maravedís*; Moral de la Reina (Infantazgo de Valladolid), 400 *maravedís*; Cigales (Campos), Cuenca de Campos (Campos), Boadilla del Camino (Castrojeriz), and Pinilla-Trasmonte (Santo Domingo de Silos), all 600 *maravedís*; Villalázara (Castilla la Vieja), 150 *maravedís*.

87. Villalázara (Castilla la Vieja), 6 *maravedís*.

88. The reference to its payment in sheep in Neila (Santo Domingo) appears to be one of a kind.

89. The Laras received 1,200 *maravedís* as *martiniega* in Cevico de la Torre (Cerrato); 1,900 in Aguilar de Campos (Infantazgo); 2,147 in Moral de la Reina (Infantazgo); 3,600 in Torrelobatón (Infantazgo); 1,800 in Cigales (Campos); 1,200 in Cuenca de Campos; 500 in Villusto (Villadiego); 400 "by force" in Villasilos (Castrojeriz); 1,800 for Lerma and its *aldeas*.

90. They are restricted—as far as the Laras are concerned—to just two settlements, Sasamón (Castrojeriz) and Basabe (Castilla la Vieja).

91. This was the case in Boadilla del Camino (Castrojeriz) and in two villages near Lerma (Villalmanzo and Ruyales del Agua). The figure for Boadilla del Camino is so low, 80 *maravedís*, that one suspects that some payment in kind from this particular village may have been ignored or overlooked by the *LBB*. In the villages near Lerma, the *infurción* seems to have been in the process of being commuted: the lord was due the monetary value of a pitcher of wine. It may be that money was in wide circulation by virtue of the villages' location near a substantial town; very unusually, means-testing by personal financial worth is used both in Villalmanzo and in Lerma.

92. In Hedesa de Montija (Castilla la Vieja), Nuño de Lara owned one house that was inhabited, says the text, by "a poor woman who pays nothing."

93. The complication here is that the nobleman in question is Martín Gil, son of Juan Alfonso de Alburquerque, whose hostility to the Laras was a central part of

the events leading up to the *LBB*; the *LBB* may not be entirely objective. This enmity appears to have colored the chronicle's description of Villasilos as a *behetría* "de mar a mar" in which the inhabitants were allegedly able to choose their lord freely. See Carlos Estepa Díez, "Las behetrías en el canciller Don Pedro López de Ayala," in María Isabel Loring, ed., *Historia social, pensamiento historiográfico y Edad Media: Homenaje al Profesor Abilio Barbero* (Madrid, 1997), 95–114.

94. In four other cases (Piñel de Abajo, Villela, Valdecañas de Abajo, and Quintanilla de Valdeolmillos) the text specifically states that Juan Núñez had customarily taken *yantar*, implying both that this was no longer paid to Nuño and that the levying of *yantar* in the past was worthy of note. There may be hints here too of the hostility to Juan Núñez's impositions which surfaces explicitly elsewhere, and of a seigneurial offensive by the Laras in the previous generation.

95. They are mentioned in only three villages (all in Cerrato) where the Laras had *solariegos:* in Hornillos, where the entry states that the inhabitants were to provide the lord with a laborer, and with an animal if they had one (perhaps for one day each month); in Moral de la Reina (where those with cattle were obliged to work the lord's demesne once every two months, and those without were to perform personal labor service); and in Manquillos, where those with oxen were to assist the lord one day each month, and those without were to provide one laborer for the harvest and another for the winemaking.

96. Álvarez Borge, "Estructura social," 789–801.

97. Claudio Sánchez Albornoz, "Las behetrías: La encomendación en Asturias, León y Castilla," *AHDE*, 1 (1924), 284–285.

98. To take just one example, the intense concentration of the Laras' *solariegos* in Castilla la Vieja was coupled with a low number of settlements in which they were lords of *behetrías* (1) or even *naturales* (9).

99. Álvarez Borge, "Estructura social," 770–779; Sánchez-Albornoz, "Las behetrías," 302–309.

100. There is at least one settlement in which this process can be seen occurring in the *LBB* at the hands of the Haro family: Santa María de Añuequez (Santo Domingo de Silos), recently purchased by Diego López de Haro.

101. It is surely this process which Esther González Crespo has in mind when she explains the relatively low number of *behetrías* in eastern Castile as being a result of the influence of the Laras ("Los Velasco en el horizonte dominical de la nobleza castellana según el libro de las behetrías," *AEM*, 14 [1984], 323–324).

102. Collantes, "Señoríos andaluces," 89, 112, argues that the reign of Alfonso XI marks the beginning of the intensive seigneurialization of Andalucía. E. Cabrera, "The Medieval Origins of the Great Landed Estates of the Guadalquivir Valley," *Economic History* Review, 2nd series, 42, no. 4 (1989), 474–481, similarly points to the enormous success of the nobility during the fourteenth century in buying land in Andalucía or using their power and influence to exploit unappropriated common lands, creating by the fifteenth century a large rural proletariat.

103. It was to the heavily fortified Busto that the vanquished defenders of Peña Ventosa fled after the latter fortress was captured by Alfonso XI; it was subsequently captured, during the siege of Lerma, by Gonzalo Ruiz de la Vega, but then returned on condition that, along with Lerma and the similarly well-fortified Villafranca de Montes de Oca (which had also been besieged), its walls and moats be destroyed (CAXI, 262, 279–280, 282–283; *GCAXI*, 2:85, 148, 161–163). The

story of Berzosa and Fuentebureba is more peaceful: both were granted to the bishop and cathedral of Burgos in fulfillment of a penalty charged by Pope Clement VI for a dispensation given for the marriage of Juan Núñez and María de Haro, relatives in the third degree (RAH 0–17, 738v–740r; *Pruebas*, 649).

104. CAXI, 264; *GCAXI*, 2:92. The *LBB* makes it clear that he had received Aguilar de Campos back, it too having been granted as surety; the inhabitants of both towns had caused particular military problems for Alfonso XI during the war (CAXI, 244; *GCAXI*, 2:28–29). Castroverde lies in the kingdom of León, beyond the region covered by the *LBB*, which does not mention Aguilar de Monteagudo.

105. Salvador de Moxó, "De la nobleza vieja a la nobleza nueva: La transformación nobiliaria castellana en la baja Edad Media," *CHE*, 3 (1969), 42–43, also claims that the Laras had properties in Andalucía at the time of the *LBB*, but I have not found evidence of this.

106. RAH C-12, 114v.

107. Isabel Beceiro Pita and Ricardo Córdoba de la Llave, *Parentesco, poder y mentalidad: La nobleza castellana, siglos XII–XV* (Madrid, 1990), 66–67.

108. The argument for such a break was expressed notably by Salvador de Moxó, "La nobleza castellano-leonesa en la Edad Media," *Hispania*, 114 (1970), esp. 50–51. María Concepción Quintanilla Raso, "El protagonismo nobiliario en la Castilla bajo medieval: Una revisión historiográfica," *Medievalismo*, 7 (1997), 197–198, surveys the trend in recent scholarship whereby this view has been challenged.

109. According to Salazar (*Casa de Lara*, 4:209), Nuño had been born in 1348; he would therefore have been no more than three years old, and was probably two. Salazar shows that Nuño had inherited the titles and offices by 25 January 1351 (*Pruebas*, 649). Nuño also appears as *alférez* and lord of Vizcaya in documents of 22 September 1351 (AHN Clero, carp. 383, no. 15); 25 September 1351 (ibid., no. 16); 8, 10, and 25 November 1351 (*Casa de Lara*, 4:210); and 10 March 1352 (Moxó, "De la nobleza vieja," 43).

110. CP, 416.

111. Ibid., 415. Also enmeshed in this crisis were Nuño's aunt, Blanca (Juan Núñez III's sister, wife of Juan Manuel), who had been imprisoned by King Pedro sometime before 21 June 1351 (RAH M-9, fols. 71v–72v); and her daughter Juana Manuel (Nuño's cousin), also imprisoned very early in the reign because of her association with the ex-mistress of Alfonso XI, Leonor, whose son Enrique de Trastámara she had married, though the marriage had not yet been consummated. The chronicle relates, rather colorfully, how Leonor encouraged her son to fulfill his marital duties secretly in the prison near Seville where both women were held, and how Enrique did so, to the great chagrin of the king (CP, 408–409).

112. As Moxó contended, Nuño's appearance in a diploma of 10 March 1352 means that he cannot have died in 1351, as Ayala claimed (Moxó, "De la nobleza vieja," 43, n. 120). In any case, he is invariably treated as lord of Lara in the *LBB*, completed in August 1352.

Conclusion

1. CP, 416.

2. Clara Estow, *Pedro the Cruel of Castile, 1350–1369* (Leiden, 1995), xiii–xxvi.

3. A point made by Jocelyn Hillgarth, *The Spanish Kingdoms, 1250–1516* (Oxford, 1976), 2 vols., 1:374–375, though the statement that "Pedro's nobles proved undependable because they saw that the king was depriving them of any power" is a little hyperbolic.

4. L. J. Andrew Villalón, "Pedro the Cruel: Portrait of a Royal Failure," in Donald J. Kagay and Joseph T. Snow, eds., *Medieval Iberia* (New York, 1997), 201–216.

5. CP, 438.

6. Ibid., 445, 481. Isabel and Juan (who was made *alférez mayor* of Castile and *adelantado de la frontera*) had two daughters, Florencia and Isabel; in a document of 1365, Juana Manuel would reward one of her maids, María González de Mendoza, for having taken care of these daughters (*Casa de Lara*, 4:214–215).

7. CP, 456, 471. She appears to have been released before very long, and gave birth to Juan (later King Juan I of Castile) on 24 August 1358 (ibid., 486). Her other children were the *infante* Pedro, who died in 1366, and the *infanta* Leonor, who married Carlos III in 1373 (*Casa de Lara*, 4:223).

8. CP, 483.

9. Ibid., 483–484.

10. In his will of 18 November 1362, Pedro styles himself lord of Vizcaya ("Señor de Vizcaya, é de Molina"; ibid., 593). Later, in 1366, he offered land in Vizcaya to Edward, the Black Prince, in return for his military assistance in the civil war, but the Prince of Wales found it impossible to establish his authority there (ibid., 566).

11. CP, 493; Zurita, *Anales*, 4:371, book IX, ch. 21, makes explicit the detail implicit in López de Ayala's account—that it was Pedro who ordered Juana to be killed.

12. CP, 494, 513; Zurita, *Anales*, 4:371 book IX, ch. 21.

13. Salvador de Moxó oddly suggests that the Laras were one of thirteen noble families to disappear as a result of a biological distinction between the reign of Alfonso XI and that of Enrique II. He refers to the biological weakness resulting from endogamy within aristocratic circles, and mentions the Laras specifically in this regard ("De la nobleza vieja a la nobleza nueva: La transformación nobiliaria castellana en la baja Edad Media," *CH*, 3 [1969], 196–200). However, it is far from self-evident that infant mortality was any higher among the aristocracy than in any other social class, and it seems clear that, in the case of the Laras, the course of biology was accelerated rather dramatically by Pedro the Cruel.

14. CP, 547.

15. Although it does not appear from the chronicle that Don Tello ever recovered the two lordships, López de Ayala later refers to "Don Tello, Conde de Vizcaya é Señor de Lara" in the context of his role in the battle of Nájera in 1367 (ibid., 552, 557), and to his presence in "his land of Vizcaya" in late 1368 (ibid., 584).

16. Ibid., 584.

17. CEII, 7–8.

18. Ibid., 19–20.

19. Ibid., 21. Two of the three sons had not only large inheritances but important ecclesiastical offices: the archiepiscopal see of Lyon and the see of Beauvais. The story also appears in a continuation of the *Crónica de 1344* (*CG1344*, 4:534).

20. The last Lara descendant in the main line, Pedro Núñez, was the illegitimate child of Juan Núñez III de Lara and Doña Mayor de Leguizamon (a noblewoman from Vizcaya); he served quietly under Juan I. He enjoyed the lordship of Castroverde, was made Count of Mayorga in 1381 (as part of a long effort to shore up the Trastámara dynasty), and the following year was granted the monastery of Begoña, in Bilbao, as a reward for his loyalty in the king's service. In 1383, he accompanied Juan I to Badajoz for the king's wedding to Queen Beatriz of Portugal (the marriage which gave rise to Castilian claims to the throne of Portugal and thus to the siege of Lisbon). Pedro also subscribed a royal charter of 20 September 1383. He died without succession in 1384, killed by the plague during a siege of Lisbon (*Casa de Lara*, 4:216–217).

21. Luís Suárez Fernández, *Nobleza y monarquía: Puntos de vista sobre la historia política castellana del siglo XV* (Valladolid, 1975), 10–13, 116–117.

22. Cristina Jular Pérez-Alfaro, *Los adelantados y merinos mayores de León, siglos XIII–XV* (León, 1990), 281–283.

23. Hillgarth, *Spanish Kingdoms*, 1:391–392; María Concepción Quintanilla Raso, "Nobleza y señoríos en Castilla durante la Baja Edad Media: Aportaciones de la historiografía reciente," *AEM*, 14, (1984), 621–622; Suárez Fernández, *Nobleza y monarquía*, 45–48.

24. Jular Pérez-Alfaro, *Adelantados y merinos mayores*, 356–375.

25. J. H. Elliott, *Imperial Spain, 1469–1716* (London, 1963), 111–114.

26. Ignacio Atienza Hernández, *Aristocracia, poder y riqueza en la España Moderna: La casa de Osuna, siglos XV–XIX* (Madrid, 1987), 50–65.

27. Ignacio Álvarez Borge, "Estructura social y organización territorial en Castilla la Vieja meridional: Los territorios entre el Arlanzón y el Duero en los siglos X al XIV" (Diss., Universidad de León, 1991), 805–806.

28. Hilda Grassotti, *Las instituciones feudo-vassalláticas en León y Castilla*, 2 vols. (Spoleto, 1969), 2:1076–1081; Suárez, *Nobleza y monarquía*, 21–27.

29. Atienza Hernández, *Aristocracia, poder y riqueza*, 24–35.

30. Isabel Beceiro Pita, "Los estados señoriales como estructura de poder en la Castilla del siglo XV," in Adeline Rucqoi, ed., *Realidad e imágenes del poder: España a fines de la Edad Media* (Valladolid, 1988), 294–296.

31. Cristina Jular Pérez-Alfaro, "La participación de una noble en el poder local a través de su clientela: Un ejemplo concreto de fines del siglo XIV," *Hispania*, 185 (1993), 861–884; Pablo Sánchez-León, "Aspectos de una teoría de la competencia señorial: Organización patrimonial, redistribución de recursos y cambio social," ibid., 891–900.

32. Beceiro Pita, "Los estados señoriales," 295–297, 302–303.

33. Álvarez Borge, "Estructura social," 806–811.

34. Elliott, *Imperial Spain*, 34, 113.

35. Julio Valdeón, "Movimientos antiseñoriales en Castilla en el siglo XIV," *CH*, 6 (1975), 357–390. Part of the reason must surely lie in the successful propagation of the symbols of power; see María Concepción Quintanilla Raso, "El orden señorial y su representación simbólica: Ritualidad y ceremonia en Castilla a fines de la Edad Media," *AEM*, 29 (1999), 843–873.

36. Henry Kamen, *Spain, 1469–1714: A Society of Conflict* (London, 1983), 20–22.

37. Perry Anderson, *The Lineages of the Absolutist State* (London, 1984), 60–61, 68.

38. This is a point made most recently by Federico Devís Márquez, *Mayorazgo y cambio político: Estudios sobre el mayorazgo de la casa de Arcos al final de la Edad Media* (Cádiz, 1999), 15–17, siding with Jaime Vicens Vives' phrase "monarquía preeminencial."

39. Américo Castro, *The Structure of Spanish History* (Princeton, 1954), 21.

The Tenancies of the Laras

Late Eleventh Century to Early Thirteenth Century

Dates following place-names are those of extant documents suggesting tenancy, during the period before the second quarter of the thirteenth century—a period when the Laras relied intensively on this form of power. The list does not aim to be fully comprehensive; when it appears certain that a tenancy was held uninterruptedly over a number of years, only the earliest and latest dates are provided. If a specific day and/or month are indicated in the documents, they are given here in parentheses. See "Abbreviations" for complete information on the sources cited.

GONZALO NÚÑEZ (D. CIRCA 1106)

Carazo: 1083 (*La Cogolla*, 257).
Huerta: 1083 (*La Cogolla*, 257).
Lara: 1081 (25 July; *Valvanera*, 137), 1083 (*La Cogolla*, 257), 1089 (25 November; *La Cogolla*, 276), 1094 (28 February; *La Cogolla*, 284–285), and 1095 (*La Cogolla*, 287–288; *Pruebas*, 506).
Osma: 1094 (28 February; *La Cogolla*, 284–285).

PEDRO GONZÁLEZ (D. 1130)

Castilla la Vieja: 1120 (2 June; *Sahagún* 4:60–61).
Dueñas: 1127 (23 May; AHN Clero, carp. 1740, nos. 18–28) and 1128 (13 May; *Palencia*, 73–74).
Lara: 1107 (6 May; José Manuel Garrido Garrido, *Documentación de la catedral de Burgos, 804–1183* [Burgos, 1983], 1:154–155), 1110 (*La Rioja*, 2:106–107; 15 October [OB, 3:139–140]), and 1115 (4 April; *Sahagún*, 4:39–40) through 1129 (2 April; *Sahagún*, 4:120–121). He was stripped of the tenancy by Alfonso VII in 1130.
"Medina": 1110 (*Valvanera*, 186, 189; *La Rioja*, 2:106–107; August [*La Cogolla*,

219–220]). The identity of Medina is hard to establish. Salazar identifies it at different points with Medina del Campo (*Casa de Lara*, 1:95) and with Medina de las Torres (ibid., 1:90), which is implausibly far south, in Extremadura. Bernard Reilly (*Urraca*, 216) suggests that it is Medinaceli, but Medinaceli had been lost to the Moors after the disastrous defeat at Uclés (Alfonso García-Gallo, "Los fueros de Medinaceli," *AHDE*, 31 [1960], 9–16). I am more inclined to believe that it is either Medina del Campo, Medina de Rioseco, or Medina de Pomar.

Palencia: 1122 (14 April; *Arlanza*, 171–173).

Peñafiel: 1113 (13 June; *Sahagún*, 4:36–37).

Portillo: 1125 (13 December; Miguel C. Vivancos Gómez, ed., *Documentos del monasterio de Santo Domingo de Silos, 954–1254* [Burgos, 1988], 51–52).

Tariego: 1127 (23 May; AHN Clero, carp. 1740, no. 18) and 1128 (13 May; *Palencia*, 73–74).

Torremormojón: 1124 (23 June; Alexandre Brel, ed., *Recueil des chartes de l'Abbaye de Cluny*, 6 vols. [Paris, 1876–1903], 5:327–328).

RODRIGO GONZÁLEZ (D. CIRCA 1143)

Aguilar de Campóo: 1120 (*Piasca*, 130–131), 1125 (*Piasca*, 135; 1 November [*Liébana*, 128]), 1127 (23 May; AHN Clero, carp. 1740, no. 18), and 1137 (1 April; *Las Dueñas*, 21–22).

Angulo: 1122 (July; *Piasca*, 132–134).

Asturias de Santillana: 1112 (29 February; AHN Clero, carp. 378, no. 1), 1119 (AHN Códices 1001B, 48v–49r) through 1129 (16 November; *Oña*, 1:193–194), and 1135 (AHN Códices 1001B, 1r).

Campóo: 1122 (July; *Piasca*, 132–134).

Campos: 1125 (26 March; *Sahagún*, 4:92–94) and 1126 (17 June; *Las Dueñas*, 21).

Castilla la Vieja: 1120 (2 June; *Sahagún*, 4:60–61), 1122 (July; *Piasca*, 132–134), and 1137 (1 April; *Las Dueñas*, 21).

Liébana: 1120 (2 June; *Sahagún*, 4:60–61), 1122 (July; *Piasca*, 132–134), and 1125 (*Piasca*, 135).

Mena: 1112 (29 February; AHN Clero, carp. 378, no. 1).

Pernía: 1125 (*Piasca*, 135).

Piedras Negras: 1122 (July; *Piasca*, 132–134).

Segovia: 1133 (3 February; *Segovia*, 59–60).

Toledo: 1122 (AHN Códices 106B, 312r–322v; *Puerto*, 329–331), 1132 (7 September; Brel, ed., *Chartes de l'Abbaye de Cluny*, 5:390–392), 1135 (*Puerto*, 332–333), and 1136 (31 March; *Sahagún*, 4:151–152).

Trasmiera: 1119 (27 June; *Puerto*, 335) and 1122 (14 June; AHN Códices 1001B, 49r–v, microfilm).

MANRIQUE PÉREZ (D. 1164)

Almería: 1157 (14 January; *Sahagún*, 4:265–266).

Atienza: 1143 (22 August; *Cartularios de Toledo*, 51n), 1160 (*El Moral*, 70–71), and 1162 (17 February [*Palencia*, 125–126] and 17 March [*Sahagún*, 4:289–290]).

Ávila: 1133 (*Casa de Lara*, 1:110), 1144 (November; *Ávila*, 6–7), 1146 (30 March [*Sahagún*, 4:192–193] and 29 May [*Ávila*, 7–8]), 1147 (*Casa de Lara*, 1:110), 1150 (31 December; *Ávila*, 8–9), and 1158 (*Casa de Lara*, 1:110).

Baeza: 1147 (18 August; *La Rioja*, 2:218–219) through 1157 (29 April; *La Rioja*, 2:275–277).

Extremadura: 1160 (31 January; *El Moral*, 67–69).

Madrid: 1144 (October; *Segovia*, 83–84) and 1145 (1 September; José Antonio García Luján, ed., *Privilegios reales de la catedral de Toledo, 1086–1462*, 2 vols. [Toledo, 1982], 2:54–56).

Medinaceli: 1146 (7 May; Minguella, *Sigüenza*, 1:380).

Osma: 1156 (5 December; Barton, *Aristocracy*, 264).

San Esteban de Gormaz: 1162 (17 February; *Palencia*, 125–126) and 1164 (18 May; *Gradefes*, 313).

Segovia: 1148 (*Segovia*, 92–93).

Toledo: 1144 (30 June; Barton, *Aristocracy*, 264, citing AHN Clero, carp. 518, no. 15) through 1149 (July; *Privilegios reales de la catedral de Toledo*, 2:61–62), 1157 (*Sahagún*, 4:271–273; and 12 November [*Sahagún*, 4:268–269]), 1158 (*Sahagún*, 4:277–279), 1160 (31 January [*El Moral*, 67–69] and 25 December [*Sahagún*, 4:282–283]), 1161 (*Benevívere*, 10–11), 1162 (*Sahagún*, 4:295–296), and 1164 (10 February; *Sahagún*, 4:304–305).

ÁLVARO PÉREZ (D. 1172)

Aguilar de Campóo: 1148 (AHN Códices 994B, charter between folios 83v and 84r), 1164 (21 June; *Aguilar de Campóo*, 2:186–187), 1165 (1 March; *Orden de San Juan*, 257–258), and 1166 (April; AHN Códices 998B, 38r–v).

Asturias de Santillana: 1156 (23 August; *SJB*, 14–16, 23 August 1132 *recte* 1156), 1160 (31 January; *El Moral*, 67–69), 1165 (1 March; *Orden de San Juan*, 257–258), 1168 (July; *Alfonso VIII*, 2:181), and 1170 (June; *Alfonso VIII*, 2:248).

Burgos: 1168 (AHN Códices 91B, 77v–78v; AHN Códices 279B, 9r–v).

Castilla: 1169 (28 December; *Sahagún*, 4:328–329).

Cervera de Pisuerga: 1172 (9 February; *Sahagún*, 4:335–337).

Grajal de Campos: 1162 (17 March; *Sahagún*, 4:289–290).

Mudá: 1172 (9 February; *Sahagún*, 4:335–337).

Piedras Negras: 1172 (9 February; *Sahagún*, 4:335–337).

Ubierna: 1173 (28 July; AHN Códices 91B, 45v).

Viesco: 1155 (29 March; *Sahagún*, 4:258–259).

Villaescusa: 1148 (AHN Códices 994B, charter between folios 83v and 84r).

NUÑO PÉREZ (D. 1177)

Abia: 1156 (*Carrión*, 1:62), 1160 (17 April; *Gradefes*, 310–311 [dating uncertain]), 1162 (17 February; *Palencia*, 125–126), 1164 (10 February; *Sahagún*, 4:304–305) through 1166 (19 July; *El Moral*, 72–73), 1168 (*Sahagún*, 4:324–325), 1170 (June; *Alfonso VIII*, 2:248), 1171 (1 February; AHN Clero, carp. 1741, no. 4), 1172 (9 February; *Sahagún*, 4:335–337), 1173 (3 April; *Alfonso VIII*, 2:229–301), 1175 (20 February; AHN Códices, 279B, 12r and 13r), and 1177 (*Carrión*, 1:74–75).

Aguilar de Campóo: 1148 (AHN Códices 994B, charter between folios 83v and 84r).

Amaya: 1173 (12 February; *El Moral*, 73–75) and 1174 (19 April; AHN Códices, 998B, 42v).

Cabezón: 1160 (*El Moral*, 70–71; 31 January [*El Moral*, 67–69]) and 1173 (AHN Clero, carp. 3439, no. 2). A document of 1210 states that he repopulated this place (cited by Reglero, *Señoríos de los Montes de Torozos*, 126).

Carrión: 1165 (9 February, half the tenancy; *Sahagún*, 4:310), 1173 (June, half the tenancy; *Carrión*, 1:67), and 1176 (22 October; *Benevívere*, 22).

Castilla: 1169 (28 December; *Sahagún*, 4:328–329), 1172 (November; *Casa de Lara*, 4:12), and 1176 (17 February; *Sobrado*, 2:68–69).

Castrojeriz: 1173 (12 February; *El Moral*, 73–75).

Cubillas de Cerrato: 1160 (*El Moral*, 70–71).

Cuenca de Campos: 1172 (27 January; *Vega*, 89) and 1176 (17 February [*Sobrado*, 2:68–69] and 8 May [*Vega*, 101]).

Dueñas: 1162 (17 February; *Palencia*, 125–126) and 1173 (AHN Clero, carp. 3439, no. 2).

Herrera de Pisuerga: 1160 (*Sahagún*, 4:284–285; 17 April [*Gradefes*, 310–311 (dating uncertain)]), 1161 (AHN Clero, carp. 1690, nos. 5 and 6), 1164 (10 February; *Sahagún*, 4:304–305) through 1166 (19 July; *El Moral*, 72–73), 1168 (*Sahagún*, 4:324–325), 1170 (June; *Alfonso VIII*, 2:248), 1172 (9 February; *Sahagún*, 4:335–337), 1174 (19 April; AHN Códices 998B, 42v), 1175 (20 February; AHN Códices 279B, 12r and 13r), and 1177 (*Carrión*, 1:74–75).

Montoro: 1154 (24 December; *Sobrado* 2:105, erroneously dated 1165) through 1156 (24 June; *Gradefes*, 308–309).

Moratinos: 1162 (17 March [*Sahagún*, 4:289–290] and 2 July [Sahagún, 4:395–396]).

Nájera: 1176 (*Vega*, 102).

Saldaña: 1173 (June, half the tenancy; *Carrión*, 1:67).

San Román de Entrepeñas: 1171 (1 February; AHN Clero, carp. 1741, no. 4) and 1172 (December; AHN Clero, carp. 1741, no. 6).

Tamariz: 1172 (27 January; *Vega*, 89) and 1176 (17 February; *Sobrado*, 2:68–69).

Tariego: 1173 (AHN Clero, carp. 3439, no. 2).

Ubierna: 1176 (8 November; AHN Clero, carp. 351, no. 19).

"Valeria": 1176 (17 February; *Sobrado*, 2:68–69). I have not been able to identify this location.

Villaescusa: 1148 (AHN Códices 994B, charter between folios 83v and 84r).

Villafáfila: 1165 (8 July, one of two tenants; *Eslonza*, 148–149).

Villagarcía de Campos: 1158 (*Sahagún*, 4:277–279).

Villanueva: 1175 (13 August; *Las Dueñas*, 24–25). Probably Villanueva de la Condesa.

Villavaquerín: 1170 (12 February; Francisco Antón, *Monasterios medievales de la provincia de Valladolid* (Valladolid, 1942), 272–273).

PEDRO RODRÍGUEZ (D. 1183)

Bureba: 1177 (*Oña*, 300) and 1179 (*Oña*, 312).

Castilla: 1174 (*Oña*, 294; 5 January [*Oña*, 292]).

Nájera: 1173 (3 April; *Alfonso VIII*, 2:299–301), 1176 (25 August, a peace treaty between Castile and Navarre stating that each king will give three castles in fidelity, the king of Navarre entrusting Nájera and "Celorigo" to Pedro Rodríguez; *Alfonso VIII*, 2:441), 1177 (*Oña*, 300), and probably 1179 (17 September; *Alfonso VIII*, 2:551) through 1180 (12 January; *Alfonso VIII*, 2:559). In the last period, 1179–1180, he appears as "Petrus Roderici de Naiera," or variants, to distinguish him from Pedro Rodríguez de Azagra.

PEDRO MANRIQUE (D. 1202)

Asturias de Oviedo: 1165 (29 January; AHN Códices 1045B, 10–11) through 1169 (28 December; *Sahagún*, 4:328–329), 1185 (16 February; AHN Clero, carp. 1506, no. 3, microfilm), and 1186 (7 March [*Sahagún*, 4:406–407], 17 March [*Sahagún*, 4:407–409], and 5 May [*Sobrado*, 2:63–64]).

Atienza: 1164 (November; AHN Clero, carp. 378, no. 8), 1165 (1 March, *Orden de San Juan*, 257–258), 1174 (27 December; AHN Clero, carp. 378, no. 16), 1181 (31 December; AHN Códices 91B, 75v–76v, and AHN Códices 279B, 15r–v), 1183 (3 June; *El Moral*, 80–81), 1184 (January or February; *Orden de San Juan*, 328–330), 1188 (AHN Ordenes Militares, Calatrava, Libros 1341-C, fol. 107r; 11 March [AHN Códices 91B, 80r–v]), and 1190 (*Oña*, 1:349–350).

Babia: 1186 (16 March; María Amparo Valcarce García, *El dominio de la Real Colegiata de San Isidro de León hasta 1189* (León, 1985), 136–137).

Cabezón: 1172 (5 November; *Alfonso VIII*, 2:291–292).

Ciudad Rodrigo: 1185 (26 September; *Sobrado*, 2:65–66) and 1186 (5 May; *Sobrado*, 2:63–64).

Cuenca: 1188 (AHN Ordenes Militares, Calatrava, Libros 1341-C, fol. 107r), 1189 (José Luís Martín Rodríguez, *Orígenes de la orden militar de Santiago, 1170–1195* [Barcelona, 1974], 430–431), 1190 (*Oña*, 1:349–350), and 1200 (José Antonio García Luján, ed., *Cartulario del monasterio de Santa María de Huerta* (Huerta, 1981), 107–108).

Dueñas: 1185 (16 February; AHN Clero, carp. 1506, no. 3, microfilm).

Extremadura: 1170 (June; Martín Rodríguez, *Orden de Santiago*, 211) and 1201 (16 June; *Casa de Lara*, 1:153).

Hita: 1181 (8 May, one of two tenants; *Cartularios de Toledo*, 184–185).

Huete: 1190 (*Oña*, 1:349–350) and 1198 (21 March; AHN Ordenes Militares, Uclés, 100, vol. 2, no. 5).

Lara: 1165 (1 March; *Orden de San Juan*, 257–258), 1166 (18 October; *Segovia*, 114) through 1168 (19 January; *Alfonso VIII*, 2:173–175), 1169 (AHN Clero, carp. 1023, no. 16); 1171 (Vivancos Gómez, ed., *Documentación del monasterio de Silos*, 94), 1171 (9 December; *Alfonso VIII*, 2:281), 1173 (*Arlanza*, 220–221), 1175 (*Arlanza*, 225–227), 1178 (2 September; *SJB*, 54), 1181 (31 December; AHN Códices 91B, 75v–76v and AHN Códices 279B, 15r–v), and 1184 (January or February; *Orden de San Juan*, 328–330). We need to be careful in interpreting the formula "Comes Petrus de Lara," which might merely denote membership of a lineage. The clearer term "Comes Petrus tenens Lara," in the diploma of 9 December 1171, is exceptional. However, members of the family were not generally referred to in diplomatic sources as "de Lara" until the early fourteenth century. It therefore seems likely that he was tenant on all the above dates. The formula "Comes Petrus de Lara" never recurred after the tenancy of Lara was transferred to one Gonzalo Ruiz in 1193.

León (fortress): 1185 (22 February; AHN Clero, carp. 825, no. 13), and 1186 (31 March [Martín Rodríguez, *Orden de Santiago*, 382–383], 1 April [Martín Rodríguez, *Orden de Santiago*, 383–384], 29 April [*Eslonza*, 172–173] and 21 May [*Gradefes*, 328]). This tenancy involved responsibility for the military defense of the city and perhaps some nonmilitary duties on behalf of the crown.

Luna: 1186 (31 March [Martín Rodríguez, *Orden de Santiago*, 382–383] and 1 April [Martín Rodríguez, *Orden de Santiago*, 383–384]).

Medinaceli: 1188 (11 March; AHN Códices 91B, 80r–v). The document refers to "Medina," probably Medinaceli because of its close proximity to Atienza, also his tenancy at this time and mentioned in the same document.

Osma: 1168 (Barton, *Aristocracy*, 282).

Salamanca: 1185 (July; *Sahagún*, 4:402–404) and 1186 (5 May; *Sobrado*, 2:63–64).

San Esteban de Gormaz: 1168 (Barton, *Aristocracy*, 282) and 1174 (27 December; AHN Clero, carp. 378, no. 16).

Toledo: 1172 (November; *Casa de Lara*, 1:140), 1173 (3 April; *Alfonso VIII*, 2:299–301), and 1179 (May; AHN Clero, carp. 3439, no. 3).

Toro: 1185 (July; *Sahagún*, 4:402–404).

Transierra: 1172 (November; *Casa de Lara*, 1:136), 1176 (17 February; *Sobrado*, 2:68–69).

ÁLVARO NÚÑEZ (D. 1218)

Abia: 1216 (*Fernando III*, 1:145).

Aguilar de Campóo: 1199 (1 March; *Aguilar de Campóo*, 2:219 *bis*).

Bureba: 1205 (*Oña*, 435, 436), 1206 (*Liébana*, 159; *Oña*, 440, 441), and 1215 (*Oña*, 500).

Castilla: 1205 (*Oña*, 435, 436) and 1206 (*Liébana*, 159; *Oña*, 440, 441).

Herrera de Pisuerga: 1208 (2 March; *Alfonso VIII*, 1:288) and 1216 (*Fernando III*, 1:145).

Lara: 1217 (DRH 197; *PCG*, 715).

Lerma: 1217 (DRH 197; *PCG*, 715).

Ojeda: 1216 (*Fernando III*, 1:145).

Tamariz: 1195 (*Sahagún*, 4:530–531).

Uceda: 1204 (November; *Alfonso VIII*, 1:288).

Note: The chronicles place Alvaro Núñez in command of Abia, Alarcón, Amaya, Belorado, Cañete, Cerezo, Nájera, Pancorbo, Tariego, and Villafranca in the year 1217, and these are represented on Map 11. However, it is not precisely clear how many of these places were bona fide tenancies and how many had simply been acquired during the preceding escalation of civil war (DRH, 198; *PCG*, 716; *CL*, 75).

FERNANDO NÚÑEZ (D. 1219)

Abia: 1174 (19 April; AHN Códices 998B, 42v), 1176 (*Vega*, 102), 1183 (3 June; *El Moral*, 80–81), 1185 (21 January; AHN Clero, carp. 1730, no. 1, microfilm), 1188 (AHN Ordenes Militares, Calatrava, Libros 1341-C, fol. 107r; 17 August [Martín Rodríguez, *Orígenes de la orden militar de Santiago*, 417–418]), and 1204 (24 May; *Aguilar de Campóo*, 2:238–239).

Aguilar de Campóo: 1173 (12 February; *El Moral*, 73–75), 1175 (1 May; *Aguilar de Campóo*, 2:192), 1183 (7 September; *Sahagún*, 4:387–388), 1185 (21 January; AHN Clero, carp. 1730, no. 1, microfilm), 1186 (*Aguilar de Campóo*, 2:200), 1188 (17 August; Martín Rodríguez, *Orígenes de la orden militar de Santiago*, 417–418), 1190 (*Aguilar de Campóo*, 2:205–206; *Oña*, 1:349–350), 1197 (*Aguilar de Campóo*, 2:215), 1198 (*Aguilar de Campóo*, 2:216), 1204 (24 May; *Aguilar de Campóo*, 2:238–239), and 1206 (*Liébana*, 160).

Amaya: 1175 (1 May; *Aguilar de Campóo*, 2:192), 1179 (6 December; AHN Códices 998B, 4r–v), 1181 (AHN Códices 279B, 15r–v; 31 December [AHN Códices 91B, 75v–76r]), 1182 (17 April; *Aguilar de Campóo*, 2:196), 1184 (January or February; *Orden de San Juan*, 328–330), 1186 (29 January; *Covarrubias*, 64–65), 1188 (11 March; AHN Códices 91B), 1190 (*Oña*, 1:349–350).

Astudillo: 1196 (6 December; Barton, *Aristocracy*, 331, incorrectly dated 9 December).

Asturias de Oviedo: 1191 (15 February; *Alfonso IX*, 2:66–67), 1192 (28 March [*Alfonso IX*, 2:82–83] through 27 December [*Alfonso IX*, 2:93–94]), and 1200 (6 January [*Alfonso IX*, 2:197–198] to 12 March [Guillermo Castán Lanaspa and Javier Castán Lanaspa, eds., *Documentos del monasterio de Santa María de Trianos, siglos XII–XIII* (Salamanca, 1992), 61]).

Asturias de Santillana: 1173 (12 February; *El Moral*, 73–75), 1176 (*Sobrado*, 2:68–69; *Vega*, 102), 1184 (January or February; *Orden de San Juan*, 328–330), and 1186 (17 August; AHN Códices, 998B, 2v–3v).

Asturias de Tineu: 1193 (3 February; *Alfonso IX*, 2:96–97).

Bureba: 1187 (*Oña*, 335; 28 July [*Oña*, 337]), 1201 (*Oña*, 407), and 1202 (*Oña*, 418, 420, 425).

Cabezón: 1178 (Reglero, *Señoríos de los Montes de Torozos*, 127).

Carrión: 1175 (half of tenancy, *Alfonso VIII*, 1:286; 30 July, half of tenancy [*Benevívere*, 20]), 1176 (half of tenancy, *Vega*, 102), 1183 (3 June; *El Moral*, 80–81), 1186 (24 April, half of tenancy [*Sahagún*, 4:410–411] and 6 June, half of tenancy [*Sahagún*, 4:412–413]), 1188 (11 March; AHN Códices 91B), and 1190 (31 March [*Liébana*, 148] and 3 October [*Sahagún*, 4:453–454]).

Castilla la Vieja: 1203 (3 March; *Pruebas*, 622) and 1209 (6 November; *Alfonso VIII*, 3:496–500).

Castrojeriz: 1218 (DRH, 198, *PCG*, 716).

Cuenca: 1181 (18 August; AHN Clero carp. 1648, no. 13, microfilm), 1188 (2 April; *Eslonza*, 174–175), 1202 (17 November; *Alfonso VIII*, 3:283), and 1203 (November; *Casa de Lara*, 4:27–28).

Herrera de Pisuerga: 1173 (3 April; *Alfonso VIII*, 2:299–301), 1176 (*Vega*, 102), 1185 (21 January; AHN Clero, carp. 1730, no. 1, microfilm), 1188 (17 August; Martín Rodríguez, *Orígenes de la orden militar de Santiago*, 417–418), and 1204 (24 May; *Aguilar de Campóo*, 2:238–239).

Huete: 1202 (17 November; *Alfonso VIII*, 3:283) and 1203 (November, *Casa de Lara*, 4:27–28).

Liébana: 1178 (one of two tenants; *Piasca*, 135).

Medina del Campo: 1210 (2 December; *Orden de San Juan*, 288–389).

Monzón de Campos: 1179 (29 December; *Benevívere*, 26) and 1218 (DRH, 198, *PCG*, 716).

Moratinos: 1184 (30 October; *Sahagún*, 4:392–393).

Ordejón: 1179 (6 December; AHN Códices 998B, 4r–v), 1182 (17 April; *Aguilar de Campóo*, 2:196), 1186 (29 January; *Covarrubias*, 64–65), and 1218 (DRH, 198, *PCG*, 716).

Saldaña: 1183 (22 June; *Benevívere*, 27–28) and 1190 (31 March [*Liébana*, 148] and 3 October [*Sahagún*, 4:453–454]).

Tamariz: 1181 (18 August; AHN Clero, carp. 1648, no. 13, microfilm) and 1195 (*Sahagún*, 4:530–531).

Toroño: 1191 (15 February; *Alfonso IX*, 2:66–67) through 1194 (15 February; *Alfonso IX*, 2:112–113).

Ubierna: 1179 (AHN Códices 91B, 46v), 1181 (March; *Catedral de Burgos*, 1:328–329), 1190 (*Oña*, 1:349–350).

Villaescusa: 1183 (7 September; *Sahagún*, 4:387–388).

GONZALO NÚÑEZ (D. 1225)

Aguilar de Campóo: 1196 (AHN Códices 994B, 23r, 38r, 25v; 6 December [Barton, *Aristocracy*, 331, incorrectly dated 9 December]).

Alba de Tormes: 1186 (10 March [*Fernando II*, 333, 506] and 21 March [*Fernando II*, 507]).

Astorga: 1220 (2 October; *Sahagún*, 5:128–130).

Asturias de Oviedo: 1185 (AHN Códices 1045B, 211), 1195 (30 April; *Alfonso IX*, 2:137–138), 1198 (20 February [AHN Códices 1002B, 26r–v] through 23 December [*Alfonso IX*, 1:173–175]), 1219 (16 June; *Alfonso IX*, 2:491–492), and 1220 (20 March; *Alfonso IX*, 2:508–509). He was also tenant of Queen Berenguela's dowry in Asturias from 15 to 29 September 1199 (*Alfonso IX*, 2:191–193).

Babia: 1198 (10 December [*ACL*, 6:100–102] to 23 December [*Alfonso IX*, 2:173–175]).

Coria: 1199 (19 March; *Alfonso IX*, 2:176–178).

El Bierzo: 1220 (2 October; *Sahagún*, 5:128–130).

Extremadura: 1197 (4 September; *Alfonso IX*, 2:155–156) and 1199 (19 March; *Alfonso IX*, 2:176–178).

Lemos: 1197 (4 September; *Alfonso IX*, 2:155–156), 1204 (19 September; *Alfonso IX*, 2:262–262) through 1206 (8 June; *Alfonso IX*, 2:296), 1210 (February [*ACL*, 6:211–212] and June [*ACL*, 6:214–215]), 1211 (21 April; *Alfonso IX*, 2:367–368), and 1221 (10 March; *ACL*, 6:383–384).

León (city): 1219 (16 June; *Alfonso IX*, 2:491–492) and 1220 (22 February; *Alfonso IX*, 2:504–505).

Limia: 1211 (21 April; *Alfonso IX*, 2:367–368).

Montenegro: 1191 (15 February [*Alfonso IX*, 2:66–67] and June [*Alfonso IX*, 2:74–75]).

Monterroso: 1204 (19 September; *Alfonso IX*, 2:261–262) through 1206 (June;

Sobrado, 1:293), 1210 (February; *ACL*, 6:211–212), 1211 (1 September; *Alfonso IX*, 2:374–376), 1220 (27 September; *Alfonso IX*, 2:518–519), and 1221 (21 September; *Fernando III*, 1:148).

Sarria: 1191 (15 February [*Alfonso IX*, 2:66–67] and 31 August [*Alfonso IX*, 2:77–78]), 1197 (*Fernando III*, 1:147–148) and 1206 (*Fernando III*, 1:147–148).

Somoza: 1219 (16 June [*Alfonso IX*, 2:491–492] and 16 July [*Fernando III*, 1:246–247]).

Tamariz: 1195 (*Sahagún*, 4:530–531).

Toroño: 1220 (27 September; *Alfonso IX*, 2:518–519) and 1221 (20 August [*Alfonso IX*, 2:523–524] and 21 September [*Fernando III*, 1:148]).

Trastámara: 1195 (18 April; Santiago Montero Díaz, *La colección diplomática de San Martín de Jubia, 977–1199* [Santiago, 1935], 111), half the tenancy from 1204 (16 September; *Alfonso IX*, 2:259–260) through 1206 (8 June; *Alfonso IX*, 2:296), 1211 (21 April; *Alfonso IX*, 2:367–368), 1220 (18 March; *Alfonso IX*, 2:506), and 1221 (21 September; *Fernando III*, 1:148).

Zamora: 1220 (22 February [*Alfonso IX*, 2:504–505] and one of two tenants in June [José Luís Martín Rodríguez, ed., *Documentos zamoranos*, vol. 1: *Documentos del Archivo Catedralicio de Zamora, 1128–1261* (Salamanca, 1982), 68–69]).

Principal Figures of the Lara Family

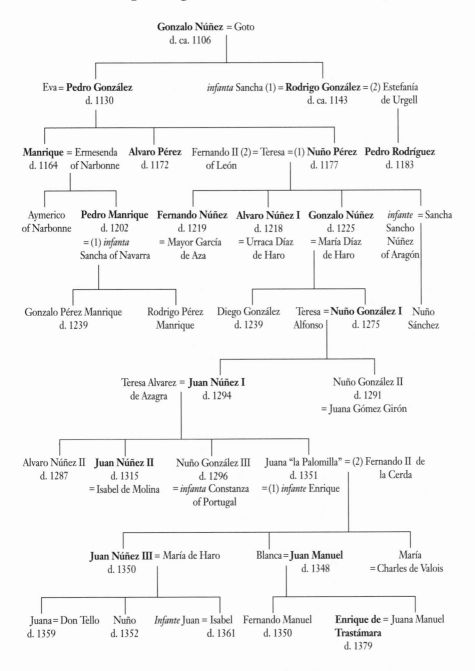

Gonzalo Núñez = Goto
d. ca. 1106

Eva = **Pedro González**
d. 1130

infanta Sancha (1) = **Rodrigo González** = (2) Estefanía
d. ca. 1143   de Urgell

Manrique = Ermesenda
d. 1164   of Narbonne

Alvaro Pérez
d. 1172

Fernando II (2) = Teresa = (1) **Nuño Pérez**
of León   d. 1177

Pedro Rodríguez
d. 1183

Aymerico
of Narbonne

Pedro Manrique
d. 1202
= (1) *infanta*
Sancha of Navarra

Fernando Núñez
d. 1219
= Mayor García
de Aza

Alvaro Núñez I
d. 1218
= Urraca Díaz
de Haro

Gonzalo Núñez
d. 1225
= María Díaz
de Haro

infante = Sancha
Sancho
Núñez
of Aragón

Gonzalo Pérez Manrique
d. 1239

Rodrigo Pérez
Manrique

Diego González
d. 1239

Teresa = **Nuño González I**
Alfonso | d. 1275

Nuño
Sánchez

Teresa Alvarez = **Juan Núñez I**
de Azagra   d. 1294

Nuño González II
d. 1291
= Juana Gómez Girón

Alvaro Núñez II
d. 1287

Juan Núñez II
d. 1315
= Isabel de Molina

Nuño González III
d. 1296
= *infanta* Constanza
of Portugal

Juana "la Palomilla" = (2) Fernando II de
d. 1351   la Cerda
= (1) *infante* Enrique

Juan Núñez III = María de Haro
d. 1350

Blanca = **Juan Manuel**
d. 1348

María
= Charles de Valois

Juana = Don Tello
d. 1359

Nuño
d. 1352

Infante Juan = Isabel
d. 1361

Fernando Manuel
d. 1350

Enrique de = Juana Manuel
Trastámara
d. 1379

Glossary of Spanish Terms

adelantado: The military and political governor of a region. Term used beginning in the 1250s.

adelantado mayor: The military and political governor of a major region (e.g., Castilla, León, Murcia, Galicia). Term supersedes *merino mayor*—probably a very similar position—beginning in the 1250s.

adelantado de la frontera: Governor of the Andalusian frontier zone.

adelantamiento: The position of *adelantado.*

alcabala: A sales tax.

alcaide: Mayor of a town, and/or castellan.

alcalde: Municipal judge.

alférez: Standard-bearer; commander of the king's military household. The position becomes honorific in the thirteenth century.

alfoz: An administrative district of fiscal dependency and obligation. Term used especially prior to the thirteenth century.

apellido: Family name.

behetría: A village or other settlement whose inhabitants legally enjoy a degree of freedom in choosing their lord.

bodega: Place where wine is made and stored.

caballeros villanos: Nonnoble knights.

camarero mayor: Head chamberlain.

canciller mayor: Head chancellor.

concejo: Municipal or village council.

Cortes: Assembly, originating in meetings of the royal court that were expanded to include larger numbers of nobles and prelates, and (beginning in 1188) municipal *procuradores.*

despensero: Treasurer.

diezmo: Tithe, or customs duties.

divisa: Share of an inheritance in a given location.

divisero: The owner of a *divisa.*

fuero: A document recording municipal or regional laws, customs, and privileges.

fonsadera: A tax paid in place of military service.

hermandad: A confederation or alliance (of nobles, towns, and so on).

hidalgo: A member of the lesser nobility.

infanta: Princess.

infantazgo: Crown lands entrusted to junior members of the royal family.

infante: Prince.

infanzón: A member of the lower nobility.

infurción: Rent paid to a lord, usually in kind, by virtue of his possession of a *solariego* or *behetría.*

justicia mayor: Chief justice.

letrados: Professional administrators and jurists.

martiniega: A feudal tax payable annually on Saint Martin's Day.

mayorazgo: An entailed estate.

mayordomo: Steward, responsible for management of the royal or other household.

mayordomo mayor: Chief steward. The position becomes honorific in the thirteenth century.

merindad: An administrative, military, and jurisdictional area. The term is used beginning in the twelfth century, but the position becomes the key instrument of royal fiscal and jurisdictional control in the thirteenth century.

merino: An official, usually (but not exclusively) of the crown, entrusted with collection of revenues, supervision of military summonses, and/or the administration of justice.

merino mayor: Chief merino, always reporting exclusively to the crown and supervising the *merinos menores.* The position dates from the early thirteenth century, but beginning in the 1250s the term appears to have been replaced by *adelantado mayor.*

merino menor: Local official in royal administration, reporting to the *merino mayor.*

moneda: A tax paid regularly in return for the preservation of a stable currency, beginning in the thirteenth century.

natural: One who by custom enjoys some form of jurisdictional authority or revenue in a given settlement.

naturaleza: The status of one who is a *natural.*

pedido: Subsidy requested, by the crown or by a local lord, for special needs.

procurador: A representative of a municipality in the Cortes.

rico hombre: An aristocrat.

servicio: A special subsidy conceded to the crown in the Cortes.

solariego: A full and hereditary seigneurial property.

tenencias: Tenancies—that is, positions of jurisdictional, military, or financial authority resulting from the temporary delegation of royal (or other) lordship in a given location. Term used beginning in the twelfth century; largely superseded by *merindades* in the thirteenth century.

tercia: Royal share (one-third) of the ecclesiastical tithe in Castile, collected beginning in the early thirteenth century and officially intended to subsidize the reconquest.

yantar: The right of a lord to hospitality (food and lodging) from those in his jurisdiction. This was increasingly commuted to monetary payment.

Index